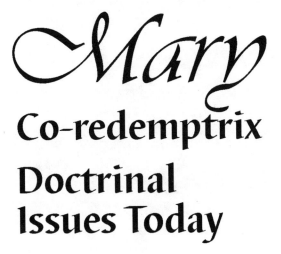

Mary
Co-redemptrix
Doctrinal Issues Today

Mary
Co-redemptrix
Doctrinal
Issues Today

Luis Cardinal Aponte Martinez

Rev. Jean Galot, S.J.

Dr. Josef Seifert

Rev. Msgr. Arthur B. Calkins

Sr. Thomas M. McBride, O.P.

Dr. John Macquarrie

Rev. Stefano Manelli, F.F.I.

Dr. Mark Miravalle S.T.D., Editor

Dr. Scott Hahn

Introduction by Edouard Cardinal Gagnon, P.S.S.

Queenship
PUBLISHING COMPANY
P.O. Box 220 • Goleta, CA 93116
(800) 647-9882 • (805) 692-0043 • Fax: (805) 967-5133

IMPRIMATUR

Cardinal Ernesto Corripio Ahumada
Mexico City
December 12, 2001

Bishop Sydney A. Charles
St. George's-in-Grenada, West Indies
December 8, 2001

Cover Art: Beato Angelico,
The Annunciation, The Crucifixion,
St. Mark's Convent, Florence.

© Copyright 2002 Mark I. Miravalle, S.T. D.
All Rights Reserved

Library of Congress Number # 2002 141054

Published by:
    Queenship Publishing
    P.O. Box 220
    Goleta, CA 93116
    (800) 647-9882 • (805) 692-0043 • Fax: (805) 967-5133
    http://www.queenship.org

Printed in the United States of America

ISBN: 1-57918-176-7

Contents

Introduction

I t is with great pleasure that I introduce you to this present theological volume dedicated to the explication and development of Church doctrine and papal teaching of Our Lady as the Co-redemptrix.

The wealth of ideas, principles, and outstanding theological exposition reflected in this volume, the work of an exceptional international team of theologians and mariologists, calls the contemporary bishop, pastor, theologian, or lay leader to dedicate time and attention to this important work and topic, so as to be properly informed and appreciative of the recent mariological development on the doctrinal issues of Marian coredemption within the Church of today. This doctrinal topic is especially relevant in light of the substantial contribution and emphasis of our present Holy Father, Pope John Paul II, on the subject of Our Lady's contribution to the Redemption, likely more than any other pontiff in Church history.

When we reflect on the mysteries of the Rosary, at times we fail to appreciate the depth of these mysteries. In the Joyful Mystery of the Presentation of Jesus in the Temple, we see Mary's call to suffer with Christ, to share in the redemptive sufferings of the Redeemer (cf. Lk 2:35). This is brought to its full completion in the Sorrowful Mystery of the Crucifixion, where Mary's sufferings with Christ are offered in union with Jesus for the redemption of the world, and the Co-redemptrix is given then to each one of us as Mediatrix of all grace and Spiritual Mother by the Redeemer: "Woman, behold your son...behold your mother" (Jn.19:26-27).

In our present world situation, in the midst of so much human suffering and global unrest, is the relevance of the doctrine of Mary Co-redemptrix not obvious to us? What doctrine better conveys the Christian mystery of the supernatural value of human suffering under any condition, including conditions beyond our earthly control, than that of Mary Co-redemptrix?

St. Paul exhorts us that if we have faith in our hearts, we should confess and proclaim publicly our faith. I believe that at this moment of history, it is very important that our faith in the role of Mary Co-redemptrix be clearly proclaimed and defined.

May the truth of Mary Co-redemptrix penetrate our hearts and lives, filling us with new strength and grace in accepting and enduring as Christian witnesses the providential suffering to which we are called personally and as a Church. May the Mediatrix of all grace bestow upon each one of us the graces to be true to the call of St. Paul to "make up what is lacking in the sufferings of Christ, for the sake of his body, which is the Church" (Col. 1:24).

Edouard Cardinal Gagnon, P.S.S.,
President Emeritus, Pontifical Council on the Family
President Emeritus,
Pontifical Committee for International Congresses
1 November 2001
Solemnity of All Saints

Mary Co-redemptrix and the New Evangelization

by Luis Cardinal Aponte Martinez

In May 2001 Pope John Paul II called to Rome the cardinals of the world in a special consistory seeking to implement the pastoral directives for the new millennium as contained in his papal document Novo Millennio Ineunte (At the Beginning of the Third Millennium).

On the first day of the consistory, as the third official presenter to the College of Cardinals and in the presence of Pope John Paul II, His Eminence, Luis Cardinal Aponte Martinez, Archbishop of Puerto Rico, offered to the consistory the following presentation concerning the decisive role of the Mother of All Peoples in the imperative of the New Evangelization for the third millennium.

Your Holiness and my dear Brother Cardinals,

As we contemplate the imperative for the New Evangelization in light of *Novo Millennio Ineunte*, the question must be posed: who was the first to "hear the word of God and keep it" (cf. Lk. 11:28)? *It was the Mother of the Lord*, who did such so completely and lovingly that the Word became flesh and dwelt among us (cf. Lk. 1:38, Jn 1:14).

Who was the first to "meet Christ"(Lk. 1:38)? *It was the Mother*. Who was the first to "see Jesus" (Jn. 12:21) and to "contemplate his face" (Lk. 2:7, NMI. 16)? *It was the Mother*. Who was the first "witness to the Gospel," to live the "life of faith," to intrinsically participate in the "depth of the mystery" of the

1

hypostatic union (NMI. 17,19,21)? *It was the Mother.*

The human face that most closely resembles and reveals "the Son's face" (NMI. 24) is the Mother's face. And no one more deeply experiences the paradoxical and redemptive "Face of Sorrow" at Calvary (NMI. 25) than the Mother Co-redemptrix (cf. Jn. 19:26-27).

As we are called in this Apostolic Letter to "direct our thoughts to the future which lies before us" and that "in the final analysis, this rooting of the Church in time and space mirrors *the movement of the Incarnation itself* (NMI. 3)," I consider that *the providential role of the Mother of the Lord in the Incarnation and the First Evangelization, as divinely determined by the heavenly Father, must be acknowledged and centrally included in our pastoral program for the New Evangelization at the outset of this new millennium.*

As a native son of the Americas, permit me to make reference to the heavenly Father's program of Evangelization that took place for our peoples of America. It was to send, as the first missionary, our Lady of Guadalupe to us as the motherly means of intercession in preparing the way for the Good News of Jesus Christ to reach the peoples of America, which resulted in the greatest single Christian evangelization since the first apostolic evangelization, producing as its spiritual catch the most populated Catholic continent in the world today.

Should we not imitate the Father's wisdom by inviting the Mother of the Lord as well into this great historic program of evangelization for the new millennium?

If we would formally invite the Virgin Mother to accompany us with those beautiful words, "do whatever he tells you" (Jn. 2:5), leading souls to the Heart of Christ as only the Mother's Heart can, then she will help us guide the peoples of the new millennium into a "New Holiness" (NMI. 30). She is the Mediatrix of all graces who "taken up into heaven did not lay aside this saving office, but by her manifold intercession continues to brings us the gifts of eternal salvation" (LG. 62).

Reverend Cardinal Brothers, which one of us, reviving the memories of our priestly and episcopal vocations, does not recognize that we owe special gratitude to the intercession of the Mother of priests and Queen of apostles for our own vocations? Let us not deny that same maternal intercession for the so desperately needed vocations in the Church and of the peoples of the new millennium (NMI. 46).

And with special concern for the great ecumenical imperative of our day (NMI. 48), is this not one of the most urgent of Christian necessities and hence in greatest need of the powerful intercession of the Mother of unity? Would now not be the time to formally invite "our common Mother" (RM. 30) to fully utilize the spiritual power of her motherly Heart in unifying the sons and daughters of God in the one Body of Christ? It is now the opportune time to definitively turn to the Mother to implore the graces necessary to fulfill the yet unfulfilled "ut unum sint" pleading of the one Lord (Jn. 17:21).

The Theotokos-Mediatrix especially awaits to be formally invited to bring the air of unity to the "two lungs of the Church" (RM. 34), where her common maternal presence in East and West can truly effect a final spiritual adhesion of these churches who have both profoundly shared the Mother's love and grace.

But the Virgin of the redemptive Fiat, always obedient to the Father's will, **awaits our personal invitation** to fully activate her titles and roles as Mediatrix for our sanctification.

How then do we properly and formally invite the Mother of the Lord and Mother of all peoples into the New Evangelization for the new millennium?

The past millennium witnessed the definition of two great Marian dogmas: the Immaculate Conception and the Assumption. Could this millennium be the moment for proclaiming Mary as Mother of all people, Mother of all grace? It is by formally recognizing the maternal gift from the Heart of the Crucified Christ to every human heart, as given on Calvary, that we would invite Mary to repeat "do as he tells you." It would be by means of this dogmatic declaration that we, those redeemed by her Son, would accept the great gift; "behold your Mother" (Jn. 19:27). It is by dogmatically declaring that we, as the people of God, do accept the maternal gift of great price and consequent instruction of the Lord Jesus to "behold our Mother" (Jn. 19:27), that we rejoice and give thanks for that great gift of her as our Intercessor, as she is clearly called in *Lumen Gentium* (LG. 61).

Is not the Christian truth of her maternal mediation (RM. III) the foundation of our Marian conciliar teaching (cf. LG. 56, 58, 61, 62), especially when it states: "Mary's maternal mission did not shadow the unique mediation of Christ, but rather shows its efficacy" (LG. 60)? Can we not state the same of the Ave Maria, of praying the rosary, of the acts of Marian entrustments, of the historic events of Guadalupe and Fatima, of the papal motto, *Totus Tuus*? To solemnly proclaim the Virgin Immaculate as the Mother of all peoples, Co-redemptrix, Mediatrix of all graces, and Advocate is to fully and officially recognize her titles and, consequently, **to activate, to bring to new life,** the spiritual functions they offer for humanity. This free act on the part of the Church, which reflects the freedom of all believers, thus releases the Mother in the order of freedom and grace to fully intercede with these spiritual and maternal roles given her by God for the sanctification of the peoples of the world. And as such, the Mother of the New Evangelization will be, so to speak, fully commissioned by humanity's exercise of free will to "bring us (once again) the gifts of eternal salvation" (cf. LG. 62), which in turn will *bring to new life the Incarnation and the Gospel* in the hearts of her earthly children.

The dogmatic proclamation of the Mother of all peoples, Co-redemptrix, Mediatrix, and Advocate would be **the gateway** to the New Evangelization. It would be the "New Cana," the renewed bridge that connects the human heart with the freshly revealed Heart of Christ through the Heart of the Mother (cf. Jn. 2:5). It would be the Star of the Sea which would serve as the compass in the great spiritual catch of the "Duc in altum."

Your Holiness, you have with filial affection said in this letter to the Mother of all peoples to "behold her children" (NMI. 58). May the Lord permit your voice to be prophetic, *that we, her children, raise our voices to solemnly and officially announce "behold our Mother" (cf. Jn. 19:27), and to positively respond to the request of over 550 episcopal brothers and over 6 million faithful worldwide to solemnly and papally define that the Virgin Immaculate is the Mother of all peoples, Co-redemptrix, Mediatrix of all graces, and Advocate.*

Let us thereby open the new millennium and its New Evangelization with a contemporary fulfillment of the Marian scriptural prophecy: "all generations will call me blessed; for he that is mighty has done great things for me" (Lk. 1:48).

Mary Co-redemptrix: Controversies and Doctrinal Questions

by Rev. Jean Galot, S.J.

Jean Galot, S.J. is a Professor of Theology at the Pontifical Gregorian University in Rome. He is internationally known for his biblical and theological scholarship, particularly in the area of Christology. He is a frequent contributor to L'Osservatore Romano. *

The way to understand the cooperation of Mary in the redemption has been the object of many discussions among theologians. Some have expressed repugnance or advanced objections against the terms "coredemption" and "Co-redemptrix." This current of opposition has had as a result the abstention of the Second Vatican Council, which, in its exposition of Marian doctrine, in chapter VIII of *Lumen gentium* (LG), avoided such terms. The Council, in fact, abstained from wishing to settle questions which did not seem sufficiently clarified and which remained sources of controversy. There is no reason to be surprised by similar controversies, which arise in many sectors of theology; in the past these characterized the development of

*Originally printed in the Italian in *Civilta Cattolica,* 1994; translated and reprinted with permission of the author.

Marian doctrine. Let it suffice to recall the title of "Mother of God," opposed by Nestorius before being proclaimed by the Council of Ephesus, and how the Immaculate Conception stirred up long and animated discussions in the course of the centuries before being defined by Pius IX in 1854.

Regarding the coredemption, some theologians maintain their reserve or state doctrinal fears. But we can affirm that, in a general manner, the cooperation of Mary in the redemptive sacrifice finds an ever greater acceptance. We would like to clarify the essential points of this doctrine, recalling the theological problems which have caused the controversies and the solution given or which it is appropriate to give them.

The Title of Co-redemptrix

The omission of the title of Co-redemptrix in the conciliar exposition of Marian doctrine is all the more significant in that a petition in favor of a definition of Mary Co-redemptrix of the human race was advanced by about fifty of the Fathers.[1] Nonetheless, while abstaining from attributing such a qualification to Mary, the Council did not at all reject the idea of a cooperation in the work of redemption. It underscored, in fact, the union of the Mother with the Son in the work of salvation, a union which "is made manifest from the time of Christ's virginal conception up to his death" (LG, n. 57). Such cooperation could be called coredemption, given that this term signifies in itself cooperation in the redemption, without further specification. The Council would have been able to use it without expressing any approval of a particular theology, as it did for the title of "mediatrix," which it introduced besides other appellations: advocate, helper, benefactress, in order not to give it precise technical meanings (LG, n. 62). Besides, it manifested a

---

[1] Cf. A. Perego, "Aperture conciliari per i titoli mariani di corredentrice e di mediatrice" in *Divus Thomas* 78 (1975) 364.

decided attachment to this title when it rejected an amendment that wanted to eliminate it because of the ambiguity which the term allowed relative to the unique mediation of Christ and to ecumenical opportuneness.[2] As compensation it rejected every use of the title Co-redemptrix.

If it avoided this title it was because the former was accused of suggesting Mary's role as too similar to that of Christ, a competition or an equality incompatible with the uniqueness of the Savior. Already in the 17th century A. Widenfeld had the Virgin say to "her indiscreet devotees": "Do not call me salvatrix or Co-redemptrix" so that nothing may be taken away from God.[3] In effect, the term "salvatrix" could stir up reservations and would require an explanation based on the nature of the Mother of the Savior; but the term "Co-redemptrix" does not allow for the same difficulty, since it clearly expresses a cooperation and does not endanger the sovereign action of Christ.

When it appeared in a hymn of the 15th century, it signaled an evolution with respect to the title of "redemptrix" which up till then was attributed to Mary as Mother of the Redeemer.[4] In this there was progress: "redemptrix" could have suggested a parallel or identical role to that of Christ, while "Co-redemptrix" indicated, in the hymn, "she who suffered with the Redeemer." At first, Mary was considered above all as the woman who gave birth to the Redeemer; by virtue of this maternity, the origin of the work of salvation was recognized in her and she was called "Mother of salvation," "Mother of the restoration of all things."[5] A more attentive doctrinal reflection had made it understood

---

[2] 61 Fathers had requested that the term "mediatrix" be omitted; cf. *Acta Synodalia Concilii Vaticani Secundi*, vol. III, 8, 163, s.

[3] A. Widenfeld, *Monita salutaria B. V. Mariae ad cultores suos indiscretos*, Gand, d'Erckel, 1673, 8-9, monitum 10.

[4] Cf. R. Laurentin, *Le titre de Corédemptrice. Étude historique*, Paris, Nouvelles Éditions Latines, 1951, 39 [and in *Marianum* 13 (1951) 395-452].

[5] Severinus of Gabala, *Or. 6 de mundi creatione* 10 (PG 54, 4); Saint Anselm, *Or. 52*, 7 (PL 158, 956 B); cf. J. Galot, *Maria la donna nell'opera di salvezza*, Roma, PUG, 1984, 362-364.

how Mary was not only the mother who had brought forth the Redeemer for mankind, but also she who had participated most especially in the sufferings of the Passion and in the offering of the sacrifice. The title of Co-redemptrix expresses this new perspective: the association of the mother in the redemptive work of the Son. One should note that this title does not challenge the absolute primacy of Christ, since it does not suggest at all an equality. Only Christ is called the Redeemer; he is not Co-redeemer, but simply Redeemer. In her role as Co-redemptrix, Mary offered her motherly collaboration in the work of her Son, a collaboration which implies dependence and submission, since only Christ is the absolute master of his own work.

The coredemption assumes a unique form in Mary, by virtue of her role as mother. Nevertheless, we must speak of coredemption in a much broader context in order to include all who are called to unite themselves to the work of redemption. In this sense all are destined to live as "coredeemers," and the Church herself is a Co-redemptrix. In this regard we cannot forget the affirmations of Paul on our participation in the redemptive path of Christ: in baptism we are "buried with Christ" (Rom. 6:4); in faith we are already "raised up with" him (Col. 2:13; 3:1); "God made us alive together with Christ ... and raised us up with him, and made us sit with him in the heavenly places in Christ Jesus" (Eph. 2:5-6). This participation results from the sovereign action of the Father, but it implies equally on our part a personal involvement. Having been made participants in the new life of Christ, we are capable of cooperating in the work of salvation. Saint Paul had a consciousness of his mission declaring: "We are God's co-workers" (I Cor. 3:9).

The affirmation is bold. The Apostle did not, however, lose his sense of divine transcendence and did not want to lay claim to an equality with God. His activity was guided by the divine design. Calling Jesus Lord, he recognized him as absolute master of his life and his activity; but this total dependence did not deprive him of the consciousness of truly cooperating with God. If all are called to be co-workers with God, according to the Pauline expression, "coredemption" assumes its broader extension. The debate stirred up over the legitimacy of the title "Co-redemptrix" helps us to better discover our own mission of coredemption.

Some have accused the Marian privileges of digging a furrow between the Mother of Jesus and us; in reality, those privileges are destined, in the divine plan, to draw Mary nearer to humanity in view of the unfolding of a more abundant grace. While with a unique character and to a level not to be equalled, Mary's cooperation in the redemption invites us to acknowledge more ardently our mission and our responsibility in a world that needs salvation. If Mary cannot be called Co-redemptrix, neither could Christians be considered as coredeemers. The condition of the whole Church in her coredeeming mission sheds light on Mary, the first model of every redemption.

The Unique Character of Coredemption

The unique character of the coredemption proper to Mary is manifested above all in the cooperation in the mystery of the Incarnation. With such cooperation Mary has exercised an influence on the entire work of salvation and on the destiny of all human beings. In her coredemption assumes a universal extension, which differentiates it from that of any other. In order to better understand such a difference, one must recall the distinction proposed by Scheeben and adopted by many theologians, between objective and subjective redemption. The first indicates the work which has acquired for mankind all the graces of salvation; such a work is accomplished with the death and glorification of Christ. In virtue of the objective redemption we can affirm that all men have been saved, even those who will be born in the future, to the end of the world. Nevertheless objective redemption concretely achieves its effect only by means of subjective redemption, that is by means of the application of the fruits of the redemptive sacrifice in individual persons. Such application is realized in the course of history, in all the men who live on earth, with the correspondence of their freedom. In Christians in particular this consists in their growth in grace which is favored by the sacraments and by the participation in the life of the Church. Redemptive grace enters into every person in order to transform him, in the measure of his openness and his responsiveness.

Mary personally cooperated in the increase of grace in her life. She likewise participated in the development of the primitive community; with her prayer, witness and action, she sustained the strength of the first disciples in their union with Christ and in their evangelizing mission. From this point of view she has been Co-redemptrix in the field of subjective redemption and her coredemption has taken the most pure and perfect form. Nonetheless, her coredemption is exercised above all in the work of the objective redemption. With her maternal cooperation in the birth of the Savior, Mary has contributed in an entirely singular manner to the gift of salvation for all mankind. She is the only creature that received the privilege of cooperating in the accomplishment of the objective redemption: her consent to the divine plan was decisive at the moment of the Annunciation.

The affirmation of the coredemption is not limited to shedding light on the maternal role which gained the Savior for humanity, but it also attributes to Mary a cooperation which has direct bearing on the redemptive sacrifice. While the greatness of the "Mother of God" has been affirmed from the first centuries, a longer time has been necessary in order to take explicitly into consideration her engagement in the redemptive sacrifice. In the East a byzantine monk at the end of the 10th century, John the Geometer, was the first to enunciate Mary's participation in the Passion with a redemptive intention.[6] In the West Saint Bernard (+ 1153) underscores with regard to the presentation of Jesus in the temple, the offering made by Mary for our reconciliation with God.[7] His disciple and friend, Arnold of Chartres (+ after 1156), in contemplating the sacrifice of Calvary discerns in the cross "two altars, one in the heart of Mary, the other in the body of Christ. Christ immolated his own flesh, Mary her own soul," "Both equally offered to God the same holocaust." In such a manner Mary "obtained with Christ the common goal of the salvation of the world."[8] Arnold has been called a protagonist of Marian coredemption, because he clearly expressed the most specific element that then would characterize the doctrine of the coredemption: a cooperation in the objective redemption not only with the maternity which gains the Savior for mankind (cooperation called mediate or indirect), but also with her association in the offering of the redemptive sacrifice (immediate or direct redemption).

Such cooperation in the redemptive work finds a solid foundation in the Gospel. The message of the Annunciation in fact enlightens Mary not only on the personality of her Son, but also on his messianic work, so that her consent implies a surrender to the service of this work. The presentation of Jesus in the Temple takes on a new meaning after the prophecy of Simeon, which gives Mary a glimpse of the sword destined to pierce her soul: the gesture of the offering of her Son is oriented toward a mysterious drama, to the point that one sees delineated here the first offering of the redemptive sacrifice, an offering more specifically maternal. The presence of Mary on Calvary, beside Christ crucified, manifests the will of the mother to unite herself to the intention of the Son and to share her suffering for the fulfillment of his work.

---

[6] Cf. ibid. 266-269.

[7] Saint Bernard, *Sermo 3 in Purif.*, 2 (PL 158, 370).

[8] Id., *De septem verbis Domini in cruce*, 3 (PL 158, 1.694); Id., *De laudibus B. M. V.* (PL 158, 1.726 s).

The Second Vatican Council clearly recognized such cooperation. In commenting on the response of Mary to the message of the angel, Vatican II affirmed that Mary "devoted herself totally, as a handmaid of the Lord, to the person and work of her Son, under and with him, serving the mystery of redemption, by the grace of Almighty God" (LG, n. 56). This places the accent on her continual union with Christ in the cooperation with his work: "She conceived, brought forth, and nourished Christ, she presented him to the Father in the temple, shared her Son's sufferings as he died on the cross. Thus, in a wholly singular way she cooperated by her obedience, faith, hope and burning charity in the work of the Savior in restoring supernatural life to souls. For this reason she is a mother to us in the order of grace" (ibid., n. 61).

Without using the term "Co-redemptrix," the Council clearly enunciated the doctrine: a cooperation of a unique kind, a maternal cooperation in the life and work of the Savior, which reaches its apex in the participation in the sacrifice of Calvary and which is oriented toward the supernatural restoration of souls. This cooperation is at the origin of Mary's spiritual maternity.

Mary Ransomed in order to be Co-redemptrix

The cooperation of Mary in the objective redemption poses with greater focus the problem of the one Savior. Jesus himself is considered as the only Redeemer, declaring that the Son of Man came to serve and "to give his life as a ransom for many" (Mk. 10:45; Mt. 20:28). There is no other ransom than his own life, no other font of salvation other than his sacrifice. This declaration finds an echo in the affirmation of the First Letter to Timothy: "For there is one God, and there is one mediator between God and men, the man Christ Jesus, who gave himself as a ransom for all" (I Tim. 2:5-6).

This last text has often been invoked in order to exclude both the coredemption and the title of mediatrix applied to Mary. Some do not cease to recall the affirmation about the unique mediator to combat the Marian doctrine. Nonetheless, as Vatican II has underscored: "the unique mediation of the Redeemer does not exclude but rather gives rise to a manifold cooperation which is but a sharing in this one source" (LG, n. 62). In her role of cooperation, Mary does not in any way enter into competition with Christ and neither does she become another fount of grace next to him. She receives from the unique Redeemer her aptitude to cooperate, hence Christ remains the unique fount. The Council enunciates more precisely this truth, which is essential for understanding the doctrine of the coredemption: the influence of the Virgin on the salvation of men "flows forth from the superabundance of the merits of Christ, rests on his mediation, depends entirely on it and draws all its power from it" (LG, n. 60).[9]

In the Letter to Timothy, clearly the principle of the oneness of the mediator does not exclude participated mediations, since the author recommends prayers and intercessions for all men, which is to say a mediation of intercession founded on the mediation of Christ. Further, it is appropriate to recall that the affirmation of the unique mediator who offers himself as a ransom for all simply transfers into terms consonant to the Greek language the word of Jesus about the Son of Man who has come to give his own life as a ransom for many.[10] Now, while enunciating his mission as that of the unique Savior, Jesus desired that his disciples share his attitude of service and sacrifice. In this sense he wanted their participation in his mission. It was not at all his intention to exclude any participation.

Nevertheless, the doctrine of participation in the objective

---

[9] On this participation in the mediation of Christ according to the doctrine of the Council, cf. John Paul II, Encyclical Letter *Redemptoris Mater*, n. 38.

[10] Cf. A. Feuillet, "Le logion sur la rançon," in *Revue des Sciences Philosophiques et Théologiques* 51 (1967) 374 s.

redemption had to face another objection. How could Mary contribute to the objective redemption when she herself needed to be redeemed? If she cooperates in such a redemption, it is because without her redemption is not yet accomplished. But in the case in which such redemption is not yet accomplished, she herself cannot benefit from it. The coredemption would suppose at the same time that the redemption is in the act of being accomplished and that it is already realized, something which is contradictory. The contradiction disappears when one understands the particular nature of the foreseen redemption which pertains to the Co-redemptrix. It is very true that Mary had to be ransomed in order to be able to collaborate actively in the work of salvation. One must also add that this condition of being ransomed contributes to give a sense to her cooperation: Mary is distinguished from Christ in her contribution to the work, not only because she is a simple creature and because she is a woman, but also because she has been ransomed. Her example helps us to understand better that even those who need to be redeemed are called to a collaboration in the work of redemption. In Mary, nevertheless, there is something unique: according to the Bull of the definition of the Immaculate Conception, she has been ransomed "in a more sublime manner."

This more elevated distinctiveness consists above all in the fact that Mary was ransomed before the redemption of all mankind was effected and in order that it be effected with her cooperation. The first intention of the redemptive sacrifice was concerned, according to the divine plan, with the ransom of Mary, accomplished in view of our ransom. Christ first ransomed his own mother, then with her collaboration the rest of mankind. Thus, while she was associated in the sacrifice of Calvary, Mary already benefited, in advance, from the fruits of the sacrifice and acted in the capacity of a ransomed creature. But she truly cooperated in the objective redemption, in the acquisition of the graces of salvation for all of mankind. Her redemption was purchased before that of other human beings. Mary was ransomed only by Christ, so that mankind could be ransomed by Christ with the collaboration of his mother. Hence there is no contradiction: coredemption implies the foreseen redemption of Mary, but not the foreseen fulfillment of the redemption of mankind; it expresses the unique situation of the mother who, while having received a singular grace from her own Son, cooperates with him in the attainment of salvation for all.

The Maternal Offering

How does one qualify exactly the attitude of Mary in the drama of Calvary? The first upholders of the coredemption in the West, Saint Bernard and Arnold of Chartres, defined this attitude as an offering: Mary offered her own Son or offered with her own Son one single holocaust. But it seems that at the time of the Council the affirmation of one offering provoked some resistance. In the draft submitted to the Council Fathers it said that Mary offered the victim whom she had brought forth, with Christ and through him; the revised text, however, was limited to saying that Mary consented with love to the immolation of the victim, because Vatican II did not wish to decide on a question which had been the object of recent discussions.

Even more particularly, some theologians preferred to speak of acceptance rather than offering. A German theologian, H. M. Köster, had published a work which had recalled to attention and presented the cooperation of Mary as a simple acceptance of the redemptive work accomplished by Christ.[11] Taking his point of reference from a theology of the Covenant, he recognized the necessity of consent in the work of salvation and affirmed that, as the representative of humanity, Mary had accepted the work accomplished by Christ, but without having

---

[11] H. M. Köster, *Die Magd des Herrn. Theologische Versuche und Überlegungen*, Limburg an der Lahn, Lahn, 1954.

associated herself actively. He wished to avoid the attribution to Mary of an action that would have been able to take away from Christ his property as being the unique Savior; hence he limited himself to the affirmation of a receptive causality.

Nevertheless, even a simple acceptance could not be assimilated to a pure passivity or receptivity. The acceptance of the message of the angel implied for Mary a commitment in the redemptive work. Further, the attitude of Mary was not limited to acceptance: in the presentation of Jesus in the temple she offers her own son knowing that this offering exposes her to the sword of sorrow. On Calvary she shows, with her deliberate presence next to the cross of her Son, that she wants to share in his sacrifice. Jesus himself accepts this intention to participate in his work conferring on her a new maternity.

While abstaining from speaking of offering, in order not to side with one theological opinion to the detriment of the other, the Council describes the participation of Mary in the drama of the Passion declaring that, in keeping with the divine design, "she suffered profoundly with her only begotten Son and associated herself with his sacrifice in her mother's heart" (LG, n. 58). The consent of love to the immolation of the victim afforded for her the deepest union with the redemptive sacrifice, meaning participation in the offering.

There is no reason to fear the affirmation of this offering, which is not a useless repetition of the offering of Christ nor in competition with it. It does not put in question the uniqueness of the sovereign offering of the Redeemer, rather it receives its reality from it. Mary does nothing but to offer her own Son and to offer herself and her personal pain only through her own Son. More particularly, the offering with which Mary is united with the redemptive sacrifice is not a priestly offering, which would imply for the mother participation in the priesthood of Jesus. It is a motherly offering, which has its particularity which differentiates it from the priestly offering. Having a maternal character, it is not a copy of the offering of Christ and has its own *raison d'être*. It offers a specific contribution to the human aspect of the drama of the Passion. This also clarifies the position of woman with regard to the priesthood. Mary is not engaged in the priestly ministry, but, in her capacity as woman, she plays an important and indispensable role in the work of salvation. She is profoundly engaged in the redemptive sacrifice by maternal right and offers a cooperation so necessary to the priestly work of Christ that the Father, in his sovereign design, required this feminine presence in order to grant salvation to the world.

Coredemptive Merit

Wholly associated with the redemptive sacrifice, Mary is united to the merit of Christ. With his offering the Redeemer merited the salvation of mankind. The maternal oblation of the Co-redemptrix has equally had a universal meritorious value, but a value which cannot diminish the proper effect of the priestly sacrifice of Christ. The Savior obtained for all men a superabundance of grace which admits of no deficiency and which cannot need a complement. Hence the problem: if Christ has merited all graces, what can be the object of the coredemptive merit of Mary?

The doctrinal studies which admit a sort of fusion between the cooperation of Mary and the redemptive activity of Jesus avoid the problem, so that the Mother and the Son form only one principle of salvific efficacy without it being necessary to distinguish between the part of the one and part of the other.[12] But such a radical way of conceiving of the association of Mary in the work of Christ is very debatable because it cannot recognize Christ as the unique Redeemer of mankind and because it

---

[12] Cf. J. Lebon, "Comment je conçois, j'établis et je défends la doctrine de la médiation mariale" in *Ephemerides Theologicae Lovanienses* 26 (1939) 655-744; R. Javelet, *L'unique médiateur Jésus et Marie*, Paris, OEIL, 1985.

tends to make of Mary a redemptrix united to the Redeemer. The majority of theologians who have reflected on the coredemption have sought that which could distinguish the merit of Mary from that of Christ. They affirmed that Mary merited by virtue of congruous merit [*di convenienza*], what Christ merited by condign merit [*di condignità*].[13] Condign merit is based on a proportion between the meritorious action and its object. Having the power of Savior, Jesus merited in strict justice (*de condigno*) the salvation of mankind since there is a proportion between the value of his redemptive offering and the benefits which revert to mankind. According to many theologians, however, Mary's merit could only be of congruity [*di convenienza*]: while not being proportioned to the salvation of mankind, it has been nevertheless elevated by divine intervention to a superior level of efficacy; thus Mary was able to contribute to meriting eternal salvation. The principle is often enunciated: "All that Christ merited in strict justice (*de condigno*), Mary merited by congruity (*de congruo*)," a principle adopted also in an encyclical of Pius X, with a slight modification of perspective.[14] Sometimes Mary's merit has also been called "supercongruous" by virtue of its exceptional excellence.[15]

Nevertheless such a solution which has been commonly proposed in order to indicate the distinction between the merit of Christ and that of Mary, encounters a fundamental difficulty: is not a merit which consists in obtaining by a lesser title what another merit has already obtained superfluous? Why should

---

[13] *Translator's note:* In rendering the terms *merito di convenienza* and *merito di condignità* into English, I have chosen to follow the convention of speaking of "congruous" and "condign" merit respectively, following the Latin rather than the Italian terminology; cf. the explanation of these terms in William G. Most, *Mary in Our Life* (New York: P. J. Kennedy & Sons, 1954) 24, n. 9 & 262. I have, however, indicated in brackets [] the original Italian terms of the author for the sake of accuracy.

[14] Pius X, Encyclical Letter *Ad diem illum* (2 February 1904) [Denz.-Schönm. 3370]: the present tense used to refer to Mary's merit (*promeret*) would seem to refer more than to the acquisition, to the distribution of grace.

[15] *De supercongruo*, an expression proposed by C. Dillenschneider, *Pour une Corédemption mariale bien comprise*, Rome, Marianum, 1949, 152.

one want to merit what has been acquired by the merit of others? All which was merited by Christ in the redemptive work must not — and cannot — constitute the object of another merit. The difficulty can be overcome only if one considers with greater attention in what consists the merit of Christ. Christ has merited with his sacrifice his glorious triumph; the first object of his merit is his resurrection. Meriting his own glorification, he merited for mankind the grace which is communicated by means of the power of the glorified Savior. The merit of Mary must be understood in the light of this merit of Christ. With her participation in the redemptive sacrifice, the Mother of Jesus merited her maternal power to collaborate in the distribution of grace. She merited the redemption under a particular aspect: the grace which reaches men by means of her maternal mediation. Here is the specific object of her merit. Mary properly merits the modality in virtue of which grace assumes a maternal aspect in order to be communicated to mankind. Thus is affirmed the difference which exists between her role and that of Christ.

From the Coredemption to the Motherhood of Grace

Recognizing the universal motherhood of Mary in the order of grace as the proper object of her merit in the cooperation in the redemptive sacrifice, one avoids every affirmation of a superfluous merit or something added over and above and is led to discern the value of the contribution of Mary to the work of salvation. More precisely it becomes possible to propose a solution which answers the doctrinal conflict on the nature of the merit, the conflict between those who limit themselves to attributing to Mary a congruous merit [*di convenienza*], by underscoring more clearly the primacy of Christ, and those who do not hesitate to affirm a condign merit [*di condignità*].

On the other hand, it is important to admit the proper congruity of the coredemptive activity of Mary. For the redemption of mankind such activity was not necessary, and the divine plan of salvation would have been able to foresee uniquely the redemptive action of the Son of God made man, without requiring the collaboration of his mother. In virtue of the redemptive sacrifice, mankind would have received in abundance the graces of salvation merited by Christ. But the divine plan provided for the maternal cooperation of Mary, assigning to the woman an essential role in the work of salvation. There was here a congruity with the divine intention of conferring on the woman all her dignity and to commit her fully in the undertaking of the restoration of the world. Such an intention was manifested in the oracle of the Protogospel, with the announcement of the struggle between the woman and the powers of evil. It was appropriate that to the association of the man and the woman in the drama of the fall there should correspond an association of the new Eve with the new Adam. From this perspective the coredemptive merit of Mary can be qualified as merit of suitability.

From the other side, in order to appreciate the value of that merit, it is also important to consider the conditions in which it reached its proper objective. One must ask above all if the property characteristic of the merit of strict justice [*di condignità*] verifies the proportion between the meritorious activity and the effect obtained. This proportion exists in Mary by virtue of her role as Mother of God, which permits her to acquire the role of mother of all men in the order of grace. As Mother of God, Mary possesses a motherhood open on the infinite, and precisely this motherhood becomes, with the coredemption, a universal motherhood for the distribution of grace. This universal motherhood — it is right to underscore this — is not simply the immediate consequence of the divine motherhood, but is the fruit of the sacrifice. The same is said in the first place for Christ, who did not become the Head of saved mankind solely in virtue of the Incarnation: it is in humiliating himself in the obedience of the cross that he merited his glorious power as Savior. Analogically, she who became the Mother of God in the mystery of the Incarnation merited, with her obedience and her maternal offering, the spiritual motherhood over all men. Jesus himself gives us to understand this truth when he pronounces the words on Calvary: "Woman, behold your son" (Jn. 19:26). Giving to Mary as son the beloved disciple, he asks her to accept the fulfillment of the sacrifice: Mary must accept losing her own only Son in order to receive another son. As the fruit of her union with the redemptive sacrifice, Mary becomes mother of the disciple, in a new motherhood which typifies a universal motherhood.

This makes clearer the proportion which characterizes the merit of the Co-redemptrix. Mother of God, Mary consented to lose her own Son, the Son of God, and received in exchange, as sons, all men destined to share the divine filiation of Jesus. She did not merit grace in its fundamental reality, but in the motherly modality with which it is communicated to mankind. Hence her coredemptive merit, while being condign merit [*di condignità*], has only a secondary value with respect to the merit of Christ. Christians cannot forget that, if they receive the affection and maternal help of Mary, they owe these to the sacrifice offered on Calvary by the Mother of the Redeemer. Mary paid a very high price, that of the coredemption, the motherhood which makes the Christian life more confident and more exultant.

The Mystery of Mary Coredemptrix in the Papal Magisterium

by Rev. Msgr. Arthur Burton Calkins

Fr. Calkins is an official of the Pontifical Commission "Ecclesia Dei" in Rome, a contributing member of the Pontifical International Marian Academy, and a corresponding member of the Pontifical Roman Theological Academy.

I. Introduction

In the course of almost two hundred years the papal Magisterium has provided ever clearer indications about Our Lady's intimate collaboration in the work of our redemption. In an earlier essay I outlined some major contributions of our present Holy Father in this regard.[1] In his general audience address of 25 October 1995 he contributed a masterful preamble on the development of this important point of doctrine. In broad strokes it sketches the historical unfolding of this doctrine in a remarkably succinct way:

> Saying that "the Virgin Mary . . . is acknowledged and honoured as being truly the Mother of God and of the Re-

---

[1] Cf. Arthur Burton Calkins, "Pope John Paul II's Teaching on Marian Coredemption" in *Foundations II*:113-147. Cf. also my study, "The Heart of Mary as Coredemptrix in the Magisterium of Pope John Paul II" in *S. Tommaso Teologo: Ricerche in occasione dei due centenari accademici* (Vatican City: Libreria Editrice Vaticana "Studi Tomistici #59," 1995) 320-335. Cf. Key to Abbreviations pp. 90-92.

deemer" (*Lumen Gentium*, n. 53), the Council draws attention to the link between Mary's motherhood and Redemption.

After becoming aware of the maternal role of Mary, who was venerated in the teaching and worship of the first centuries as the virginal Mother of Jesus Christ and therefore as the Mother of God, in the Middle Ages the Church's piety and theological reflection brought to light her cooperation in the Saviour's work.

This delay is explained by the fact that the efforts of the Church Fathers and of the early Ecumenical Councils, focused as they were on Christ's identity, necessarily left other aspects of dogma aside. Only gradually could the revealed truth be unfolded in all its richness. Down the centuries, Mariology would always take its direction from Christology. The divine motherhood of Mary was itself proclaimed at the Council of Ephesus primarily to affirm the oneness of Christ's person. Similarly, there was a deeper understanding of Mary's presence in salvation history.

At the end of the second century, St. Irenaeus, a disciple of Polycarp, already pointed out Mary's contribution to the work of salvation. He understood the value of Mary's consent at the time of the Annunciation, recognizing in the Virgin of Nazareth's obedience to and faith in the angel's message the perfect antithesis of Eve's disobedience and disbelief, with a beneficial effect on humanity's destiny. In fact, just as Eve caused death, so Mary, with her "yes," became "a cause of salvation" for herself and for all mankind (cf. *Adv. Haer.*, III, 22, 4; *SC* 211, 441). But this affirmation was not developed in a consistent and systematic way by the other Fathers of the Church.

Instead, this doctrine was systematically worked out for the first time at the end of the 10th century in the *Life of Mary* by a Byzantine monk, John the Geometer. Here Mary is united to Christ in the whole work of Redemption, sharing, according to God's plan, in the Cross and suffering for our salvation. She remained united to the Son "in every deed, attitude and wish" (cf. *Life of Mary*, Bol. 196, f. 123 v.).

In the West St. Bernard, who died in 1153, turns to Mary and comments on the presentation of Jesus in the temple: "Offer your Son, sacrosanct Virgin, and present the fruit of your womb to the Lord. For our reconciliation with all, offer the heavenly victim pleasing to God" (*Serm. 3 in Purif.*, 2: *PL* 183, 370).

A disciple and friend of St. Bernard, Arnold of Chartres, shed light particularly on Mary's offering in the sacrifice of Calvary. He distinguished in the Cross "two altars: one in Mary's heart, the other in Christ's body. Christ sacrificed his flesh, Mary her soul." Mary sacrificed herself spiritually in deep communion with Christ, and implored the world's salvation: "What the mother asks, the Son approves and the Father grants" (cf. *De septem verbis Domini in cruce*, 3: *PL* 189, 1694).

From this age on other authors explain the doctrine of Mary's special cooperation in the redemptive sacrifice.[2]

As the Holy Father, then, has already traced the high points of this theme in its theological development, I will attempt to indicate the major developments of this subject in the papal magisterium itself. Following the slow course of this theological development, the specific focus of the papal magisterium on Mary's collaboration in the work of the redemption is a relatively recent one.[3] Only after pondering over this mystery at length, like Mary herself,[4] does the Church begin to teach about it in a more solemn way.

---

[2] *Inseg* XVIII/2 (1995) 934-935 [*ORE* 1414:11; *MCat* 25-27].
[3] Cf. Carol, "Our Lady's Coredemption," *Mariology* 2:382; Robichaud, "Mary, Dispensatrix of All Graces," *Mariology* 2:429.
[4] Cf. Lk. 2:19, 51.

A. Modern Period: 1740 to Present

It would, no doubt, be highly instructive and interesting to search out the first adumbrations of the doctrine of Marian mediation in the teaching of the popes in the earlier periods of the Church's life, but we must leave this to other researchers.[5] According to widely accepted convention, the modern period of the codification of the papal magisterium begins with the pontificate of Benedict XIV (1740-1758)[6] while a further notable concentration and consolidation of Marian doctrine begins with the pontificate of Blessed Pius IX (1846-1878). It is precisely this modern period of the papal Magisterium that we intend to study here.

B. Intimate Connection between Coredemption and Mediation

Finally, we must clarify one further point before we begin to analyze the papal texts themselves. From at least the beginning of the twentieth century authors have consistently treated Marian coredemption and mediation together under the general title of "mediation."[7] The founder of the Marianum, the Roman theological faculty specializing in the study of Mariology, Father Gabriele M. Roschini, O.S.M., for instance, stated that some Mariologists restrict the title of "Mediatrix" to the second

---

[5] Armand J. Robichaud, S.M. supplies only one reference for this early period, that to Sixtus IV (1471-1484), in "Mary, Dispensatrix of All Graces," *Mariology* 2:429.

[6] This is the standard practice of compilations such as *Our Lady: Papal Teachings*, trans. Daughters of St. Paul (Boston: St. Paul Editions, 1961); Claudia Carlen, I.H.M., *The Papal Encyclicals, 1740-1980* (Ann Arbor: The Pierian Press, 1990, c. 1981); ibid., *Papal Pronouncements: A Guide, 1740-1978* (Ann Arbor: The Pierian Press, 1990) and Ugo Bellochi (ed.), *Tutte le encicliche e i principali documenti pontifici emanati dal 1740* (Vatican City State: Libreria Editrice Vaticana, 1993 —) I —.

[7] Cf. the classic work of E. Druwé, S.J., "La Médiation universelle de Marie," in *Maria* I in which the first part of the study (pp. 427-537) deals with the doctrine of Mary's collaboration in the work of redemption and the second part (pp. 538-568) treats Our Lady's mediation or distribution of grace.

phase of mediation (to the cooperation of Mary in the distribution of grace), reserving the title "Coredemptrix" to the first phase, but even this first phase, he argues, is a true and proper mediation since it is a participation in the mediatorial work of Christ.[8] This follows logically from the fact that both of these phases may be seen as subdivisions of the broad category of "Marian mediation" or what the late Father Giuseppe Besutti had consistently described in his *Bibliografia Mariana* since 1968 as "Mary in salvation history [*historia salutis*]."[9] These two phases of the redemption are often differentiated as "objective" and "subjective," as well as by other distinctions.[10] Indeed, many of the pontifical documents which we will examine clearly teach that Our Lady's cooperation in the distribution of grace flows directly from her coredemptive role.[11] For this reason we will find that not a few of the papal texts which we will cite in support of Marian coredemption may also be justly cited in support of Mary's role in the distribution of the graces of the redemption.

II. A Matter of Terminology

The term Coredemptrix usually requires some initial explanation in the English language because often the prefix "co" immediately conjures up visions of complete equality. For instance a co-signer of a check or a co-owner of a house is considered a co-equal with the other signer or owner. Thus the first

---

[8] Gabriele M. Roschini, O.S.M., *Dizionario di Mariologia* (Rome: Editrice Studium, 1961) 323.

[9] Cf. Giuseppe M. Besutti, O.S.M., *Bibliografia Mariana 1958-1966* (Roma: Edizioni «Marianum», 1968) 194-205; *Bibliografia Mariana 1967-1972* (1974) 164-167; *Bibliografia Mariana 1973-1977* (1980) 155-158; *Bibliografia Mariana 1978-1984* (1988) 256-259; *Bibliografia Mariana 1985-1989* (1993) 328-333.

[10] These distinctions are carefully delineated in Carol, "Our Lady's Coredemption," *Mariology* 2:380-381.

[11] Cf. Mark I. Miravalle, S.T.D., *Mary: Coredemptrix, Mediatrix, Advocate* (Santa Barbara, CA: Queenship Publishing, 1993) xvi.

fear of many is that describing Our Lady as Coredemptrix puts her on the same level as her Divine Son and implies that she is "Redeemer" in the same way that he is, thus reducing Jesus "to being half of a team of redeemers."[12] In the Latin language from which the term Coredemptrix comes, however, the meaning is always that Mary's cooperation or collaboration in the redemption is secondary, subordinate, dependent on that of Christ — and yet for all that — something that God "freely wished to accept . . . as constituting an unneeded, but yet wonderfully pleasing part of that one great price"[13] paid by His Son for the world's redemption. As Mark Miravalle points out:

> The prefix "co" does not mean equal, but comes from the Latin word, *"cum"* which means "with." The title of *Coredemptrix* applied to the Mother of Jesus *never places Mary on a level of equality with Jesus Christ, the divine Lord of all, in the saving process of humanity's redemption*. Rather, it denotes Mary's singular and unique *sharing with her Son* in the saving work of redemption for the human family. The Mother of Jesus *participates* in the redemptive work of her *Saviour Son, who alone could reconcile humanity with the Father in his glorious divinity and humanity*.[14]

While one might argue about the use of the term Coredemptrix[15] because of the possible confusion which might result from it and propose Pius XII's term of predilection, *alma socia Christi* (beloved associate of Christ),[16] it is equally argu-

---

[12] Eamon R. Carroll, O.Carm., *Understanding the Mother of Jesus* (Wilmington, DE: Michael Glazier, Inc., 1979) 93.

[13] William G. Most, "Reparation to the Immaculate Heart," *Cross and Crown* 8 (1956) 139.

[14] Miravalle xv.

[15] On its origin, diffusion and the *status quæstionis* on its use up to 1969, cf. *Prob* 14-23.

[16] Cf. *Prob* 75; *Theotokos* 54. Pius' preference had to do with the theological disputes on this question which only came to a resolution at the Mariological Congress at Lourdes in 1958 shortly before his death. On this matter, cf. *Il "calvario"* 13.

able that there is no other word which places the participation of the Mother of God in our redemption in such sharp and bold relief.[17] Furthermore, as we shall see, it has been hallowed by use, especially by magisterial use both in the past and in the present.

A. First Uses in the Magisterium

The word "Coredemptrix" makes its preliminary appearance on the magisterial level by means of official pronouncements of Roman Congregations during the reign of Pope Saint Pius X (1903-1914) and then enters into the papal vocabulary.

1. The term first occurs in the *Acta Apostolicæ Sedis* in a response to a request made by Father Giuseppe M. Lucchesi, Prior General of the Servites (1907-1913), requesting the elevation of the rank of the feast of the Seven Sorrows of Our Lady to a double of the second class for the entire Church. The Sacred Congregation of Rites, in acceding to the request, expressed the desire that thus "the cultus of the Sorrowful Mother may increase and the piety of the faithful and their gratitude toward *the merciful Coredemptrix* of the human race may intensify."[18]

2. Five years later the Sacred Congregation of the Holy Office in a decree signed by Cardinal Mariano Rampolla expressed its satisfaction with the practice of adding to the name of Jesus that of Mary in the greeting "Praised be Jesus and Mary" to which one responds "Now and forever":

> There are Christians who have such a tender devotion toward her who is the most blessed among virgins as to be unable to recall the name of Jesus without accompanying it with the glorious name of the Mother, *our Coredemptrix*, the Blessed Virgin Mary.[19]

---

[17] Cf. Juniper Carol's able handling of the objections in his masterful article, "Our Lady's Coredemption," *Mariology* 2:422-424.

[18] *AAS* 1 (1908) 409; my trans. (emphasis my own); cf. Laurentin 23; *Prob* 21.

[19] *AAS* 5 (1913) 364; my trans. (emphasis my own); cf. Laurentin 24; *Prob* 21.

3. Barely six months after this declaration, on 22 January 1914, the same Congregation granted a partial indulgence of 100 days for the recitation of a prayer of reparation to Our Lady beginning with the Italian words *Vergine benedetta*. Here is the portion of that prayer which bears on our argument:

> O blessed Virgin, Mother of God, look down in mercy from Heaven, where thou art enthroned as Queen, upon me, a miserable sinner, thine unworthy servant. Although I know full well my own unworthiness, yet in order to atone for the offenses that are done to thee by impious and blasphemous tongues, from the depths of my heart I praise and extol thee as the purest, the fairest, the holiest creature of all God's handiwork. I bless thy holy Name, I praise thine exalted privilege of being truly Mother of God, ever Virgin, conceived without stain of sin, *Coredemptrix of the human race*.[20]

On the basis of these last two instances Monsignor Brunero Gherardini comments that

> The authority of that dicastery [the Sacred Congregation of the Holy Office], now designated as 'for the Doctrine of the Faith', is such as to confer on its interventions a certain definitive character for Catholic thought.[21]

4. The first papal usage of the term occurs in an allocution by Pope Pius XI (1922-1939) to pilgrims from Vicenza on 30 November 1933:

> From the nature of His work the Redeemer ought to have

---

[20] *AAS* 6 (1914) 108; Joseph P. Christopher, Charles E. Spence and John F. Rowan (eds.), *The Raccolta* (Boston: Benziger Brothers, Inc., 1957) #329, pp. 228-229 (it should be noted that the English translation is rendered in the first person plural whereas the Italian is in the first person singular; emphasis my own); cf. Laurentin 24-25; *Prob* 21.

[21] Brunero Gherardini, *La Madre: Maria in una sintesi storico-teologica* (Frigento [AV]: Casa Mariana Editrice, 1989) 271 (my trans.).

associated His Mother with His work. For this reason *We invoke her under the title of Coredemptrix*. She gave us the Savior, she accompanied Him in the work of Redemption as far as the Cross itself, sharing with Him the sorrows of the agony and of the death in which Jesus consummated the Redemption of mankind.[22]

5. On 23 March 1934, the Lenten commemoration of Our Lady of Sorrows, Pius XI received two groups of Spanish pilgrims, one of which was composed of members of Marian Congregations of Catalonia. *L'Osservatore Romano* did not publish the text of the Pope's address, but rather reported his principal remarks to these groups. Noting with pleasure the Marian banners carried by these pilgrims, he commented that they had come to Rome to celebrate with the Vicar of Christ

not only the nineteenth centenary of the divine Redemption, but also *the nineteenth centenary of Mary, the centenary of her Coredemption, of her universal maternity.*[23]

He continued, addressing himself especially to the young people, saying that they must:

follow the way of thinking and the desire of Mary most holy, who is *our Mother and our Coredemptrix: they, too, must make a great effort to be coredeemers and apostles*, according to the spirit of Catholic Action, which is precisely the cooperation of the laity in the hierarchical apostolate of the Church.[24]

6. Finally, Pope Pius XI referred to Our Lady as

---

[22] Domenico Bertetto, S.D.B., ed., *Discorsi di Pio XI* 2:1013; *OL* #326 (emphasis my own); cf. Laurentin 26; Carol, "Our Lady's Coredemption," *Mariology* 2:384.
[23] *OR* 25 marzo 1934, p. 1 (my trans.; emphasis my own).
[24] *OR* 25 marzo 1934, p. 1 (my trans.; emphasis my own); cf. *Prob* 21; Laurentin 26-27. Laurentin comments that coredeemer here is simply a synonym for apostle in the larger sense of the word!

Coredemptrix on 28 April 1935 in a Radio Message for the closing of the Holy Year at Lourdes:

> Mother most faithful and most merciful, who as *Coredemptrix and partaker of thy dear Son's sorrows* didst assist Him as He offered the sacrifice of our Redemption on the altar of the Cross . . . preserve in us and increase each day, we beseech thee, the precious fruits of our Redemption and thy compassion.[25]

Because of this usage of the term Coredemptrix in magisterial documents and addresses by the Supreme Pontiff, Canon René Laurentin wrote thus in 1951 about its employment:

> Used or protected by two popes, even in the most humble exercise of their supreme magisterium, the term henceforth requires our respect. It would be gravely temerarious, at the very least, to attack its legitimacy.[26]

Since that rather nuanced statement the well known French scholar has long since altered his position, saying that:

> The title of "Coredemptrix" which was coined for her [Mary] and widely attributed to her by Mariologists, though not retained by the papal magisterium or by Vatican II, would fit the Holy Spirit in the primary and strictest sense of the term.[27]

Nonetheless, we believe that his earlier defense of the legitimacy of the term may stand on its own. We shall subsequently

---

[25] *OR* 29-30 aprile 1935, p. 1; *OL* #334 (emphasis my own); cf. Laurentin 27; Carol, "Our Lady's Coredemption," *Mariology* 2:384.

[26] Laurentin 27-28 (my trans.); emphasis my own.

[27] René Laurentin, *A Short Treatise on the Virgin Mary* trans. Charles Neumann, S.M. (Washington, NJ: AMI Press, 1991) 242-243. For an extensive analysis and refutation of this claim, cf. Alessandro Apollonio, F.I., "The Holy Spirit and Mary Coredemptrix" in *Mary at the Foot of the Cross: Acts of the International Symposium on Marian Coredemption* (New Bedford, MA: Academy of the Immaculate, 2001) 61-83 (esp. 77-80).

note that the term has been retained by the papal magisterium.

B. *The Second Vatican Council*

A further argument brought up against the use of this term is that it was specifically avoided by the Second Vatican Council. While this statement is true, it requires a number of clarifications. First, it must be remembered that the Council was convoked just at a time when Marian doctrine and piety had reached an apex[28] which had been building on a popular level since the apparition of Our Lady to Saint Catherine Labouré in 1830[29] and on the magisterial level since the time of the dogmatic definition of the Immaculate Conception on 8 December 1854.[30] This Marian orientation had accelerated notably during the nineteen-year reign of the Servant of God Pope Pius XII (1939-1958) with the Consecration of the world to the Immaculate Heart of Mary on 31 October 1942,[31] the dogmatic definition of the Assumption of Our Lady on 1 November 1950,[32] the establishment of the Feast of the Immaculate Heart of Mary in 1944[33] and of the Queenship of Mary in the Marian Year of 1954.[34]

Secondly, and as a consequence of this comprehensive "Marian movement," much study, discussion and debate had

---

[28] Cf. Michael O'Carroll, C.S.Sp., "Still Mediatress of All Graces?" *Miles Immaculatæ* 24 (1988) 121-122; *Theotokos* 351-352.

[29] This apparition of Our Lady would be succeeded by a number of others in the nineteenth and twentieth centuries which would eventually be recognized by the Church as worthy of credence. Two popular books which trace these events are Don Sharkey, *The Woman Shall Conquer* (Milwaukee: The Bruce Publishing Company, 1952) and John Beevers, *The Sun Her Mantle* (Westminster, MD: The Newman Press, 1954).

[30] Cf. *Theotokos* 179-180. Interestingly, Father O'Carroll acknowledges an impetus for the definition in the apparition of 1830, cf. *Theotokos* 182.

[31] Cf. *Totus Tuus* 98-101.

[32] Cf. *Theotokos* 55-56.

[33] Cf. *Totus Tuus* 100.

[34] Cf. *Totus Tuus* 104-105.

been devoted to Mary's role in salvation history, specifically to the topics of coredemption and mediation.[35] While there had been vigorous disputation regarding Mary's active collaboration in the work of our redemption during the reign of Pope Pius XII, by the the time of the International Mariological Congress in Lourdes in 1958 there was a fairly unanimous consensus regarding Our Lady's true cooperation in acquiring the universal grace of redemption.[36] Not surprisingly, then, a good number of bishops entered the Council with the desire to see a comprehensive treatment of these questions. Father Michael O'Carroll, C.S.Sp. informs us that of the 54 bishops at the Council who wanted a conciliar pronouncement on Mary as Coredemptrix, 36 sought a definition and 11 a dogma of faith on this matter.[37] On the related question of Mary's mediation, he tells us that 362 bishops desired a conciliar statement on Mary's mediation while 266 of them asked for a dogmatic definition.[38] Father Besutti, on the other hand, holds that over 500 bishops were asking for such a definition.[39] A fundamental reason why no such definition emanated from the Council was the expressed

---

[35] Instances of such study may be seen in the International Mariological Congresses held in Rome in 1950 and in Lourdes in 1958. The second volume of the proceedings of the 1950 congress and the fourth volume of the 1958 congress are almost completely devoted to the theme of Marian coredemption and mediation. Cf. *De cooperatione B. V. Mariæ in acquisitione et distributione gratiarum* Vol. II of *Alma Socia Christi: Acta Congressus Internationalis Mariologici-Mariani, Romæ Anno MCML celebrati* (Rome: Academia Mariana, 1952) and *Cooperatio B. V. Mariæ et Ecclesiæ ad Christi redemptionem* Vol IV of *Maria et Ecclesia: Acta Congressus Internationalis Mariologici-Mariani, in civitate Lourdes Anno MCMLVIII celebrati* (Rome: Academia Mariana, 1959).

[36] Cf. *Il "calvario"* 7-8.

[37] Cf. *Theotokos* 308.

[38] Cf. Michael O'Carroll, C.S.Sp., "Mary's Mediation: Vatican II and John Paul II" in *Virgo Liber Verbi: Miscellanea di studi in onore di P. Giuseppe M. Besutti, O.S.M.* (Rome: Edizioni «Marianum», 1991) 543; *Theotokos* 352. In the latter article Father O'Carroll gives the number of Fathers asking for a statement on Mary's mediation as 382.

[39] G. Besutti, O.S.M., *Lo schema mariano al Concilio Vaticano II* (Rome: Edizioni Marianum-Desclée, 1966) 17.

will of Blessed Pope John XXIII that the Council was to be primarily pastoral in its orientation, specifically excluding any new dogmatic definitions.[40]

Thirdly, at the very same time another current was entering into the mainstream of Catholic life, that of "ecumenical sensitivity." While Father Besutti confirms that the word "Coredemptrix" did appear in the original *schema* of the Marian document prepared in advance for the Council,[41] the *Prænotanda* to the first conciliar draft document or *schema* on Our Lady contained these words:

> Certain expressions and words used by Supreme Pontiffs have been omitted, which, in themselves are absolutely true, but which may only be understood with difficulty by separated brethren (in this case Protestants). Among such words may be numbered the following: "Coredemptrix of the human race" [Pius X, Pius XI] . . .[42]

This original prohibition was rigorously respected and hence the term "Coredemptrix" was not used in any of the official documents promulgated by the Council and, undeniably, "ecumenical sensitivity" was a prime factor in its avoidance[43] along with a dissatisfaction for the general language of mediation on the part of more progressive theologians.[44] We remain free to debate about the wisdom and effectiveness of such a strategy.[45]

---

[40] Cf. *Il "calvario"* 14.

[41] *Lo schema* 28-29.

[42] . . . *Acta Synodalia Sacrosancti Concilii Oecumenici Vaticani Secundi*, Vol., I, Pt. IV (Typis Polyglottis Vaticanis, 1971) 99; my trans. Cf. Gabriele M. Roschini, O.S.M., *Maria Santissima nella Storia della Salvezza* II (Isola del Liri: Tipografia M. Pisani, 1969) 111-112.

[43] Cf. Thomas Mary Sennott, O.S.B., "Mary Mediatrix of All Graces, Vatican II and Ecumenism," *Miles Immaculatæ* 24 (1988) 151-167; *Theotokos* 242-245.

[44] Cf. Ralph M. Wiltgen, S.V.D., *The Rhine Flows Into the Tiber: A History of Vatican II* (Rockford, IL: Tan Books and Publishers, Inc., 1985, c. 1967) 90-95, 153-159.

[45] Cf. my article "'Towards Another Marian Dogma?' A Response to Father Angelo Amato," *Marianum* LIX (1997) 163-165.

C. Lumen Gentium Chapter 8

Given these disparate currents present on the floor of the Council, one might have expected a doctrinal minimalism to prevail on the entire question of Marian coredemption/mediation. While the climate at the Second Vatican Council was not auspicious for its full assimilation, solid groundwork was laid, especially with regard to the topic of Marian coredemption or Mary's collaboration in the work of the redemption. Here is how Pope John Paul II summarized the matter in his general audience of 13 December 1995:

> During the Council sessions, many Fathers wished further to enrich Marian doctrine with other statements on Mary's role in the work of salvation. *The particular context in which Vatican II's Mariological debate took place did not allow these wishes, although substantial and widespread, to be accepted,* but the Council's entire discussion of Mary remains vigorous and balanced, and the topics themselves, though not fully defined, received significant attention in the overall treatment.
>
> Thus, the hesitation of some Fathers regarding the title of Mediatrix did not prevent the Council from using this title once, and *from stating in other terms Mary's mediating role from her consent to the Angel's message to her motherhood in the order of grace* (cf. *Lumen Gentium*, n. 62). Furthermore, the Council asserts her cooperation "in a wholly singular way" in the work of restoring supernatural life to souls (ibid., n. 61).[46]

This is an astute observation made by one who has continued to meditate on and develop these very themes. To my knowledge, it is the first official public acknowledgement on the part of a Pope of the currents at the Council which shaped the writing of chapter 8 of *Lumen Gentium*. It also makes graceful and

---

[46] *Inseg* XVIII/2 (1995) 1369-1370 [*ORE* 1421:13; *MCat* 51-52]; emphasis my own.

unprejudiced reference to the Fathers who "wished further to enrich Marian doctrine with other statements on Mary's role in the work of salvation."

While the term "Coredemptrix" does not occur anywhere in the Council documents, it must be recognized that the concept was nonetheless conveyed. In fact, the Council taught much more clearly and coherently about Mary's coredemptive role than about her role in the distribution of grace, even if the word "Mediatrix" was used once in #62. Thus *Lumen Gentium* #56 speaks forthrightly of Mary's collaboration in the work of redemption:

> Committing herself whole-heartedly to God's saving will and impeded by no sin, she devoted herself totally, as a handmaid of the Lord, to the person and work of her Son, under and with him, serving the mystery of redemption, by the grace of Almighty God.[47]

In the same paragraph there is further specification about the active nature of Mary's service:

> Rightly, therefore, the Fathers see Mary not merely as passively engaged by God, but as freely cooperating in the work of man's salvation through faith and obedience. For, as St. Irenaeus says, she "being obedient, became the cause of salvation for herself and for the whole human race." Hence not a few of the early Fathers gladly assert with him in their preaching: "the knot of Eve's disobedience was untied by Mary's obedience: what the virgin Eve bound through her disbelief, Mary loosened by her faith." Comparing Mary with Eve, they call her "Mother of the living," and frequently claim: "death through Eve, life through Mary."[48]

---

[47] *CDD* 195; Flannery 416 (I have altered the word order of the translation found in Flannery).

[48] *CDD* 195; Flannery 416.

Quite clearly, then, the Council Fathers speak of an active collaboration of Mary in the work of the redemption and they illustrate this with the Eve/Mary parallel, found already in the writings of the sub-Apostolic Fathers, Saint Justin Martyr (+165), Irenaeus (+ after 193) and Tertullian (+ 220).[49]

Further, the Council Fathers move on from the establishment of the general principle of Mary's collaboration in the work of the redemption to underscore the personal nature of the "union of the mother with the Son in the work of salvation" [*Matris cum Filio in opere salutari coniunctio*] throughout Jesus' hidden life (#57) and public life (#58). Finally, in #58 they stress how she

> faithfully persevered in her union with her Son unto the cross, where she stood, in keeping with the divine plan, enduring with her only begotten Son the intensity of his suffering, associated herself with his sacrifice in her mother's heart, and lovingly consenting to the immolation of this victim which was born of her.[50]

Not only, then, does the Council teach that Mary was generally associated with Jesus in the work of redemption throughout his life, but that she associated herself with his sacrifice and consented to it. Furthermore, the Council Fathers state in #61 that Mary:

> shared her Son's sufferings as he died on the cross. Thus, in a wholly singular way she cooperated by her obedience, faith, hope and burning charity in the work of the Savior in restoring supernatural life to souls.[51]

Not only did Mary consent to the sacrifice, but she also united herself to it. In these final two statements we find a synthesis of

---

[49] Cf. *Theotokos* 139-141.
[50] *CDD* 197; Flannery 417.
[51] *CDD* 199; Flannery 418.

the previous papal teaching on the coredemption as well as a stable point of reference for the teaching of the postconciliar Popes.

Monsignor Brunero Gherardini points out that, with or without the use of the term Coredemptrix, the Protestant observers recognized just as readily the Catholic position on Mary's participation in the redemption. They see any human participation in the work of man's salvation, however secondary and subordinate, as contrary to Luther's principle of *solus Christus* and thus "a robbery from God and from Christ."[52] Hence in elaborating the magisterial teaching on Mary's collaboration in the redemption, we are dealing with more than just the possible justification of the term Coredemptrix, but a fundamental datum of Catholic theology, a matter which will not be facilely dealt with in ecumenical dialogue by simply substituting one word or phrase with another which seems more neutral.[53]

D. Usage of the Term by John Paul II

Given this recent history, it is of no little significance that without fanfare, but quite publicly, John Paul II has rehabilitated the word Coredemptrix and has used it or a cognate form at least six times in published statements, not to mention his far more numerous references to the concept which this term represents. Let us quickly review his usage of Coredemptrix.[54]

1. In his greetings to the sick after the general audience of 8 September 1982 the Pope said:

Mary, though conceived and born without the taint of sin, participated in a marvelous way in the sufferings of her di-

---

[52] Gherardini 281.

[53] Cf. Roschini, *Maria Santissima nella Storia della Salvezza* II:113.

[54] For the sake of consistency in usage I have regularly capitalized the word Coredemptrix and spelled it without a hyphen. The translations in the weekly English edition of *L'Osservatore Romano* [*ORE*] have varied with regard to capitalization and have regularly rendered it Co-redemptrix.

vine Son, in order to be *Coredemptrix of humanity.*[55]

2. On the Feast of his patron saint, Charles Borromeo, in 1984 the Pope offered these thoughts in his Angelus address in Arona:

> To Our Lady — *the Coredemptrix* — St. Charles turned with singularly revealing accents. Commenting on the loss of the twelve-year-old Jesus in the Temple, he reconstructed the interior dialogue that could have run between the Mother and the Son, and he added, "You will endure much greater sorrows, O blessed Mother, and you will continue to live; but life will be for you a thousand times more bitter than death. You will see your innocent Son handed over into the hands of sinners . . . You will see him brutally crucified between thieves; you will see his holy side pierced by the cruel thrust of a lance; finally, you will see the blood that you gave him spilling. And nevertheless you will not be able to die!" (From the homily delivered in the Cathedral of Milan the Sunday after the Epiphany, 1584).[56]

3. On 31 January 1985, in an address at the Marian shrine in Guayaquil, Ecuador, he spoke thus:

> Mary goes before us and accompanies us. The silent journey that begins with her Immaculate Conception and passes through the "yes" of Nazareth, which makes her the Mother of God, finds on Calvary a particularly important moment. There also, *accepting and assisting at the sacrifice of her son,* Mary is the dawn of Redemption; . . . *Crucified spiritually with her crucified son* (cf. Gal. 2:20), she contemplated with heroic love the death of her God, she "lovingly consented to the immolation of this Victim which she herself had brought forth" (*Lumen Gentium,* 58). . . .

---

[55] *Inseg* V/3 (1982) 404; my trans.; emphasis my own.
[56] *Alla Madonna — la Corredentrice — San Carlo si rivolge con accenti singolarmente rivelatori. Inseg* VII/2 (1984) 1151 [*ORE* 860:1]; emphasis my own.

In fact, at Calvary *she united herself with the sacrifice of her Son that led to the foundation of the Church; her maternal heart shared to the very depths the will of Christ "to gather into one all the dispersed children of God"* (Jn. 11:52). *Having suffered for the Church*, Mary deserved to become the Mother of all the disciples of her Son, the Mother of their unity. . . .

The Gospels do not tell us of an appearance of the risen Christ to Mary. Nevertheless, as she was in a special way close to the Cross of her Son, she also had to have a privileged experience of his Resurrection. In fact, *Mary's role as Coredemptrix* did not cease with the glorification of her Son.[57]

In the above text we have a fine illustration of the various ways in which Mary's collaboration in the redemption is described by the Pope, culminating in his reference to her "role as Coredemptrix." It should be noted that he presents Mary's coredemptive role here with reference to Paul's statement, "I have been crucified with Christ" (Gal. 2:20) and also with reference to the mystery of her Heart.

4. On 31 March 1985, Palm Sunday and World Youth Day, the Pope spoke in this vein about Mary's immersion in the mystery of Christ's Passion:

At the Angelus hour on this Palm Sunday, which the Liturgy calls also the Sunday of the Lord's Passion, our thoughts run to Mary, immersed in the mystery of an immeasurable sorrow.

Mary accompanied her divine Son in the most discreet concealment pondering everything in the depths of her heart. On Calvary, at the foot of the Cross, in the vastness and in the depth of her maternal sacrifice, she had John, the youngest Apostle, beside her. . . .

May, Mary our Protectress, *the Coredemptrix*, to whom we offer our prayer with great outpouring, make our desire

---

[57] *Inseg* VIII/1 (1985) 318-319 [*ORE* 876:7]; emphasis my own.

generously correspond to the desire of the Redeemer.[58]

5. On 24 March 1990 the Holy Father addressed volunteer participants in the pilgrimage of the Federated Alliance of Transportation of the Sick to Lourdes (OFTAL) as well as the sick to whom they minister with these words:

> May Mary most holy, *Coredemptrix of the human race beside her Son*, always give you courage and confidence![59]

6. Likewise in commemorating the sixth centenary of the canonization of St. Bridget of Sweden on 6 October 1991 he said:

> Birgitta looked to Mary as her model and support in the various moments of her life. She spoke energetically about the divine privilege of Mary's Immaculate Conception. She contemplated her astonishing mission as Mother of the Saviour. She invoked her as the Immaculate Conception, Our Lady of Sorrows, and *Coredemptrix*, exalting Mary's singular role in the history of salvation and the life of the Christian people.[60]

In a completely natural way and without calling undue attention to his use of the word Coredemptrix, the Pontiff has simply resumed the use of terminology which has been employed in the liturgy and by theologians since the late Middle Ages[61] and which was also utilized by the magisterium earlier in this century, and specifically by Pope Pius XI, as we have already seen.

Pope John Paul II has also used the word "coredeemer" or "coredemption" at least three times in speaking of the on-going

---

[58] *Inseg* VIII/1 (1985) 889-890 [*ORE* 880:12]; emphasis my own.

[59] *Inseg* XIII/1 (1990) 743:1; my trans.; emphasis my own.

[60] *Inseg* XIV/2 (1991) 756 [*ORE* 1211:4]; emphasis my own.

[61] Cf. Laurentin 15-16; Carol, "Our Lady's Coredemption," *Mariology* 2: 398-409.

collaboration of Christians in the work of Redemption. Traditionally, theologians have distinguished between Mary's unique collaboration in the redemption as it was taking place *in actu primo* from the application of the graces of the redemption to individual persons which takes place *in actu secundo*. Redemption *in actu primo* or "objective redemption" or the ascending phase of redemption may be defined as the acquisition of universal salvation by means of the sacrifice willed by God to reconcile the world to himself. Redemption *in actu secundo* or "subjective redemption" or the descending phase of redemption or the mediation of grace may be defined as the application of the fruits of the redemption to particular individuals by means of the mediation willed by God.[62] It has been consistently held that Our Lady participates in both of these phases of the work of redemption while all other Christians can participate in the application of the graces of redemption to specific persons and situations. Hence we can all be coredeemers *in actu secundo*. Here is how the Holy Father illustrated these distinctions in his general audience address of 9 April 1997 without employing the classical technical terminology we used above:

> *The collaboration of Christians in salvation takes place after the Calvary event, whose fruits they endeavour to spread by prayer and sacrifice. Mary, instead, cooperated during the event itself and in the role of mother; thus her cooperation embraces the whole of Christ's saving work.* She alone was associated in this way with the redemptive sacrifice that merited the salvation of all mankind. In union with Christ and in submission to him, she collaborated in obtaining the grace of salvation for all humanity.
>
> The Blessed Virgin's role as cooperator has its source in her divine motherhood. By giving birth to the One who was

---

[62] Cf. Alessandro Apollonio, F.I., "I 'Punti Fermi' della Corredenzione Mariana" in *Maria Corredentrice: Storia e Teologia I* (Frigento [AV]: Casa Mariana Editrice «Bibliotheca Corredemptionis B. V. Mariæ» Studi e Richerche 1, 1998) 23.

destined to achieve man's redemption, by nourishing him, presenting him in the temple and suffering with him as he died on the Cross, "in a wholly singular way she cooperated . . . in the work of the Saviour" (*Lumen Gentium*, n. 61). *Although God's call to cooperate in the work of salvation concerns every human being, the participation of the Saviour's Mother in humanity's Redemption is a unique and unrepeatable fact.*[63]

Now let us briefly review the Holy Father's use of the word "coredeemer" and "coredemption" as it applies to all Christians.

1. In addressing the sick at the Hospital of the Brothers of St. John of God (Fatebenefratelli) on Rome's Tiber Island on 5 April 1981, he asked:

> Is it necessary to remind all of you, sorely tried by suffering, who are listening to me, that your pain unites you more and more with the Lamb of God, who "takes away the sin of the world" through his Passion (Jn. 1:29)? And that therefore *you, too, associated with him in suffering, can be coredeemers of mankind?* You know these shining truths. Never tire of offering your sufferings for the Church, that all her children may be consistent with their faith, persevering in prayer and fervent in hope.[64]

2. On 13 January 1982 the Pope addressed himself thus to the sick after giving his general audience address:

> To the sick who are present and to those who are in hospital wards, in nursing homes and in families I say: never feel alone, because the Lord is with you and will never abandon you. *Be courageous and strong: unite your pains and sufferings to those of the Crucified and you will become coredeemers of humanity, together with Christ.*[65]

---

[63] *Inseg* XX/1 (1997) 621-622 [*ORE* 1487:7; *MCat* 185-186]; emphasis my own.

[64] *Inseg* IV/1 (1981) 896 [*ORE* 679:6]; emphasis my own.

[65] *Inseg* V/1 (1982) 91 [my trans.]; emphasis my own.

It should be pointed out that this is a constantly recurring theme in the pastoral discourses of Pope John Paul II, a theme which he treated with remarkable depth and insight in his Apostolic Letter *Salvifici Doloris* of 11 February 1984 in which he expounds at length on Marian coredemption *in actu primo* and in Christian coredemption *in actu secundo* without using the words "Coredemptrix," "coredemption" or "coredeemer."

3. On 8 May 1988 the Holy Father addressed these significant words about candidates for the priesthood to the Bishops of Uruguay who had assembled at the Apostolic Nunciature in Montevideo:

> "The candidate should be irreproachable" (Tit. 1:6), Saint Paul admonishes again. *Personal spiritual direction* should cultivate in them [candidates for the priesthood] *an unlimited love for Christ and his Mother, and a great desire to unite themselves closely to the work of coredemption.*[66]

Despite all of the facts which I have carefully outlined above, there has been what seems an orchestrated attempt to state that none of these instances are of any theological value.

First of all there was the "Declaration of the Theological Commission of the Pontifical International Marian Academy" made in Czestochowa, Poland in August of 1996 made by an "ad hoc" commission composed of 18 Catholics, 3 Orthodox, an Anglican and a Lutheran and released by *L'Osservatore Romano* on 4 June 1997. Dealing with the titles Coredemptrix, Mediatrix and Advocate, it states:

> The titles, as proposed, are ambiguous, as they can be understood in very different ways. Furthermore, the theological direction taken by the Second Vatican Council, which did not wish to define any of these titles, should not be abandoned. The Second Vatican Council did not use the title

---

[66] *Inseg* XI/2 (1988) 1216 [*ORE* 1041:4]; emphasis my own.

"Coredemptrix," and uses "Mediatrix" and "Advocate" in a very moderate way (cf. *Lumen Gentium*, n. 62). In fact, from the time of Pope Pius XII, the term "Coredemptrix" has not been used by the papal Magisterium in its significant documents. There is evidence that Pope Pius XII himself intentionally avoided using it.[67]

From what I have already stated and documented, it is apparent that this declaration is not above criticism for the way it attempts to deal with facts and that it has no magisterial value. It dismisses the use of the term by Pope John Paul II as not occurring in significant magisterial documents.

Together with the declaration in *L'Osservatore Romano* two commentaries appeared in the same edition: one unsigned with the title "A new Marian dogma?"[68] and the other under the signature of Salvatore M. Perrella, O.S.M. entitled "Mary's cooperation in the work of Redemption: Present state of the question."[69] The unsigned commentary offers a further specification with regard to the usage of this term by the present Pontiff:

> With respect to the title of *Coredemptrix*, the Declaration of Czestochowa notes that "from the time of Pope Pius XII, the term *Coredemptrix* has not been used by the papal Magisterium *in its significant documents*" and there is evidence that he himself intentionally avoided using it. An important qualification, because here and there, in papal writings which are marginal therefore devoid of doctrinal weight, one can find such a title, be it very rarely. In substantial documents, however, and in those of some doctrinal importance, this term is absolutely avoided.[70]

In the light of these statements we must ask: What is the

---

[67] *OR* 4 Giugno 1997, p. 10 [*ORE* 1494:12].
[68] *OR* 4 Giugno 1997, p. 10 [*ORE* 1497:10].
[69] *OR* 4 Giugno 1997, p. 10-11 [*ORE* 1498:9-10].
[70] *OR* 4 Giugno 1997, p. 10 [*ORE* 1497:10].

doctrinal value of Pope John Paul II's usages of the term "Coredemptrix" and "coredemption"? I would certainly not argue that his use of the word Coredemptrix occurs in papal documents of the highest teaching authority or that he has proclaimed the doctrine or used the word in the most solemn manner. I do believe, however, that the instances of his use of the term Coredemptrix to characterize Our Lady's collaboration in the work of our redemption — especially in the light of previous magisterial usage — do not deserve to be cavalierly dismissed as "marginal [and] therefore devoid of doctrinal weight."[71] While it is true that five usages of the term may be regarded as passing references, I do not believe that they deserve to be ignored. The instance of 31 January 1985 at Guayaquil, however, constitutes a very significant commentary on the meaning of Marian coredemption and deserves to be pondered very carefully. At the conclusion of this essay it will be possible to make a more comprehensive analysis of the doctrinal weight of the collective papal teaching on the entire question.

A final terminological question: How does one explain the Pope's refraining from the use of the words "Coredemptrix," "coredemption" and "coredeemer" since 1991? Here I am pleased to have recourse to a response given by Father Alessandro Apollonio:

> The Pope, from the time when the echoes of the theological controversy raised in the Church as a result of Dr. Miravalle's *Vox populi* movement have arrived at the highest levels of the hierarchy, has not in fact further used the title *Coredemptrix*. Such a prudential stance on the part of the Holy Father is entirely comprehensible because his explicit pronouncement on coredemption, given the circumstances, would have been like a clear and direct approval of the request, while prudence would require that, before pronouncing definitively

---

[71] The original Italian speaks of *documenti pontifici secondari, e quindi senza peso dottrinale.*

on a new dogma, the Pope would convoke commissions of experts, promote studies and the devotion, illustrate the doctrine exhaustively and consult with the entire episcopate. The Wednesday catecheses [from 6 September 1995 to 12 November 1997], while never mentioning the explicit title *Coredemptrix*, clearly illustrate the doctrine and thus prepare the terrain for the new dogma. Hence if the Pope, after having prudently done all of this, proclaims the new dogma, he would be doing nothing contrary to his magisterium, but would crown it in the most splendid way, for the edification and exultation of all of the faithful.[72]

Pope John Paul II has, in fact, done much more than simply to rehabilitate the use of a word and show that it has a legitimate use. He has made another gracious gesture in the direction of those "many Fathers [of the Second Vatican Council who] wished further to enrich Marian doctrine with other statements on Mary's role in the work of salvation,"[73] even as he did in re-proposing the discussion of Marian mediation in his Encyclical *Redemptoris Mater*[74] after it had largely passed out of theological circulation.[75] He has shown once again that the magisterium is above mere "theological correctness" and is conscious of continuity with the Tradition. Further, he continues to draw out the manifold aspects of Mary's coredemptive role, as we shall see.

III. Mary's Collaboration in the Work of the Redemption

Now it remains to indicate the consistent perspective of the papal magisterium on Mary's coredemptive role, a matter far greater than the mere use of the term Coredemptrix. While it would prolong our study unduly to cite every papal text avail-

---

[72] *Il "calvario"* replace with (my trans.).
[73] *OR* 14 dicembre 1995, p. 4 [*ORE* 1421:13].
[74] Cf. #22, 38-41.
[75] Cf. *Totus Tuus* 184-187.

able on this vast topic, I nonetheless intend to illustrate each of the major points with representative passages from the various pontificates. In doing so, I shall strive to follow the basic orientation which we have already noted in chapter 8 of *Lumen Gentium*, which also follows the historical order indicated by Pope John Paul II in his general audience address of 25 October 1995[76] i.e., first establishing Mary's collaboration in the work of redemption as the "New Eve" and "Associate of the Redeemer" and then treating her active participation in the offering of the sacrifice of our redemption. It will be immediately apparent, however, that any given text cited will often fit into more than one category.

A. *The "New Eve" — Associate of the "New Adam"*

We have already noted above the Holy Father's reference to St. Irenaeus's teaching about Mary as the "New Eve" in his catechesis of 25 October 1995. Indeed, St. Justin Martyr (+ 165), St. Irenaeus (+ after 193) and Tertullian (+ after 220), all of whom belong to the sub-Apostolic period, signalled the parallelism and contrast between Mary and Eve. This fascinating parallelism, never absent from the Church's liturgy[77] and magisterium,[78] was highlighted in *Lumen Gentium* #56 and in the *Catechism of the Catholic Church* #411. This theme sheds notable light on Mary's role in our redemption and has been amply illustrated by the papal magisterium in modern times. Here is an instance which comes from the teaching of Pope Benedict XV (1914-1922). In his homily of 13 May 1920 for the canonization of St. Gabriel of the Sorrowful Virgin and St. Margaret Mary Alacoque he declared:

---

[76] *Inseg* XVIII/2 (1995) 934-937 [*ORE* 1414:11; *MCat* 25-28]; cf. footnote 2 above.
[77] Cf. my treatment of this theme in "Mary as Coredemptrix, Mediatrix and Advocate in the Contemporary Roman Liturgy," *Foundations* I:55-57.
[78] Cf. my treatment of this theme in *MMC* 179-187.

But the sufferings of Jesus cannot be separated from the sorrows of Mary. *Just as the first Adam had a woman for accomplice in his rebellion against God, so the new Adam wished to have a woman share in His work of re-opening the gates of heaven for men. From the cross, He addressed His own Sorrowful Mother as the "woman," and proclaimed her the new Eve*, the Mother of all men, for whom He was dying that they might live.[79]

Pope Pius XII took up the theme on a number of occasions. Here is an excerpt from his allocution to pilgrims from Genoa of 22 April 1940:

In fact, are not Jesus and Mary the two sublime loves of the Christian people? *Are they not the new Adam and the new Eve whom the Tree of the Cross unites in pain and love to atone for the sin of our first parents in Eden?*[80]

In his Encyclical Letter *Mystici Corporis* of 29 June 1943 he describes Mary as "like a new Eve"[81] and in his Apostolic Constitution *Munificentissimus Deus* of 1 November 1950, by which he solemnly defined the dogma of Mary's assumption into heaven, he draws our attention to the antiquity of this theme:

We must remember especially that, *since the second century, the Virgin Mary has been designated by the holy Fathers as the new Eve, who, although subject to the new Adam, is most intimately associated with Him in that struggle against the infernal foe which, as foretold in the protoevangelium, would finally result in that most complete victory over the sin and death* which are always mentioned together in the writings of the Apostle of the Gentiles.[82]

---

[79] *AAS* 12 (1920) 224 [Bro. Richard Zehnle, S.M. (trans.), "Marian Doctrine of Benedict XV," *Marian Reprint* 70:9], emphasis my own.

[80] *OR* 22-23 aprile 1940, p. 1; Domenico Bertetto, S.D.B. (ed.), *Il Magistero Mariano di Pio XII* (Rome: Edizioni Paoline, 1956) #43 [*OL* #359]; emphasis my own.

[81] *nova veluti Eva. AAS* 35 (1943) 247 [*OL* #383].

[82] *AAS* 42 (1950) 768 [*OL* #519]; emphasis my own.

As Eve was subject to Adam, the Pontiff underscores, so is the new Eve to the new Adam. Nevertheless, he continues, she is "most intimately associated with Him in that struggle against the infernal foe which . . . would finally result in that most complete victory over sin and death." Thus he keeps in balance the Catholic truth which both recognizes Jesus as the only Redeemer and Mary as subordinate and yet "most intimately associated with Him" in the work of redemption.

In his Encyclical Letter *Ad Cæli Reginam* of 11 October 1954 Pius XII continued to enlarge upon this analogy between Eve and Mary, calling upon the testimony of Saint Irenaeus:

> From these considerations we can conclude as follows: *in the work of redemption Mary was by God's will joined with Jesus Christ, the cause of salvation, in much the same way as Eve was joined with Adam, the cause of death.* Hence it can be said that the work of our salvation was brought about by a "restoration" (St. Irenaeus) in which *the human race, just as it was doomed to death by a virgin, was saved by a virgin.*[83]

In his *Professio Fidei* or "Credo of the People of God" of 30 June 1968, Pope Paul VI united the closely related themes of "Associate of the Redeemer" and "New Eve" in formulating the Church's belief in the Virgin Mary:

> *Joined by a close and indissoluble bond to the mystery of the Incarnation and Redemption,* the Blessed Virgin Mary, the Immaculate, was raised body and soul to heavenly glory at the end of her earthly life, and was made like her risen Son in anticipation of the future lot of all the just; and We believe that the Blessed Mother of God, *the New Eve,* Mother of the Church, continues in heaven her maternal role with regard to Christ's members, cooperating with the birth and growth of divine life in the souls of the redeemed.[84]

---

[83] *AAS* 46 (1954) 634-635 [*OL* #705]; emphasis my own.
[84] *AAS* 60 (1968) 438-439 [*TPS* 13:278]; emphasis my own.

This article is truly a masterpiece in synthesizing the principal Marian dogmas i.e., that Mary is Mother of God, ever-Virgin, conceived immaculate, assumed into heaven, while at the same time underscoring her spiritual maternity, and her coredemptive and mediatory roles.

Finally, let us note a graceful allusion which Paul VI made to the "New Eve" theme in his Apostolic Exhortation *Marialis Cultus* of 2 February 1974, stating that: "Mary, the New Woman, stands at the side of Christ, the New Man, within whose mystery the mystery of man alone finds true light."[85]

Virtually inseparable from the concept of Mary as "New Eve" is that of her intimate association with the life, suffering and death of Christ. Hence describing her as associate or companion of the Redeemer [*socia Redemptoris*][86] has become another way of recognizing her unique active role in the Redemption. The first explicit use of this terminology with regard to Mary occurs in the writings of Ambrose Autpert (+784), but he uses the verbal form *sociata* to express the idea. "As present knowledge goes, it is Ekbert of Schönau (+1184) who first uses the noun *socia* of Mary."[87]

Blessed Pius IX (1846-1878) in his Apostolic Constitution *Ineffabilis Deus* of 8 December 1854 enunciated a principle of capital importance for Mariology, which had long been held by the Franciscan school of theology,[88] namely that "God, by one

---

[85] *AAS* 66 (1974) 166 [St. Paul Editions 49]. The Latin title of the 20th mass formulary in the *Collection of Masses of the Blessed Virgin Mary* [*Collectio Missarum de Beata Maria Virgine*] is also *Sancta Maria, Mulier Nova*, but it was rendered into English as "Holy Mary, the New Eve".

[86] Cf. my article in *Foundations I*:52-54.

[87] *Theotokos* 53. Cf. entire article 53-55 and also Michael O'Carroll, C.S.Sp., "Socia: the word and idea in regard to Mary," *Ephemerides Mariologicæ* 25 (1975) 337-357.

[88] The cornerstone of this school is the so-called Franciscan thesis: the absolute primacy of the Word Incarnate (Kingship of Christ) and his Blessed Mother's association *uno eodemque decreto* in that primacy. The late Father Juniper B. Carol, O.F.M., in his last major work, put the Franciscan thesis succinctly thus: that "Christ and His Blessed Mother were efficaciously predestined to existence with a logical priority to all others." *Why Jesus Christ? Thomistic, Scotistic and Conciliatory Perspectives* (Manassas, VA: Trinity Communications, 1986) 4.

and the same decree, had established the origin of Mary and the Incarnation of Divine Wisdom."[89] On the basis of this principle, frequently confirmed by the magisterium,[90] Mary's intimate association with Jesus as the "New Eve" in the work of the redemption is axiomatic and, thus, Pius IX declares in the same Apostolic Constitution:

> Hence, just as Christ, the Mediator between God and man, assumed human nature, blotted the handwriting of the decree that stood against us, and fastened it triumphantly to the cross, so the most holy Virgin, *united with Him by a most intimate and indissoluble bond*, was, with Him and through Him, eternally at enmity with the evil serpent, and most completely triumphed over him, and thus crushed his head with her immaculate foot.[91]

Pope Leo XIII (1878-1903) in his rosary encyclical of 1 September 1883, *Supremi Apostolatus*, argues on the same basis that Mary is the "associate with Jesus in the work of man's salvation" [*servandi hominum generis consors*]:

> The Blessed Virgin was exempt from the stain of original sin and chosen to be the Mother of God. For this very reason *she was associated with Him in the work of man's salvation*, and enjoys favor and power with her Son greater than any man or angel has ever attained or could attain.[92]

---

[89] *Pii IX Acta* I:599 [*OL* #34].

[90] It was reiterated by Pius XII in *Munificentissimus Deus* [*AAS* 42 (1950) 768 [*OL* #520] and by the Second Vatican Council which stated in *LG* #61 that Mary was predestined to be the Mother of God from eternity by that decree of divine Providence which determined the incarnation of the Word. Paul VI also cited this text in *Marialis Cultus* #25 [*AAS* 66 (1974) 136; St. Paul Editions 23]. In *Redemptoris Mater* John Paul II says: "In the mystery of Christ she is *present* even 'before the creation of the world,' as the one whom the Father 'has chosen' as *Mother* of his Son in the Incarnation. . . . In an entirely special and exceptional way Mary is united to Christ, and similarly she *is eternally loved in this 'beloved Son'.*" *Inseg* X/1 (1987) 687 [St. Paul Editions 14].

[91] *Pii IX Acta* I:607 [*OL* #46]; emphasis my own.

[92] *ASS* 16 (1883) 114 [*Rosary* #19]; emphasis my own.

This brief text which speaks so clearly of Mary as the Associate of Christ in the work of our salvation, also lays the foundation for her mediation. He develops exactly the same line of argumentation in his rosary encyclical of 5 September 1895, *Adiutricem Populi*, literally calling Mary the "minister for effecting the mystery of human redemption" [*sacramenti humanæ redemptionis patrandi administra*][93] and thus emphasizing her role as Coredemptrix in the past and Mediatrix in the present:

> From her heavenly abode, she began, by God's decree, to watch over the Church, to assist and befriend us as our Mother; so that *she who was so intimately associated with the mystery of human salvation* is just as closely associated with the distribution of the graces which from all time will flow from the Redemption.[94]

Finally, in his Apostolic Constitution *Ubi primum* of 2 October 1898 he states that Mary was "*the cooperatrix in man's Redemption* and always the chief and sovereign refuge of Catholics in the trials they underwent."[95]

Pope Saint Pius X (1903-1914), in his Encyclical Letter *Ad Diem Illum* of 2 February 1904, commemorating the fiftieth anniversary of the proclamation of the Immaculate Conception, refers to Mary as "Jesus' constant companion" [*assidua comes*] in asking this question:

> Will it not appear to all that it is right and proper to affirm that Mary, whom Jesus made *His constant companion from the house of Nazareth to the place of Calvary*, knew, as no other knew, the secrets of his heart, distributes as by a mother's right the treasures of His merits, and is the surest help to the

---

[93] On Mary as "Minister of Grace according to the magisterium," cf. Arthur Burton Calkins, "Mary as Coredemptrix, mediatrix and Advocate in the Contemporary Roman Liturgy" in *Foundations I:*70-82.
[94] *ASS* 28 (1895-1896) 130 [*OL* #169]; emphasis my own. Cf. *Prob* 84-85.
[95] *ASS* 31 (1898-1899) 257 [*OL* #212]; emphasis my own.

knowledge and love of Christ?[96]

In the same encyclical the saint goes on to refer to Mary as "a partaker in the sufferings of Christ and the associate in His Passion" [*particeps passionum Christi sociaque*].[97] Following the line of thought developed by Blessed Pius IX and Leo XIII, Pius XI presents Mary's Immaculate Conception as a necessary preparation for her role as "associate in the redemption of mankind" [*generis humani consors*] in his Letter of 28 January 1933 *Auspicatus profecto* to Cardinal Binet:

> In fact, the august Virgin, conceived without original sin, was chosen to be the Mother of Christ in order to be *associated with Him in the Redemption of mankind*. For that reason she was adorned with such abundant grace and such great power in her Son's sight that neither human nor angelic nature can ever acquire a like grace or power.[98]

During his pontificate the Servant of God Pope Pius XII (1939-1958) would show particular favor to describing Mary as the beloved associate of Christ [*alma socia Christi*].[99] In his Radio Message to Fatima of 13 May 1946 he used the verbal form to describe Mary's intimate collaboration in the redemption:

> He, the Son of God, gave His heavenly Mother a share in His glory, His majesty, His kingship; because, *associated as Mother and Minister to the King of martyrs in the ineffable work of man's Redemption*, she is likewise associated with Him forever, with power so to speak infinite, in the distribution

---

[96] *ASS* 36 (1903-1904) 454-455 [*OL* #235]; emphasis my own.

[97] *ASS* 36 (1903-1904) 457 [*OL* #241].

[98] *AAS* 25 (1933) 80 [*OL* #319]; emphasis my own.

[99] As Cardinal Secretary of State under Pius XI, he had used the term Coredemptrix in speaking of Our Lady (cf. *OR* 8 dicembre 1937, p. 3-4), but abstained from its use as Pope, preferring instead to speak of Mary as *socia Christi*. Cf. *Theotokos* 54; *Prob* 22.

of the graces which flow from Redemption.[100]

In the above text we once again notice the accustomed linkage of coredemption with mediation in papal teaching.

In his Apostolic Constitution *Munificentissimus Deus* of 1 November 1950, by which he declared Mary's assumption into a heaven a dogma of the faith, Pius referred to her as "the noble associate of the divine Redeemer" [*generosa Divini Redemptoris socia*].[101] He would underscore this association also in his Encyclical on the Queenship of Mary, *Ad Cæli Reginam* of 11 October 1954, explaining that "in this work of Redemption the Blessed Virgin Mary was closely associated with Christ,"[102] that she is "His associate in the work of redemption"[103] and then quoting from Francisco Suarez to the effect that:

> Just as Christ, because He redeemed us, is by a special title our King and our Lord, so too is Blessed Mary [our Queen and our Mistress] because of the unique way in which she cooperated in our redemption.[104]

Finally, in his great Encyclical Letter on the Sacred Heart of Jesus, *Haurietis Aquas* of 15 May 1956, he described Mary as "His [our Redeemer's] associate in recalling the children of Eve to the life of divine grace."[105]

Blessed John XXIII (1958-1963) made two allusions to Our Lady as associated with the work of redemption. In a Radio Message to the faithful of Ecuador, he referred to Mary as "She who, in her earthly life, was so intimately associated in the work of Christ"[106] and on 9 December 1962 at the canonization of

---

[100] *AAS* 38 (1946) 266 [*OL* #413]; emphasis my own.
[101] *AAS* 42 (1950) 768 [*OL* #520]; for commentary cf. Carol, "Our Lady's Coredemption," *Mariology* 2:385-386.
[102] *AAS* 46 (1954) 634 [*OL* #704].
[103] *AAS* 46 (1954) 635 [*OL* #706].
[104] *AAS* 46 (1954) 634 [*OL* #704].
[105] *AAS* 48 (1956) 332.
[106] *AAS* 52 (1960) 53 [my trans.]; cf. *Prob* 77.

Peter Julian Eymard, Anthony Pucci and Francesco da Camporosso he stated:

> Beside Jesus is found His Mother — *Regina sanctorum omnium* — she who stirs up holiness in God's Church and is the first flower of His grace. *Intimately associated with the Redemption in the eternal plans of the Most High,* Our Lady, as Severianus of Gabala sang forth, "is the mother of salvation, the source of the light that has become visible" (*PG* 56, 498).[107]

The Servant of God Pope Paul VI (1963-1978), in the course of his pontificate, followed closely the lines developed in the eighth chapter of *Lumen Gentium.* In his major address at the conclusion of the third session of the Second Vatican Council, the one in which he declared Mary Mother of the Church and entrusted the Church to her once again,[108] he said:

> For the Church is not constituted just by her hierarchical order, her sacred liturgy, her sacraments, her institutional structure. Her inner vitality and peculiar nature, the main source of her effectiveness in sanctifying men, is to be found in her mystical union with Christ. *We cannot conceive of this union apart from her who is the Mother of the Incarnate Word, and whom Christ so intimately associated with Himself in bringing about our salvation.*[109]

He spoke similarly of Mary in his Apostolic Exhortation *Signum Magnum* of 13 May 1967, calling her "the Mother of Christ and His most intimate associate"[110] and "the cooperator of the Son in the work of restoration of supernatural life in souls."[111] Likewise in his Apostolic Exhortation *Marialis Cultus*

---

[107] *AAS* 55 (1963) 10 [*TPS* 8:375]; emphasis my own. Cf. *Prob* 77.
[108] Cf. *Totus Tuus* 106-107.
[109] *AAS* 56 (1964) 1014 [*TPS* 10:138]; emphasis my own.
[110] *AAS* 59 (1967) 467 [St. Paul Editions (NCWC trans.) 3].
[111] *AAS* 59 (1967) 473 [St. Paul Editions (NCWC trans.) 10].

of 2 February 1974 he spoke of Mary as "the associate of the Redeemer"[112] and "Mother and associate of the Savior."[113]

In his message to the Bishops and people of Chile of 24 November 1974, Paul VI characterized Mary as "associated mysteriously and for ever with the work of Christ."[114] But perhaps his most original use of the term was in his Letter of 13 May 1975, *E' con sentimenti,* to Cardinal Leo Jozef Suenens on the occasion of the 14th International Marian Congress. In that letter he stated:

> The Catholic Church, moreover, has always believed that the Holy Spirit, intervening personally, even though in indivisible communion with the other Persons of the Holy Trinity, in the work of human salvation (cf. G. Philips, *L'Union personelle avec le Dieu vivant. Essai sur l'origine et le sens de la grâce crée,* 1974), has associated the humble virgin of Nazareth with Himself.[115]

What is of particular interest here is that Paul VI speaks in effect of Mary as the "associate of the Holy Spirit in the work of human salvation." While he is careful to justify his statement theologically, he nonetheless introduces here a new nuance in conceptualizing Mary's unique collaboration in the work of salvation.

Pope John Paul has continued in the line of his predecessors to highlight Mary's role as the "New Eve" and "Associate of the Redeemer." In a notable general audience address given on 4 May 1983 the Holy Father spoke thus with an emphasis on the concept of "Associate":

> Dearest brothers and sisters, in the month of May we raise our eyes to *Mary, the woman who was associated in a unique*

---

[112] *AAS* 66 (1974) 134 [St. Paul Editions 21].
[113] *AAS* 66 (1974) 142 [St. Paul Editions 28].
[114] *AAS* 66 (1974) 728 [*MGMO* 176].
[115] *AAS* 67 (1975) 355-356 [*MGMO* 190].

way in the work of mankind's reconciliation with God. According to the Father's plan, Christ was to accomplish this work through his sacrifice. However, *a woman would be associated with him, the Immaculate Virgin who is thus placed before our eyes as the highest model of cooperation in the work of salvation.* . . . The "Yes" of the Annunciation constituted not only the acceptance of the offered motherhood, but signified above all Mary's commitment to service of the mystery of the Redemption. *Redemption was the work of her Son; Mary was associated with it on a subordinate level. Nevertheless, her participation was real and demanding.* Giving her consent to the angel's message, *Mary agreed to collaborate in the whole work of mankind's reconciliation with God,* just as her Son would accomplish it.[116]

Let us now consider some more recent instances in which he underscores Mary, in particular, as the "New Eve." Here is an exposition from his catechesis of 15 October 1997:

> St. Justin and St. Irenaeus speak of Mary as the new Eve who by her faith and obedience makes amends for the disbelief and disobedience of the first woman. According to the Bishop of Lyons, it was not enough for Adam to be redeemed in Christ, but "it was right and necessary that Eve be restored in Mary" (*Demonstratio apostolica,* 33). In this way he stresses the importance of woman in the work of salvation and lays the foundation for the inseparability of Marian devotion from that shown to Jesus, which will endure down the Christian centuries.[117]

He further speaks of Mary as the "new woman desired by God to atone for Eve's fall."[118] He says that:

---

[116] *Inseg* VI/1 (1983) 1135-1136 [*ORE* 783:1]; emphasis my own.
[117] *Inseg* XX/2 (1997) 565 [*ORE* 1513:11; *MCat* 246].
[118] *Inseg* XIX/1 (1996) 116 [*ORE* 1426:11; *MCat* 62].

The parallel, established by Paul between Adam and Christ, is completed by that between Eve and Mary: the role of woman, important in the drama of sin, is equally so in the Redemption of mankind.

St. Irenaeus presents Mary as the new Eve, who by her faith and obedience compensated for the disbelief and disobedience of Eve. Such a role in the economy of salvation requires the absence of sin.[119]

Again he tells us that:

The universal motherhood of Mary, the "Woman" of the wedding at Cana and of Calvary, recalls Eve, "mother of all living" (Gen. 3:20). However, while the latter helped to bring sin into the world, the new Eve, Mary, cooperates in the saving event of Redemption. Thus in the Blessed Virgin the figure of "woman" is rehabilitated and her motherhood takes up the task of spreading the new life in Christ among men.[120]

As Eve was given to Adam as his helpmate (cf. Gen. 2:18-20), so the Pope tells us:

Having created man "male and female" (cf. Gen. 1:27), the Lord also wants to place the New Eve beside the New Adam in the Redemption. Our first parents had chosen the way of sin as a couple; a new pair, the Son of God with his Mother's cooperation, would re-establish the human race in its original dignity.[121]

In teaching about Mary's glorious Assumption into heaven, the Pope further specifies that, while we may speak of Jesus and Mary as "a couple, a new pair," we must also recognize that there is an important difference as well:

---

[119] *Inseg* XIX/1 (1996) 1392 [*ORE* 1444:11; *MCat* 96].
[120] *Inseg* XX/1 (1997) 750-751 [*ORE* 1489:11, *MCat* 189-190].
[121] *Inseg* XX/1 (1997) 622 [*ORE* 1487:7; *MCat* 186].

In a way analogous to what happened at the beginning of the human race and of salvation history, in God's plan the eschatological ideal was not to be revealed in an individual, but in a couple. Thus in heavenly glory, beside the risen Christ there is a woman who has been raised up, Mary; the new Adam and the new Eve, the first-fruits of the general resurrection of the bodies of all humanity.

The eschatological conditions of Christ and Mary should not, of course, be put on the same level. Mary, the new Eve, received from Christ, the new Adam, the fullness of grace and heavenly glory, having been raised through the Holy Spirit by the sovereign power of the Son.[122]

Classical mariology has long known and taught that there is an analogy, a certain "likeness in difference" between Christ and Mary, a certain symmetry and complementarity, though not identity, between them.[123] This principle of analogy is very germane to the topic under discussion and, indeed, the entire discourse on Mary's role in the work of our redemption cannot be understood without it. Thus in the above catechesis the Holy Father is careful to underscore and illustrate this principle. He does so as well as in the following catechesis in which he treats of the Kingship of Christ and the Queenship of Mary:

My venerable Predecessor Pius XII, in his Encyclical *Ad coeli Reginam* to which the text of the Constitution *Lumen Gentium* refers, indicates as the basis for Mary's queenship in addition to her motherhood, her cooperation in the work of the Redemption. The Encyclical recalls the liturgical text: "There was St. Mary, Queen of heaven and Sovereign of the world, sorrowing near the Cross of our Lord Jesus Christ" (*AAS* 46 [1954] 634). It then establishes an analogy between Mary and Christ, which helps us understand the significance of the Blessed Virgin's royal status. *Christ is King not only*

---

[122] *Inseg* XX/2 (1997) 35 [*ORE* 1500:7; *MCat* 208]; emphasis my own.
[123] Cf. my treatment of this matter in *Totus Tuus* 162-168.

because he is Son of God, but also because he is the Redeemer; Mary is Queen not only because she is Mother of God, but also because, associated as the new Eve with the new Adam, she co-operated in the work of the redemption of the human race (AAS 46 [1954] 635).[124]

Let us note well the "likeness in difference": Christ is King because (1) he is Son of God and (2) because he is Redeemer; Mary is Queen because (1) she is Mother of God and (2) because she cooperated in the work of the redemption.[125]

IV. Mary's Active Participation in the Sacrifice of Calvary

Now we move on to consider the apex of Our Lady's coredemptive activity, her participation in the Passion and Death of her Son. Pope John Paul II, in the very significant catechesis which he gave on 25 October 1995, provides us a glimpse of the growth of the Church's insight into Mary's active participation in the redemption. He comments that Irenaeus' intuition that Mary "with her 'yes,' became 'a cause of salvation' for herself and for all mankind"

was not developed in a consistent and systematic way by the other Fathers of the Church.

Instead, this doctrine was systematically worked out for the first time at the end of the 10th century in the *Life of Mary* by a Byzantine monk, John the Geometer.[126] *Here Mary is united to Christ in the whole work of Redemption, sharing, according to God's plan, in the Cross and suffering for our salvation.* She remained united to the Son "in every deed, attitude and wish" (cf. *Life of Mary*, Bol. 196, f. 123 v.).[127]

---

[124] *Inseg* XX/2 (1997) 56 [*ORE* 1502:7; *MCat* 210]; emphasis my own.

[125] For the magisterial background and foundation for this analogy, cf. *Totus Tuus* 85-86; 102-105.

[126] On John the Geometer's contribution to Mariology, cf. *Theotokos* 203-204.

[127] *Inseg* XVIII/2 (1995) 935 [*ORE* 1414:11; *MCat* 26]; except for titles, emphasis my own.

Mary's abiding union with Jesus "in every deed, attitude and wish" is a datum that the Church would come to grasp ever more clearly with the passage of time as she continued to ruminate on the person and role of Mary under the guidance of the Holy Spirit. John the Geometer seems to have been the first to have left us written reflections on the inseparable bond between Jesus and Mary in the work of our salvation. He explicitly states that "The Virgin, after giving birth to her Son, was never separated from him in his activity, his dispositions, his will."[128] This obviously implies Mary's willing assent to (1) the sacrifice of her Son, which also, of necessity, implies (2) the sacrifice of herself in union with him. While in the following subsections, I will make a logical distinction between these two offerings, in reality they were simultaneous and the papal texts which I cite will often treat them so.

A. Her Offering of the Victim

Under the guidance of the Holy Spirit the Church came to understand with ever greater conviction that Mary's "fiat" at the moment of the Annunciation blossomed into her "fiat" under the Cross and that her consent to the offering of the sacrifice of her Son constituted on her part a real offering of the sacrifice. Here is a text of capital importance from Leo XIII's Encyclical Letter *Jucunda Semper* of 8 September 1894 which associates these two "fiats":

> When she professed herself the handmaid of the Lord for the mother's office, and when, at the foot of the altar, she offered up her whole self with her child Jesus — then and thereafter she took her part in the painful expiation offered by her son for the sins of the world. It is certain, therefore, that she suffered in the very depths of her soul with His most bitter

---

[128] *Theotokos* 204.

sufferings and with His torments. Finally, *it was before the eyes of Mary that the divine Sacrifice for which she had borne and nurtured the Victim was to be finished.* As we contemplate Him in the last and most piteous of these mysteries, we see that "there stood by the cross of Jesus Mary His Mother" (Jn. 19:25), who, in a miracle of love, so that she might receive us as her sons, *offered generously to Divine Justice her own Son,* and in her Heart died with Him, stabbed by the sword of sorrow.[129]

What I wish to point out here is that Leo links the two "fiats" by means of Mary's presentation of Jesus in the temple (Lk. 2:22-24), which is seen as an anticipation of his presentation on the Cross. He speaks explicitly of Mary as the one who "generously nurtured the Victim" and who "offered [Him] to Divine Justice."

Pope Saint Pius X follows in the same line, but with even more conciseness, in his Encyclical Letter *Ad Diem Illum* of 2 February 1904:

The most holy Mother of God, accordingly, *supplied the "matter for the flesh* of the Only-begotten Son of God to be born of human members" so that a Victim for man's salvation might be available. But this is not her only title to our praise. In addition, *she was entrusted with the duty of watching over the same Victim, of nourishing Him, and even of offering Him upon the altar* at the appointed time.[130]

While there is no direct reference here to the sacrifice of Abraham (Gen. 22), the language employed suggests a striking parallel. Mary is described here as preparing the divine Victim for sacrifice even as Abraham prepared Isaac. The difference, of course, is that Abraham was spared having to carry through with the sacrifice while Mary was not.

---

[129] *ASS* 27 (1894-1895) 178 [*OL* #151]; emphasis my own.
[130] *ASS* 36 (1903-1904) 453 [Burke 55 (alt.)]; emphasis my own.

Pope Benedict XV made a very emphatic affirmation about Mary's offering in his Letter *Inter Sodalicia* of 22 March 1918. He stated that:

> According to the common teaching of the Doctors *it was God's design* that the Blessed Virgin Mary, apparently absent from the public life of Jesus, should assist Him when He was dying nailed to the Cross. Mary suffered and, as it were, nearly died with her suffering Son; *for the salvation of mankind she renounced her mother's rights and, as far as it depended on her, offered her Son to placate divine justice*; so we may well say that she with Christ redeemed mankind.[131]

It should be noted here that Benedict indicates that Mary's presence beneath the Cross of Christ was "not without divine design" [*non sine divino consilio*], the very same language is reproduced verbatim in *Lumen Gentium* #58, although with no reference to this text. Seemingly deriving from the principle that "God, by one and the same decree, had established the origin of Mary and the Incarnation of Divine Wisdom,"[132] Benedict XV holds that God had also predestined Mary's union with her Son in his sacrifice to the extent of making the sacrifice with him *quantum ad se pertinebat*.

The next papal statement which we consider came ten years after that of Benedict XV and was destined for the universal Church. It occurs at the conclusion of Pope Pius XI's encyclical on reparation to the Sacred Heart of Jesus, *Miserentissimus Redemptor* of 8 May 1928:

> May the most gracious Mother of God, who gave us Jesus as Redeemer, who reared Him, and *at the foot of the Cross offered Him as Victim*, who by her mysterious union with Christ

---

[131] *AAS* 10 (1918) 181-182 [*OL* #267]; emphasis my own. For commentary on this text, cf. *Prob* 90-91; Carol, "Our Lady's Coredemption," *Mariology* 2:383-384.
[132] *Pii IX Acta* I:599 [*OL* #34].

and by her matchless grace rightly merits the name *Reparatrix*, deign to smile upon Our wishes and Our undertakings.[133]

Here Pius XI speaks clearly of Mary's offering of Jesus to the Father as a victim. Furthermore, by virtue of her intimate union with Christ and her altogether unique grace, he says that she may rightly be called "Reparatrix." This title had already been attributed to Mary by Blessed Pius IX who called her "Reparatrix of the first parents" in his Apostolic Constitution *Ineffabilis Deus*,[134] by Leo XIII who cited Saint Tharasius of Constantinople[135] as his authority for calling her "Reparatrix of the Whole World" in his Encyclical Letter *Adiutricem Populi*[136] and by Saint Pius X who quoted Eadmer of Canterbury[137] as calling her "the Reparatrix of the lost world" in his Encyclical Letter *Ad Diem Illum*.[138] The title is obviously significant in that it speaks, as Pius XI testifies, of Mary's intimate union with Christ and of the reparation which she makes to the Father in union with the Redeemer (*Reparator*).

Mary's offering of Christ to the Father is given classic expression in Pius XII's Encyclical Letter *Mystici Corporis* of 29 June 1943:

> *She it was who, immune from all sin, personal or inherited, and ever most closely united with her Son, offered Him on Golgotha to the Eternal Father together with the holocaust of her maternal rights and motherly love, like a new Eve, for all the children of Adam contaminated through this unhappy fall,* and thus she, who was the mother of our Head according to the flesh, be-

---

[133] *AAS* 20 (1928) 178 [*OL* #287]; emphasis my own.

[134] *Pii IX Acta* I:610 [*OL* #52].

[135] Cf. *Theotokos* 336-337.

[136] *ASS* 28 (1895-1896) 130-31 [*OL* #170].

[137] Cf. *Theotokos* 125-126.

[138] *ASS* 36 (1903-1904) 454 [*OL* #233].

came by a new title of sorrow and glory the spiritual mother of all His members.[139]

Once again we have a clear affirmation that Mary offered Jesus to the Father. Pius XII adds that Our Lady made this offering "together with the holocaust of her motherly rights and motherly love." Benedict XV in *Inter Sodalicia* had put it that Mary had "renounced (or abdicated) her motherly rights." The Fathers of the Second Vatican Council effectively echoed him when they stated in *Lumen Gentium* #58 that Mary "lovingly consented to the immolation of this victim which was born of her."

Blessed Pope John XXIII developed the theme of Mary's "offering of the Divine Victim" in his Radio Message to Bishops of Italy in Catania on occasion of the 16th National Eucharistic Congress and the Consecration of Italy to the Immaculate Heart of Mary of 13 September 1959:

> We trust that, as a result of the homage they have just paid to the Virgin Mary, all Italians will be strengthened in their fervor and veneration of the Blessed Virgin as Mother of the Mystical Body, of which the Eucharist is the symbol and vital center. *We trust that they will imitate in her the most perfect model of union with Jesus, our Head; We trust that they will join Mary in her offering of the Divine Victim*, and that they will ask for her motherly mediation to obtain for the Church the gifts of unity, of peace, and especially of a new luxuriant blossoming of religious vocations.[140]

Here Pope John made an application linking Mary's offering of Jesus to the participation of the faithful in the Mass. This co-offering, of course, does not at all take away from the fact that Jesus himself is the primary priest of the sacrifice. Rather it is

---

[139] *AAS* 35 (1943) 247-248 [*OL* #383]; emphasis my own. Pius XII quoted the first part of this text again in his Encyclical Letter *Ad Cæli Reginam* of 11 October 1954, *AAS* 46 (1954) 635 [*OL* #705].

[140] *AAS* 51 (1959) 713 [*TPS* 6:94]; emphasis my own.

an acknowledgement that Mary was the primary co-offerer of the sacrifice along with Jesus himself,[141] just as all members of the faithful present at Mass are called to be co-offerers of the sacrifice along with the priest who acts *in persona Christi*.[142]

In #20 of his Apostolic Exhortation *Marialis Cultus* of 2 February 1974 Pope Paul VI proposed Mary to the faithful as "the Virgin presenting offerings" [*Virgo offerens*]:

> *The Church herself, in particular from the Middle Ages onwards, has detected in the heart of the Virgin taking her Son to Jerusalem to present Him to the Lord (cf. Lk. 2:22) a desire to make an offering, a desire that exceeds the ordinary meaning of the rite.* A witness to this intuition is found in the loving prayer of Saint Bernard: "Offer your Son, holy Virgin, and present to the Lord the blessed fruit of your womb. Offer for the reconciliation of us all the holy Victim which is pleasing to God."
>
> This union of the Mother and the Son in the work of redemption reaches its climax on Calvary, where Christ "offered himself as the perfect sacrifice to God" (Heb. 9:14) and where Mary stood by the cross (cf. Jn. 19:25), "suffering grievously with her only-begotten Son. There she united herself with a maternal heart to His sacrifice, and lovingly consented to the immolation of this victim which she herself had brought forth" *and also was offering to the eternal Father.*[143]

Here I shall limit myself to comments on the Pope's sources. First, he cites the text of Saint Bernard which Pope John Paul II

---

[141] Cf. Colman E. O'Neill, O.P., *Meeting Christ in the Sacraments* (Staten Island, N. Y.: Alba House, 1991; rev. ed. Romanus Cessario, O.P.) 221-231.

[142] On the distinction between the manner in which priests and the faithful offer the divine victim in the Mass, Cf. Pius XII's Encyclical Letter *Mediator Dei* of 20 November 1947, *AAS* 39 (1947) 553-555 [Pierre Veuillot (ed.), *The Catholic Priesthood According to the Teaching of the Church: Papal Documents from Pius X to Pius XII (1939-1954)* (Dublin: Gill and Son, 1957), Book I, Vol. 2, #229-232] and *Meeting Christ in the Sacraments* 209-214.

[143] *AAS* 66 (1974) 131-132 [St. Paul Editions 19].

also used in his catechesis on Mary's collaboration in the work of redemption of 25 October 1995.[144] Secondly, he quotes from the text of *Lumen Gentium* #58, adding for emphasis that Mary, too, "was offering [the victim] to the eternal Father" and giving as his reference the text of Pius XII in *Mystici Corporis*.[145]

Pope John Paul II is the heir of the magisterial teaching of all his predecessors and shows this in an Angelus address of 5 June 1983, the Feast of Corpus Christi:

> Born of the Virgin to be a pure, holy and immaculate oblation, Christ offered on the Cross the one perfect Sacrifice which every Mass, in an unbloody manner, renews and makes present. *In that one Sacrifice, Mary, the first redeemed, the Mother of the Church, had an active part.* She stood near the Crucified, suffering deeply with her Firstborn; with a motherly heart she associated herself with his Sacrifice; with love she consented to his immolation (cf. *Lumen Gentium*, 58; *Marialis Cultus*, 20): *she offered him and she offered herself to the Father.* Every Eucharist is a memorial of that Sacrifice and that Passover that restored life to the world; every Mass puts us in intimate communion with her, the Mother, whose sacrifice "becomes present" just as the Sacrifice of her Son "becomes present" at the words of consecration of the bread and wine pronounced by the priest.[146]

Let us note that the Pope links Mary's offering of Christ with her offering of herself, as so many of his predecessors have done. Again, this follows from the theology of the Mass: the faithful are called to offer themselves to the Father in union with their offering of Christ.

On 7 December 1983 in his general audience address the Holy Father linked Mary's offering of Christ to her Immaculate Conception:

---

[144] Cf. footnote #2 above.

[145] *AAS* 35 (1943) 247.

[146] *Inseg* VI/1 (1983) 1447 [*ORE* 788:2]; emphasis my own.

We must above all note that Mary was created immaculate in order to be better able to act on our behalf. *The fullness of grace allowed her to fulfill perfectly her mission of collaboration with the work of salvation*; it gave the maximum value to her cooperation in the sacrifice. *When Mary presented to the Father her Son nailed to the cross, her painful offering was entirely pure.*[147]

Hence we can say that, even though on an entirely subordinate level, Mary's offering, like Christ's, is a perfect offering, totally pure. In this she is a model for all the faithful.

On Saint Joseph's Day in 1995 at the Shrine of Our Lady of Sorrows in Castelpetroso the Pope made these comments:

Dear brothers and sisters, may you also offer the Lord your daily joys and labours in communion with Christ and through the intercession of his Mother venerated here as *she offers to the Father the Son who sacrificed himself for our salvation.*[148]

Note here the Pope's theological precision: he speaks of Mary offering the Son to the Father, but further qualifies the Son as he "who sacrificed himself for our salvation." Mary's offering of Christ always implies his own offering of himself.

In his Encyclical Letter *Evangelium Vitæ* of 25 March 1995 he links Mary's offering of Jesus to her *fiat* and to her spiritual maternity:

"Standing by the cross of Jesus" (Jn. 19:25), Mary shares in the gift which the Son makes of himself: *she offers Jesus, gives him over, and begets him to the end for our sake. The "yes" spoken on the day of the Annunciation reaches full maturity on the day of the Cross, when the time comes for Mary to receive and beget as her children all those who become disciples,* pouring out upon them the saving love of her Son: "When Jesus

---

[147] *Inseg* VI/2 (1983) 1265 [*ORE* 813:1]; emphasis my own.
[148] *Inseg* XVIII/1 (1995) 542 [*ORE* 1384:3]; emphasis my own.

saw his mother, and the disciple whom he loved standing near, he said to his mother, 'Woman, behold, your son!'" (Jn. 19:26).[149]

This passage also subtly evokes the text of Revelation 12:17 which refers to "the rest of the offspring" of "the Woman clothed with the sun" (Rev. 12:1): while Mary gave birth to Jesus in a painless way, her intense sufferings in union with Jesus on Calvary were the birth pangs by which she "begets as her children all those who become [his] disciples."

B. Her Offering of Herself

We have already seen numerous papal texts which speak of Mary offering herself and her sorrows on Calvary to the Eternal Father for our salvation. This is so because distinguishing between Mary's offering of her Son and herself to the Father is a legitimate logical distinction — and it is certainly made by the magisterium because it involves the offering of two distinct persons, one divine and one human — but, in fact, it is difficult to separate the one offering from the other. Nonetheless, I believe that there is also particular value in underscoring Mary's offering of herself which became part of the one price of our salvation.

This, in fact, is precisely the point of a text which comes to us from Pope Pius VII (1800-1823):

Certainly, it is the duty of Christians towards the Blessed Virgin Mary, as children of so good a Mother, to honor unceasingly and with affectionate zeal the memory of *the bitter sorrows which she underwent with admirable courage and invincible constancy especially when she stood at the foot of the Cross and offered those sorrows to the Eternal Father for our salvation.*[150]

---

[149] *AAS* 87 (1995) 520 [*ORE* 1385:XIX]; emphasis my own.
[150] *Summa Aurea* 7:495 [*OL* #12]; emphasis my own.

Leo XIII effectively makes the same point in his Rosary Encyclical *Iucunda Semper* of 8 September 1894 when he speaks of the mystery of the presentation of the child Jesus in the Temple:

> When she professed herself the handmaid of the Lord for the mother's office, and when, at the foot of the altar, she offered up her whole self with her child Jesus — *then and thereafter she took her part in the painful expiation offered by her son for the sins of the world.*[151]

Saint Pius X speaks eloquently in *Ad Diem Illum* of the "communion of sorrows and of will" shared by Jesus and Mary on Calvary:

> Hence the ever united life and labors of the Son and the Mother which permit the application to both of the words of the Psalmist: "My life is wasted with grief and my years in sighs." When the supreme hour of the Son came, beside the cross of Jesus there stood Mary, His Mother, not merely occupied in contemplating the cruel spectacle, but rejoicing that her only Son was offered for the salvation of mankind; and *so entirely participating in His Passion that, if it had been possible "she would have gladly borne all the torments that her Son underwent."*
>
> From *this community of will and suffering between Christ and Mary* "she merited to become most worthily the reparatrix of the lost world" (Eadmer, *De Excellentia Virg. Mariæ*, c. 9) and dispensatrix of all the gifts that our Savior purchased for us by his death and by his blood.[152]

We have already considered the famous text of Benedict XV's *Inter Sodalicia* from the perspective of Mary's offering of Christ, but it behooves us now to examine that text from the perspective of Mary's self-offering and of her "paying the price of

---

[151] *ASS* 27 (1894-1895) 178 [*OL* #151]; emphasis my own.
[152] *ASS* 36 (1903-1904) 453-454 [*OL* #232-233].

mankind's redemption" along with Christ.

> *Mary suffered and, as it were, nearly died with her suffering Son*; for the salvation of mankind she renounced her mother's rights and, as far as it depended on her, offered her Son to placate divine justice; *so we may well say that she with Christ redeemed mankind.*[153]

Benedict speaks as if our redemption were a joint effort. This, of course, takes nothing away from the fact that Jesus' merits were all-sufficient or that Mary, as a human creature, could never equal her divine Son. Rather he recognizes that Mary's presence on Calvary was "not without divine design,"[154] that it was willed by God as a consequence of his decree predestining Jesus and Mary for the work of salvation. As if by way of commentary, two years later, in his homily at the canonization of St. Gabriel of the Sorrowful Virgin and St. Margaret Mary Alacoque, he said that "the sufferings of Jesus cannot be separated from the sorrows of Mary":[155] they can be logically distinguished, but God sees them as one.

In an allocution which he gave to newly-weds on 30 October 1933 Pius XI spoke in a similar vein. He had just given these young couples a rosary and medal of Our Lady and commented on the latter gift:

> The image of the Virgin, of the Mother of God reminds and gently admonishes that one must not pass a day without remembering the heavenly Mother, who was entrusted to us under the cross and *united her sufferings and those of the Redeemer for the salvation of her children.*[156]

---

[153] *AAS* 10 (1918) 182 [*OL* #267]; emphasis my own.

[154] Benedict's terminology also appears in *LG* #58.

[155] *AAS* 12 (1920) 224 [Bro. Richard Zehnle, S.M. (trans.), "Marian Doctrine of Benedict XV," *Marian Reprint* 70:9].

[156] Domenico Bertetto, S.D.B. (ed.), *Discorsi di Pio XI* 2:988 [my trans.]; emphasis my own.

He spoke in like manner to pilgrims from Vicenza a month later:

> By the very nature of their relationship the Redeemer could not have not associated His Mother with His work. For this reason We invoke her under the title of Co-redemptrix. She gave us the Savior, she accompanied Him in the work of Redemption as far as the Cross itself, *sharing with Him the sorrows of the agony and of the death in which Jesus consummated the Redemption of mankind.*[157]

This latter text is most interesting not only because of his use of the term Co-redemptrix, but also because the Pope speaks of a kind of inner necessity [*per necessità di cose*] requiring Mary's participation in Jesus' passion and death. He seems to be echoing here Benedict XV's conviction that Mary's involvement was necessary according to God's inscrutable plan, that it was "not without divine design" [*non sine divino consilio*] i.e., flowing from the "logic of the Incarnation" [*uno eodemque decreto*].

We seem to have an echo of this same theme in a statement which Pius XII made in his Radio Message to the Marian Congress of the Union of South Africa on 4 May 1952:

> Yes, dearly beloved, *in the loving providence of God, it was Mary's "be it done unto me according to thy word" that made possible the passion and death and resurrection of the divine Redeemer of the world. That is why we dare not separate the Mother from the son.* His death on Golgotha was her martyrdom; His triumph is her exaltation.[158]

Pius XII's most brilliant and succinct assertion of Mary's joint share in the work of the redemption, however, occurs in

---

[157] Domenico Bertetto, S.D.B. (ed.), *Discorsi di Pio XI* 2:1013 [*OL* #326 (alt.)]; emphasis my own.

[158] *AAS* 44 (1952) 429 [*OL* #568]; emphasis my own.

his great Sacred Heart encyclical of 15 May 1956, *Haurietis Aquas*:

> *By the will of God,* the most Blessed Virgin Mary was insepa-
> rably joined with Christ in accomplishing the work of man's
> redemption, so that *our salvation flows from the love of Jesus
> Christ and His sufferings intimately united with the love and
> sorrows of His Mother.*[159]

In this classic passage every word is carefully weighed and mea-
sured in order to make a declaration on the redemption and
Mary's role in it which remains unparalleled for its clarity and
precision. No doubt for this reason it is included in Denzinger-
Hünermann's *Enchiridion Symbolorum.*[160] Pius professes that
"our salvation flows from the love of Jesus Christ and His sufferings" [*ex Iesu Christi caritate eiusque cruciatibus*] which are
"intimately united with the love and sorrows of His Mother"
[*cum amore doloribusque ipsius Matris intime consociatis*]. The
Latin preposition *ex* indicates Jesus as the source of our redemption while three other Latin words, *cum* and *intime consociatis*
indicate Mary's inseparability from the source.[161] Finally, let us
note Pius' insistence on the fact that this union of Jesus with
Mary for our salvation has been ordained "by the will of God"
[*ex Dei voluntate*].

In a sermon which John XXIII preached at the conclusion
of the solemn novena in honor of the Immaculate Conception
at Santi Apostoli on 7 December 1959 he also dwelt on the
inner logic of Mary's "fiat" which found its conclusion on Cal-

---

[159] *AAS* 48 (1956) 352 [*OL* #778]; emphasis my own.

[160] *D-H* #3926.

[161] On Pius XII's treatment of the Hearts of Jesus and Mary, cf. my commentary in
*Foundations I:*67 and my article, "The Cultus of the Hearts of Jesus and Mary in the
Papal Magisterium from Pius IX to Pius XII" *Acta Congressus Mariologici-Mariani
Internationalis in Sanctuario Mariano Kevelaer (Germania) Anno 1987 Celebrati* II:
*De Cultu Mariano Saeculis XIX et XX usque ad Concilium Vaticanum II Studia Indolis
Generalioris* (Rome: Pontificia Academia Mariana Internationalis, 1991) 381-392.

vary. Speaking of the joy which came into the world at Mary's birth, he said:

> This joy, however, is also a scarlet flower of sacrifice: the sacrifice of the Blessed Mother of Jesus, who, having spoken her timely "*fiat*," at the same time agreed to share in the fate of her Son, the poverty of Bethlehem, in the self-denial of a hidden life, and in the martyrdom of Calvary.[162]

Continuing in the line of his predecessors, Paul VI also attested to Mary's participation in the sacrifice of Jesus to the point of sacrificing herself. In a Radio Message to invalid priest pilgrims at Lourdes on 30 July 1966 he spoke thus:

> May *the Immaculate Virgin, who pronounced the "fiat" of perfect conformity to the divine will and who, agreeing to become the Mother of the Incarnate Word, chose voluntary participation in the sufferings of her Son, the Redeemer,* look kindly on the suffering yet confident band of these her sons, having been made worthy to follow Christ, with her, on the royal road of the holy Cross.[163]

Here he underscores the familiar theme that the "fiat" of the Annunciation leads to the cross, but — even more — insists that Mary's "fiat" represented a deliberate choice to participate in the sufferings of her Son. In his Apostolic Exhortation *Signum Magnum* of 13 May 1967 he emphasized Our Lady's

> charity, strong and constant in the fulfillment of her mission *to the point of sacrificing herself, in full communion of sentiments with her Son who immolated Himself on the Cross to give men a new life.*[164]

---

[162] *Discorsi, messaggi, Colloqui del Santo Padre Giovanni XXIII* II:52 [*TPS* 6:176].

[163] *Inseg P* IV (1966) 825 [my trans.]; emphasis my own.

[164] *AAS* 59 (1967) 470 [St. Paul Editions (NCWC trans.) 6]; emphasis my own.

Eight years later, on 13 May 1975, he wove these two themes together in his Letter to Cardinal Suenens on the occasion of the 14th International Marian Congress:

> It was the Holy Spirit that sustained the Mother of Jesus, present at the foot of His cross, inspiring her, as already in the Annunciation, with the *Fiat* to the will of the heavenly Father, *who wished her to be maternally associated with the sacrifice of her Son for the redemption of mankind* (cf. Jn. 19:25).[165]

Like his predecessors, Pope John Paul II consistently maintains that Mary's assent to the bloody sacrifice of the cross was the drawing out of all of the implications of her "yes" at the Annunciation. The joyful *fiat* spoken to the Angel Gabriel becomes on Calvary the reason why the Pope could say in Guayaquil on 31 January 1985:

> *Crucified spiritually with her crucified son* (cf. Gal. 2:20), she contemplated with heroic love the death of her God, she "lovingly consented to the immolation of this Victim which she herself had brought forth" (*Lumen Gentium*, 58).[166]

While it may seem audacious to some that the Pope should speak of Mary as "crucified spiritually with her crucified son," we note that in his text the Pope supplies us with his point of reference. It is Saint Paul's Epistle to the Galatians 2:20 where he asserts "I have been crucified with Christ." If Paul could claim this of himself, there is all the more reason to say this of Mary on Calvary. In an extemporaneous address to youth in Vicenza, Italy on 8 September 1991 the Pope offered a further commentary on what he had said in Guayaquil:

> Then there is the moment of the crucifixion. *Certainly, when*

---

[165] *AAS* 67 (1975) 356 [*MGMO* 192]; emphasis my own.
[166] *Inseg* VIII/1 (1985) 318-319 [*ORE* 876:7]; emphasis my own.

Jesus died on the cross, her very self, her heart, her motherhood, all was crucified. When I wrote the Encyclical *Redemptoris Mater* I compared this moment in Mary's life to a dark night, darker than all the nights which the souls of mystics have experienced throughout the Church's history.[167]

Here we find the Pauline terminology of coredemption applied to Mary's sacrifice of "her very self, her heart, her motherhood" in a way that is at once original and striking. Again, speaking to youth, this time on 9 May 1993 in the sports stadium in Agrigento, Sicily the Holy Father spoke of Our Lady's self-offering in this way:

The Virgin of Nazareth *precedes you on your way,* the *woman made holy by the passover* of the Son of God, *she who offered herself with Christ for the redemption of all humanity.*[168]

In this final quote the Pope deftly speaks of the offering of Mary as united to the offering of Christ. Without taking away at all from the fact that the sacrifice of Christ is more than sufficient for the salvation of the world, the Pope's statement indicates that our salvation has effectively come about through the sacrificial offering of Christ to which is joined the self-offering of Mary.[169]

While it would be possible to quote numerous other texts from the teaching of John Paul II in support of Mary's sacrifice of herself on Calvary in union with Jesus, I wish to cite just one more, which comes from his Apostolic Letter *Salvifici Doloris* of 11 February 1984 and which can also serve as a marvelous recapitulation of his magisterium and that of his predecessors on this point:

---

[167] *Inseg* XIV/2 (1991) 530 [*ORE* 1207:4 (alt.)]; emphasis my own.

[168] *Inseg* XVI/1 (1993) 1136 [*ORE* 1292:7]; final emphasis my own.

[169] On the theme of the united sacrifice of Jesus and Mary in the magisterium and in the liturgy, cf. my article, "Mary as Coredemptrix, Mediatrix and Advocate in the Contemporary Roman Liturgy," *Foundations I*:66-68.

It is especially consoling to note — and also accurate in ac-
cordance with the Gospel and history — that at the side of
Christ, in the first and most exalted place, there is always His
Mother through the exemplary testimony that she bears *by
her whole life* to this particular Gospel of suffering. *In her,
the many and intense sufferings were amassed in such an interconnected way that they were not only a proof of her unshakable
faith but also a contribution to the Redemption of all.* . . . *It was
on Calvary that Mary's suffering, beside the suffering of Jesus,
reached an intensity which can hardly be imagined from a human point of view but which was mysteriously and supernaturally fruitful for the Redemption of the world.* Her ascent of
Calvary and her standing at the foot of the cross together
with the beloved disciple were a special sort of sharing in the
redeeming death of her Son.[170]

Another citation from *Salvifici Doloris* may help to
contextualize the truths which underlie the mystery of Mary as
Co-redemptrix: "The sufferings of Christ created the good of
the world's Redemption. This good in itself is inexhaustible
and infinite. No man can add anything to it."[171] But at the
same time "Mary's suffering [on Calvary], beside the suffering
of Jesus . . . was mysteriously and supernaturally fruitful for the
Redemption of the world." Thus the Pope strikes that careful
balance which is always a hallmark of Catholic truth: he up-
holds the principle that the sufferings of Christ were all-sufficient for the salvation of the world, while maintaining that Mary's
sacrifice was nonetheless "a contribution to the Redemption of
all."

C. The Joint Offering of Jesus and Mary

Having amply reviewed how the papal magisterium pre-

---

[170] *Inseg* VII/1 (1984) 308-309 [St. Paul Editions 40-41]; except for "by her whole
life," emphasis my own.
[171] *Inseg* VII/1 (1984) 307 [St. Paul Editions 37-38].

sents Mary's offering of Jesus and her offering of herself on Calvary, let us now consider texts in which Pope John Paul II emphasizes how Mary's sacrifice is inseparable from that of Jesus, how, it is a "joint but subordinate action with Christ the Redeemer."[172] Let us begin with the beautiful commentary the Pope made on *Lumen Gentium* #58 in his catechesis of 2 April 1997:

> With our gaze illumined by the radiance of the resurrection, we pause to reflect on *the Mother's involvement in her Son's redeeming passion, which was completed by her sharing in his suffering.* Let us return again, but now in the perspective of the Resurrection, to the foot of the Cross where the Mother endured "with her only-begotten Son the intensity of his suffering, associated herself with his sacrifice in her mother's heart, and lovingly consented to the immolation of this victim which was born of her" (ibid., n. 58).
>
> *With these words, the Council reminds us of "Mary's compassion";* in her heart reverberates all that Jesus suffers in body and soul, emphasizing her willingness to share in her Son's redeeming sacrifice and to join her own maternal suffering to his priestly offering.
>
> *The Council text also stresses that her consent to Jesus' immolation is not passive acceptance but a genuine act of love, by which she offers her Son as a "victim" of expiation for the sins of all humanity.*
>
> Lastly, *Lumen Gentium* relates the Blessed Virgin to Christ, who has the lead role in Redemption, making it clear that in associating herself "with his sacrifice" she remains subordinate to her divine Son.[173]

Let us note briefly how the Holy Father brings both of these dimensions of Mary's offering together by referring to her "compassion" or "suffering with" Jesus as well as insisting that her

---

[172] *Inseg* XX/1 (1997) 621 [*ORE* 1487:7; *MCat* 185].

[173] *Inseg* XX/1 (1997) 572 [*ORE* 1486:11; *MCat* 183]; emphasis my own.

"consent to Jesus' immolation" was "a genuine act of love, by which she offers her Son as a 'victim' of expiation for the sins of all humanity." Another point to be noted is how beautifully and carefully the Pope puts "the Mother's involvement in her Son's redeeming passion" into the proper theological perspective: it is always to be understood as "subordinate," but at the same time "her sharing in his suffering" completes "her Son's redeeming passion."

These two dimensions of Mary's offering are gracefully intermingled by the Holy Father in his catechesis of 10 September 1997 in which he presents Mary as "the Church's model for generously participating in sacrifice":

> In presenting Jesus in the temple and, especially, at the foot of the Cross, Mary completes the gift of herself which associates her as Mother with the suffering and trials of her Son.[174]

The gift of herself is seen as completed in her association with the suffering of her Son whom she offered in the temple as an infant and now offers again on Calvary.

This intermingling of Mary's offering of Jesus and of herself was magnificently expressed in the Pope's homily at the Commemoration of Abraham "Our Father in Faith" during the Great Jubilee of the Year 2000:

> Daughter of Abraham in faith as well as in the flesh, Mary personally shared in this experience. *Like Abraham, she too accepted the sacrifice of her Son, but while the actual sacrifice of Isaac was not demanded of Abraham, Christ drank the cup of suffering to the last drop. Mary personally took part in her Son's trial,* believing and hoping at the foot of the Cross (cf. Jn. 19:25).
>
> This was the epilogue of a long wait. Having been taught to meditate on the prophetic texts, Mary foresaw what

---

[174] *Inseg* XX/2 (1997) 297 [*ORE* 1508:7; *MCat* 232].

awaited her and in praising the mercy of God, faithful to his people from generation to generation, *she gave her own consent to his plan of salvation; in particular, she said her "yes" to the central event of this plan, the sacrifice of that Child whom she bore in her womb. Like Abraham, she accepted the sacrifice of her Son.*[175]

Here the reference to the amalgamating of the two sacrifices on the part of Mary is subtle but real. Mary is compared to Abraham in that both of them gave their consent to the sacrifice of their only son, but in the case of Abraham, the consent was all that was required. In the case of Mary, however, the sacrifice was carried out, effectively requiring of her the sacrifice of her maternal heart,[176] indeed of her very life.

The "joint but subordinate" sacrifice on the part of Mary has profound ecclesial reverberations. In treating of the "woman clothed with the sun," who appears in the twelfth chapter of the Book of Revelation, as being an image of the Church and of Mary, the Pope makes this comment in his catechesis of 29 May 1996:

Identified by her motherhood, the woman "was with child and she cried out in her pangs of birth, in anguish for her delivery" (12:2). This note refers to the Mother of Jesus at the Cross (cf. Jn. 19:25), where she shares in anguish for the delivery of the community of disciples with a soul pierced by the sword (cf. Lk. 2:35). Despite her sufferings, she is "clothed with the sun" — that is, she reflects the divine splendour —

---

[175] *OR* 24 febbraio 2000, p. 7 [*ORE* 1632:11]; emphasis my own.

[176] Cf. my treatment of the sacrifice of Mary's maternal Heart in *MMC* 213-218; *Foundations II:* 140-144. For a more detailed study of the Heart of Mary as a symbol of her collaboration in the work of our salvation, cf. my article, "The Heart of Mary as Coredemptrix in the Magisterium of Pope John Paul II" in *S. Tommaso Teologo: Ricerche in occasione dei due centenari accademici* (Città del Vaticano: Libreria Editrice Vaticana "Stdi Tomistici #59," 1995) 320-335; An Italian trans. "Il Cuore di Maria Corredentrice nel Magistero di papa Giovanni Paolo II" was published in *Corredemptrix: Annali Mariani 1996 del Santuario dell'Addolorata* (Castelpetroso, Isernia, 1997) 97-114.

and appears as a "great sign" of God's spousal relationship with his people.[177]

Here the Pope, in effect, proposes a datum of the tradition i.e., that while Mary gave birth to Jesus in a painless way, her intense sufferings in union with Jesus on Calvary were the birth pangs by which she "begets as her children all those who become [his] disciples."

At the foot of the cross, then, Mary is not only a partner in the passion (*socia passionis*)[178] but is instrumental in giving birth to the Church. Note well that there are two striking symbols for the generation of the Church on Calvary: the pierced Heart of Jesus from which flows blood and water, "the fountain of sacramental life in the Church"[179] and the Heart of Mary to which the Holy Father makes an allusion in the above text by referring to Lk. 2:35.

Quite clearly, there is a partnership for the sake of our salvation, but it is not a partnership of strict equality, as the Holy Father tells us in the same catechesis of 29 May 1996:

> It was fitting that like Christ, the new Adam, Mary too, the new Eve, did not know sin and was thus capable of co-operating in the Redemption.
>
> Sin, which washes over humanity like a torrent, halts before *the Redeemer and his faithful Collaborator*. With a substantial difference: *Christ is all holy by virtue of the grace that in his humanity derives from the divine person: Mary is all holy by virtue of the grace received by the merits of the Saviour.*[180]

Developing the notion of Mary's labor pains on Calvary for the birth of the Church (cf. Rev. 12:2), the Pope stated in his

---

[177] *Inseg* XIX/1 (1996) 1391 [*ORE* 1444:11; *MCat* 95].

[178] On the concept of Mary as associate or partner in the work of salvation according to the liturgy, cf. my study in *Foundations I*:52-54. On this same concept according to the magisterium, cf. my studies in *MMC* 167-179 and in *Foundations II*:126-127.

[179] *Roman Missal*, Preface of the Sacred Heart of Jesus.

[180] *Inseg* XIX/1 (1996) 1392 [*ORE* 1444:11; *MCat* 96]; emphasis my own.

catechesis of 17 September 1997:

> *On Calvary, Mary united herself to the sacrifice of her Son and*
> *made her own maternal contribution to the work of salvation,*
> *which took the form of labour pains, the birth of the new hu-*
> *manity.*
>
> In addressing the words "Woman, behold your son" to
> Mary, the Crucified One proclaims her motherhood not only
> in relation to the Apostle John but also to every disciple.
> The Evangelist himself, by saying that Jesus had to die "to
> gather into one the children of God who are scattered abroad"
> (Jn. 11:52), indicates *the Church's birth as the fruit of the re-*
> *demptive sacrifice with which Mary is maternally associated.*[181]

Always subordinate and secondary, nonetheless Mary's "maternal contribution to the work of salvation" is unique and the
sacrifice by which the Church was born cannot be separated
from her maternal collaboration.

V. Evaluation

At this point I deem it indispensable to introduce into this
discussion #25 of the Second Vatican Council's Dogmatic Constitution on the Church *Lumen Gentium*, a text of capital importance on the Pope's magisterium or teaching office:

> This loyal submission of the will and intellect must be given,
> in a special way, to the authentic teaching authority
> [*magisterium*] of the Roman Pontiff, even when he does not
> speak *ex cathedra* in such wise, indeed, that his supreme teach-
> ing authority be acknowledged with respect, and that one
> sincerely adhere to decisions made by him, conformably with
> his manifest mind and intention, which is made known prin-
> cipally either (1) by the character of the documents in ques-
> tion, or (2) by the frequency with which a certain doctrine is

---

[181] *Inseg* XX/2 (1997) 331 [*ORE* 1509:11; *MCat* 234]; emphasis my own.

proposed, or (3) by the manner in which the doctrine is for-mulated.[182]

On the basis of a careful analysis of this passage I have argued in my book *Totus Tuus* that the Pope's teaching on consecration or entrustment to Mary forms an important component of his "or-dinary magisterium"[183] and that he has brought this doctrine to a new level of importance.

I believe that an identical case may be made for his teaching on Mary's altogether unique role in the work of our redemption and even for his use of the term Co-redemptrix. I would cer-tainly not argue that his use of the word Co-redemptrix occurs in papal documents of the highest teaching authority or that he has proclaimed the doctrine or used the word in the most sol-emn manner. I do believe, however, that my presentation here and in the other essays that I have written on this topic demon-strates beyond the shadow of a doubt that the Holy Father's teaching on Mary's unique collaboration in and contribution to the work of our redemption has brought the teaching to a new clarity and is an unmistakable component of his ordinary magisterium — precisely on the basis of the second criterion indicated in *Lumen Gentium* #25, the frequency with which he has proposed this doctrine. I will go further and argue that six instances of his use of the term Co-redemptrix to characterize Our Lady's collaboration in the work of our redemption — es-pecially in the light of previous magisterial usage — do not de-serve to be easily dismissed as "marginal [and] therefore devoid of doctrinal weight."[184]

I am grateful to Father Ignazio Calabuig, O.S.M., one of the signers of the Czestochowa Declaration and President of the Pontifical Faculty Marianum, and his colleagues who have recently acknowledged that my study of the use of the term Co-

---

[182] Flannery 379. I have added the numbers.

[183] Cf. *Totus Tuus* 266-269.

[184] The Italian speaks of *documenti pontifici secondari, e quindi senza peso dottrinale*.

redemptrix published in *Maria Corredentrice: Storia e Teologia I* was done with praiseworthy precision and clearly indicates that the title is not proscribed and is susceptible of a correct reading. I still respectfully disagree with them, however, when they state that the word occurs only in documents of a non-magisterial character.[185]

A final question and response: "How do we best describe this secondary and subordinate, but nonetheless active and unique role willed by God for Mary in the work of our redemption?" Our Holy Father has used a good number of descriptive titles such as collaborator and cooperator, associate and ally. He has called her "the perfect co-worker in Christ's sacrifice" (*perfetta cooperatrice del sacrificio di Cristo*)[186] and "the perfect model for those who seek to be united with her Son in his saving work for all humanity."[187]

This is a matter on which neither our present Holy Father nor any of his predecessors have pronounced and we are quite free to debate it. Quite obviously scholars, theologians and persons of good will have varying opinions in this regard. My argument would simply be that none of the one-word titles such as collaborator, cooperator, co-worker, associate, partner and ally sufficiently accentuates the uniqueness of Mary's role whereas others seem to me to be either lengthy phrases or cumbersome circumlocutions.[188]

While granting that five of Pope John Paul II's usages of the term Co-redemptrix were passing references, I do not believe that these should be undervalued any more than the three us-

---

[185] Ignazio M. Calabuig, O.S.M. e il Comitato di redazione della rivista Marianum, "Riflessione sulla richiesta della definizione dogmatica di Maria corredentrice, mediatrice, avvocata," *Marianum* LXI (1999) 157 n. 50.

[186] *Inseg* XIX/1 (1996) 1344 [*ORE* 1446:6].

[187] *Inseg* XVIII/2 (1995) 54 [*ORE* 1399:3].

[188] With apologies to Father Aidan Nichols, O.P. I would put his proposal of "The Redemptive Collaboratrix" among these. Cf. his article "Von Balthasar and the Coredemption" in *Mary at the Foot of the Cross: Acts of the International Symposium on Marian Coredemption* (New Bedford, MA: Academy of the Immaculate, 2001) 314.

ages by Roman Congregations at the beginning of the last century or the three usages by Pope Pius XI. These are a testimony to the Church's living tradition and to the legitimate employment of the term. What I would simply present here is that, once it has been made clear that the "co" in Co-redemptrix does not mean equal to the Redeemer, but subordinate to him,[189] it is arguable that it expresses the reality of Mary's altogether unique and active participation better than any other.

In any case, the study of the magisterium on this matter convinces me that the Holy Spirit is moving the Church ineluctably and ever more compellingly in the direction of highlighting Mary's active role in our redemption. We have seen that the papal teaching has become ever more vigorous and insistent in this regard — and I have by no means been able to present all of it. In fact, the output from this pontificate alone exceeds that of all the previous pontificates taken together!

The more this teaching is studied, understood and proclaimed, the more powerful positive results we can expect for the Church and the world. Indeed, the more we grasp Mary's divinely ordained role in our salvation, the more we are motivated to call upon her who is the Mediatrix of all graces and the Advocate of God's people. In this dramatic hour of crisis it will certainly be argued by many that there are far more urgent matters to be dealt with and yet in the struggle with the powers of darkness which continues unabated, who has the Father given as our defense along with the "New Adam," if not the "New Eve"? I believe that this is a profound truth which the Spirit has been speaking to the Church in modern times — and never more than in our own day through our present Holy Father.

Laus Cordibus Jesu Virginisque Matris Eius

---

[189] Cf. Mark I. Miravalle, S.T.D., *Mary: Coredemptrix, Mediatrix, Advocate* (Santa Barbara, CA: Queenship Publishing, 1993) xv; *MMC 147-148*; *Foundations II,* 117-118.

KEY TO ABBREVIATIONS

AAS   *Acta Apostolicæ Sedis* (1909 —).

ASS   *Acta Sanctæ Sedis* (1865-1908).

Burke   Thomas J. M. Burke, S.J., ed., *Mary and the Popes:*
                 Five Great Marian Letters (New York: The
                 America Press, 1954).

CDD   Sacrosanctum Oecumenicum Concilium
                 Vaticanum II: *Constitutiones, Decreta,*
                 Declarationes cura et studio Secretariæ Generalis
                 Concilii Oecumenici Vaticani II (Vatican City:
                 Typis Polyglottis Vaticanis, 1974).

D-H   Heinrich Denzinger, S.I., *Enchiridion Symbolorum*
                 Definitionum et Declarationum de Rebus Fidei et
                 Morum: Edizione Bilingue (XXXVII) a cura di
                 Peter Hünermann (Bologna: Edizioni Dehoniane,
                 2000).

Flannery   Austin Flannery, O.P., ed., *Vatican Council II: The*
                 Conciliar and Post Conciliar Documents
                 (Collegeville, MN: Liturgical Press, 1975).

Foundations I Mark I. Miravalle, S.T.D., (ed.), *Mary —*
                 Coredemptrix, Mediatrix, Advocate — Theological
                 Foundations — Towards a Papal Definition?
                 (Santa Barbara, CA: Queenship Publishing, 1995).

Foundations II Mark I. Miravalle, S.T.D., (ed.), *Mary*
                 Coredemptrix, Mediatrix, Advocate—Theological
                 Foundations II: Papal, Pneumatological,
                 Ecumenical (Santa Barbara, CA: Queenship
                 Publishing Company, 1997).

Foundations III	Mark I. Miravalle, S.T.D., (ed.), *Contemporary insights on a Fifth Marian Dogma; Mary Coredemptrix, Mediatrix, Adocate: Theological Foundation III* (Santa Barbara, CA: Queenship Publishing Company, 2000).
Il "calvario"	Alessandro M. Apollonio, *Il "calvario teologico" della Coredenzione mariana* (Castelpetroso, IS: Casa Mariana Editrice, 1999).
Inseg	*Insegnamenti di Giovanni Paolo II*, I (1978-) (Città del Vaticano: Libreria Editrice Vaticana, 1979--).
Inseg P	*Insegnamenti di Paolo VI*, I-XVI (1963-1978) (Vatican City: Libreria Editrice Vaticana, 1963-1978).
Laurentin	René Laurentin, *Le titre de Corédemptrice: Étude historique* (Roma: Marianum, 1951).
Maria	Hubert du Manoir, S.J. (ed.), *Maria: Études sur la Sainte Vierge* 8 vols. (Paris: Beauchesne et Ses Fils, 1949-1971).
Mariology	Juniper B. Carol, O.F.M. (ed.), *Mariology* 3 vols. (Milwaukee: Bruce Publishing Co., 1955-1961).
MGMO	Pope Paul VI, *Mary — God's Mother and Ours* (Boston: St. Paul Editions, 1979).
OL	*Our Lady: Papal Teachings*, trans. Daughters of St. Paul (Boston: St. Paul Editions, 1961).
MCat	Pope John Paul II, *Theotókos - Woman, Mother, Disciple: A Catechesis on Mary, Mother of God* with a Foreword by Eamon R. Carroll, O.Carm, S.T.D. (Boston: Pauline Books and Media, 2000).

MMC	Arthur Burton Calkins, "Il Mistero di Maria Corredentrice nel Magistero Pontificio" in Autori Vari, *Maria Corredentrice: Storia e Teologia I* (Frigento [AV]: Casa Mariana Editrice «*Bibliotheca Corredemptionis B. V. Mariæ*» Studi e Ricerche 1, 1998) 141-220.
OR	*L'Osservatore Romano*, daily Italian edition.
ORE	*L'Osservatore Romano*, weekly edition in English. First number = cumulative edition number; second number = page.
Pii IX Acta	*Pii IX Pontificis Maximi Acta* (Graz, Austria: Akademische Druck- u. Verlagsanstelt, 1971).
Prob	Gabriele M. Roschini, O.S.M., *Problematica sulla Corredenzione* (Roma: Edizioni "Marianum," 1969).
Rosary	*The Rosary: Papal Teachings*, trans. Paul J. Oligny, O.F.M. (Boston: St. Paul Editions, 1980).
Summa Aurea	Jean-Jacques Bourassé, *Summa Aurea de Laudibus Beatissimæ Virginis Mariæ* Vols. 1-12 (Paris: J.-P. Migne, 1862); Vol. 13 (Paris: J.-P. Migne, 1866).
TPS	*The Pope Speaks*, 1 - (1954 -)
Theotokos	Michael O'Carroll, C.S.Sp., *Theotokos: A Theological Encyclopedia of the Blessed Virgin Mary* (Wilmington: Michael Glazier, Inc.; Dublin: Dominican Publications, 1982).
Totus Tuus	Arthur Burton Calkins, *Totus Tuus: John Paul II's Program of Marian Consecration and Entrustment* (New Bedford, MA: Academy of the Immaculate "Studies and Texts," No. 1, 1992).

Mary Co-redemptrix:
A Response to 7 Common Objections

Dr. Mark I. Miravalle, S.T.D.

Dr. Miravalle is a Professor of Theology and Mariology at the Franciscan University of Steubenville and President of the international Catholic movement, Vox Populi Mariae Mediatrici. He is author and editor of several books and anthologies in Mariology.

On December 23, 2000, the *New York Times* ran a cover story in its "Arts and Ideas" section on the *Vox Populi Mariae Mediatrici* movement, which seeks the papal definition of the Blessed Virgin Mary as the Co-redemptrix, Mediatrix of all graces and Advocate. This article was in turn reprinted in a great number of U.S. major newspapers, thereby sparking renewed and high-spirited debate across the country over the concept of Our Lady as "Co-redemptrix," both inside and outside the Catholic circles of thought.

Although diverse in their formulation, most objections to Our Lady's title of Co-redemptrix and her subsequent role in Coredemption fall into the same foundational categories (many of which were debated in recent publications in response to the *New York Times* piece). There is a critical need to articulate to the general public (let alone to the growing genus of uncatechized Catholic faithful), the basic doctrinal truths contained in the

Church's use of Co-redemptrix and its ongoing discussion pertinent to a possible papal definition.

The call of the Second Vatican Council to "bring Christ to the world", with an evangelical focus not simply within the confines of the Church, but to the entire world, applies as well to the Christian truth regarding the Mother of Christ. This conciliar call to proclaim Christian truth to the world, inclusive of *Christian truth about Mary,* is at the same time an evangelical call that must be free from any doctrinal compromise in presenting the full truth about Mary as officially taught by the Catholic Church—a doctrinal truth which essentially includes Marian coredemption.

What follows then is a synthesis of seven common objections to Mary Co-redemptrix and the doctrinal role of Marian coredemption, taken principally from recent publications, both secular and Christian. A fundamental summary response will be offered to each objection, with general mind for the Catholic and non-Catholic reader alike. In an effort to allow each response to stand independently of the other responses, some content is repeated within responses where appropriate.

> Objection 1. *Calling Mary a "Co-redemptrix" places her on an equal level with Jesus Christ, the Divine Son of God, making her something like a fourth person of the Trinity, a goddess or quasi-divine goddess, which is blasphemy for any true Christian.*

The Catholic Church's use of the title "Co-redemptrix" as applied to the Mother of Jesus in no sense places Mary on a level of equality with Jesus Christ, the divine Redeemer. There is an infinite difference between the divine person of Jesus Christ and the human person, Mary. Rather, papal teaching has used the title "Co-redemptrix" to refer to the unique participation of the Mother of Jesus with and under her divine son in the work of human redemption.

The term "co-redemptrix" is properly translated "the woman with the redeemer" or more literally "she who buys back with [the redeemer]." The prefix, "co," comes from the Latin term "cum," which means "with" and not "equal to." Co-redemptrix therefore as applied to Mary refers to her exceptional cooperation with and under her divine son, Jesus Christ, in the redemption of the human family, as manifested in Christian Scripture.

With Mary's free and active "fiat" to the invitation of the angel Gabriel to become the mother of Jesus, "Be it done unto me according to your word" (Lk. 1:38), she uniquely cooperated with the work of redemption by giving the divine Redeemer his body, which was the very instrument of human redemption. "We have been sanctified by the offering of the body of Jesus Christ once for all" (Heb. 10:10), and the body of Jesus Christ is given to him through the free, active, and unique cooperation of the Virgin Mary. By virtue of giving flesh to the "Word made flesh" (Jn.1:14), who in turn redeems humanity, the Virgin of Nazareth uniquely merits the title Co-redemptrix. In the words of the late Mother Teresa of Calcutta, "Of course Mary is the Co-redemptrix—she gave Jesus his body, and his body is what saved us."[1]

The New Testament prophecy of Simeon in the temple also reveals the suffering, co-redemptive mission of Mary in direct union with her Redeemer son in their one unified work of redemption: "Simeon blessed them, and said to Mary, his mother, 'Behold, this child is set for the fall and rise of many in Israel, and will be a sign of contradiction, and a sword shall pierce through your own soul, too.'" (Lk. 2:34-35)

But the climax of Mary's role as Co-redemptrix under her divine son takes place at the foot of the Cross, where the total suffering of the mother's heart is obediently united to the suffering of the Son's heart in fulfillment of the Father's plan of

---

[1] Mother Teresa of Calcutta, Personal Interview, Calcutta, August 14, 1993.

redemption (cf. Gal. 4:4). As the fruit of this redemptive suffering, Mary is given by the crucified Savior as the spiritual mother of all peoples, "'Woman, behold your son!' Then he said to the disciple, 'behold, your mother!'" (Jn.19:27). As described by Pope John Paul II, Mary was "spiritually crucified with her crucified son" at Calvary, and "her role as Co-redemptrix did not cease with the glorification of her Son."[2] Even after the accomplishment of the acquisition of the graces of redemption at Calvary, Mary's co-redemptive role continues in the distribution of those saving graces to the hearts of humanity.

The earliest Christian writers and Fathers of the Church explained Marian coredemption with great profundity in simplicity in the first theological model of Mary as the "New Eve." Essentially, they articulated that as Eve, the first "mother of the living" (Gen. 3:20) was directly instrumental with Adam, the father of the human race, in the loss of grace for all humanity, so too Mary, the "New Eve," was directly instrumental with Jesus Christ, whom St. Paul calls the "New Adam" (Cf. 1 Cor. 15:45-48), in the restoration of grace to all humanity. In the words of 2nd century Church Father, St. Irenaeus: "Just as Eve, wife of Adam, yet still a virgin, became by her disobedience the cause of death for herself and the whole human race, so Mary, too, espoused yet a virgin, became by her obedience the *cause of salvation for herself and the whole human race*." [3]

In light of her unique and direct cooperation with the Redeemer in the restoration of grace for the human family (cf. Gen. 3:15), Mary became universally known in the early Church as the "New Mother of the Living," and her instrumental coredemption with Christ was well summed up in the succinct expression of 4th century Church Father, St. Jerome: "Death through Eve, life through Mary."[4]

---

[2] John Paul II, Papal Address, Jan. 31, 1985, Guayaquil, Ecuador, (O.R., March 13, 1985).

[3] St. Irenaeus of Lyons, *Adversus haeresus*, III, 22, emphasis author's.

[4] St. Jerome. *Epist.* 22, 21.

Explicit references to Marian coredemption as Mary's unique participation with and under Jesus Christ in redeeming or "buying back" humanity from the slavery of Satan and sin is present throughout Christian Tradition. For example, the 7th century Church writer, Modestus of Jerusalem, states that through Mary, we "are redeemed from the tyranny of the devil."[5] St John Damascene (8th century) greets her: "Hail thou, through whom we are redeemed from the curse."[6] St. Bernard of Clairvaux (12th century) preaches that, "through her, man was redeemed."[7] The great Franciscan Doctor, St. Bonaventure (13th century) aptly summarizes Christian Tradition in this teaching: "That woman (namely Eve), drove us out of Paradise and sold us; but this one (Mary) brought us back again *and bought us*."[8]

Although there was never any question of the total and radical dependency of the Virgin Mary's participation in redemption upon the divine work and merits of Jesus Christ in the minds of the Church fathers and doctors, nonetheless early Christian Tradition did not hesitate to teach and preach the unparalleled intimate participation of the woman, Mary, in the "buying back" or redeeming of the human race from the slavery of Satan. As humanity was sold by a man and a woman, so it was God's will that humanity would be bought back by a Man and a woman.

It is upon this rich Christian foundation that 20th century popes and saints have used the title Co-redemptrix for Mary's unique role in human redemption, as exemplified in the contemporary use of Co-redemptrix for Mary by Pope John Paul II on six occasions during his present pontificate.[9] "Co-redemptrix" as used by the popes means no more that Mary is a goddess

---

[5] Modestus of Jerusalem, Migne PG 86; 3287.

[6] St. John Damascene, PG 86; 658.

[7] St. Bernard of Clairvaux, Ser. III, *super Salve*.

[8] St. Bonaventure, de don. Sp. 6; 14., emphasis author's.

[9] Cf. Calkins, *The Mystery of Mary Co-redemptrix in the Papal Magisterium* in this present volume.

equal with Jesus Christ than St. Paul's identification of all Christians as "God's co-workers"(1 Cor. 3:9) means that Christians are gods equal to the one God.

All Christians are rightly called to be co-workers or "co-redeemers" with Jesus Christ (cf. Col. 1:24) in the reception and cooperation with grace necessary for our own redemption and the redemption of others—personal, subjective redemption made possible by the historic objective redemption or "buying back" accomplished by Jesus Christ, the "New Adam," the *Redemptor*, and Mary, the "New Eve," the *Co-redemptrix*.

Objection 2: *Calling the Blessed Virgin Mary "Co-redemptrix" is against proper Christian ecumenism, as it leads to division between Catholics and other Christians.*

Arguably the most commonly posed objection to the use of Co-redemptrix (let alone any potential definition of the doctrine) is its perceived opposition to Christian ecumenism. Therefore we must begin with an accurate definition of authentic Christian ecumenism and its appropriate corresponding activity as understood by the Catholic Church.

In his papal document on ecumenism, *Ut Unum Sint* ("That They May Be One"), Pope John Paul II defines authentic Christian ecumenism in terms of prayer "as the soul" and dialogue "as the body" working towards the ultimate goal of true and lasting Christian unity.[10] At the same time, the Catholic imperative to work and strive for Christian unity does not permit *in any degree* the reduction or dilution of Catholic doctrinal teaching, as such would both lack Catholic integrity and concurrently be misleading in dialogue with other non-Catholic Christians as to what the Catholic Church truly believes.

As the Second Vatican Council clearly teaches in terms of ecumenical dialogue: "It is, of course, essential that doctrine be

---

[10] Cf. John Paul II, *Ut Unum Sint*, 21, 28.

clearly presented in its entirety. Nothing is so foreign to the spirit of ecumenism as a false conciliatory approach which harms the purity of Catholic doctrine and obscures its assured genuine meaning."[11]

John Paul II further explains: "With regard to the study of areas of disagreement, the Council requires that the whole body of doctrine be clearly presented. At the same time, it asks that the manner and method of expounding the Catholic faith should not be a hindrance to dialogue with our brothers and sisters ... Full communion of course will have to come about through the acceptance of the whole truth into which the Holy Spirit guides Christ's disciples. Hence all forms of reductionism or facile 'agreement' must be absolutely avoided."[12]

An accurate understanding then of ecumenism from the Catholic perspective is the critical Church mandate to pray, to dialogue, and to work together in charity and in truth in the seeking of true Christian unity among all brothers and sisters in Christ, but without compromise in presenting the full doctrinal teachings of the Church. The present pope, so personally dedicated to authentic Christian unity, again affirms: "The unity willed by God can be attained only by the adherence of all to the content of revealed faith in its entirety. In matters of faith, compromise is in contradiction with God who is Truth. In the Body of Christ, 'the way, the truth, and the life' (Jn.14:6), who could consider legitimate a reconciliation brought about at the expense of the truth?"[13]

Let us now apply this understanding of ecumenism to the question of Mary Co-redemptrix. The Co-redemptrix title for Mary has been used in repeated papal teaching, and the doctrine of Marian coredemption as Mary's unique participation with and under Jesus Christ in the redemption of humanity

---

[11] Second Vatican Council, *Unitatis Redintegratio*, n.11.
[12] John Paul II, *Ut Unum Sint*, n. 36.
[13] John Paul II, *Ut Unum Sint*, 18.

constitutes the repeated doctrinal teaching of the Second Vatican Council:

> ...She devoted herself totally, as handmaid of the Lord, to the person and work of her Son, under and with him, serving the mystery of redemption, by the grace of Almighty God. Rightly, therefore, the Fathers see Mary not merely as passively engaged by God, but as freely cooperating in the work of man's salvation through faith and obedience.[14]

And further:

> Thus the Blessed Virgin advanced in her pilgrimage of faith, and faithfully persevered in union with her Son unto the cross, where she stood, in keeping with the divine plan, enduring with her only begotten Son the intensity of his suffering, associating herself with his sacrifice in her mother's heart, and lovingly consenting to the immolation of this victim which was born of her.[15]

And further:

> She conceived, brought forth, and nourished Christ, she presented Him to the Father in the Temple, shared her Son's suffering as He died on the cross. Thus, in a wholly singular way she cooperated by her obedience, faith, hope, and burning charity in the work of the Savior in restoring supernatural life to souls. For this reason she is a mother to us in the order of grace.[16]

Thereby, there is no question that Marian coredemption constitutes the doctrinal teaching of the Catholic Church and as such must be presented in any true articulation of Catholic teaching, which critically includes the domain of true ecumenical dialogue.

---

[14] Second Vatican Council, *Lumen Gentium*, n. 56.
[15] *Lumen Gentium*, n. 58.
[16] *Lumen Gentium*, n. 61.

Hence to claim that Mary Co-redemptrix in title and doctrine is in any way contrary to the ecumenical mission of the Church is fundamentally to misunderstand the ecumenical mission of the Church itself. Full Catholic doctrine, including the doctrine of Marian coredemption, must be included for any true dialogue seeking Christian unity. Moreover, the purposeful absence of Mary Co-redemptrix in full ecumenical dialogue and in the overall ecumenical mission of the Church would lack integrity and justice for the Catholic ecumenist towards non-Catholic Christians who have presumably, on their part, brought the full teachings of their particular ecclesial body to the tables of dialogue. To return to the Christian admonition of John Paul II: "In the Body of Christ, 'the way, the truth, and the life' (Jn.14:6), who could consider legitimate a reconciliation brought about at the expense of the truth?"[17]

In fact, if the doctrine of Co-redemptrix presently constitutes a source of confusion for some Christians, connoting for some an image of goddess or other concepts of Marian excesses, then it appears all the more appropriate that a clear articulation of this Marian doctrine be given to brother and sister Christians in ecumenical dialogue. Here lies the potential benefit of a formal papal definition providing the greatest possible clarity from the highest possible Catholic authority. In the words of the late John Cardinal O'Connor of New York: "Clearly, a formal papal definition would be articulated in such precise terminology that other Christians would lose their anxiety that we do not distinguish adequately between Mary's unique association with Christ and the redemptive power exercised by Christ alone."[18]

Properly understood as the Spiritual Mother of all peoples, the consequence of her Coredemption, Mary can be properly recognized as the principal intercessor for Christian unity among

---

[17] John Paul II, *Ut Unum Sint*, 18.
[18] John Cardinal O'Connor, Endorsement Letter For Papal Definition of Mary, Co-redemptrix, Mediatrix, Advocate, February 14, 1994.

Christian brothers and sisters, rather than as its prime obstacle. Lutheran pastor, Rev. Dr. Charles Dickson, calls on Protestant Christianity to re-examine the documented positive Marian defense and devotion of many of its own founders, as manifested, for example, in the words of Martin Luther in his *Commentary on the Magnificat*: "May the tender Mother of God herself procure for me the spirit of wisdom profitably and thoroughly to expound this song of hers...May Christ grant us a right understanding...through the intercession and for the sake of His dear Mother Mary...."[19] Luther goes on to call Mary the "workshop of God," the "Queen of heaven," and states: "The Virgin Mary means to say simply that her praise will be sung from one generation to another so that there will never be a time when she will not be praised."[20]

On the role of Mary's universal spiritual motherhood as an instrument of Christian unity, Dr. Dickson further comments:

> In our time, we are still faced with the tragic divisions among the world's Christians. Yet, standing on the brink of a bright new ecumenical age, Mary as model of catholicity, or universality, becomes even more important. In the course of many centuries from the beginning of the Church, from the time of Mary and the Apostles, the motherhood of the Church was one. This fundamental motherhood cannot vanish, even though divisions occur. Mary, through her motherhood, maintains the universality of Christ's flock. As the entire Christian community turns to her, the possibility of a new birth, a reconciliation, increases. So Mary, the mother of the Church, is also a source of reconciliation among her scattered and divided children.[21]

---

[19] Martin Luther, *Commentary on the Magnificat*, 1521, as quoted in Dr. Charles Dickson, *A Protestant Pastor Looks at Mary*, 1996, Our Sunday Visitor Press, p. 41, 42.

[20] Ibid.

[21] Dickson, *A Protestant Pastor Looks at Mary*, p. 48-49.

Objection 3 : *Calling the Mother of Jesus "Co-redemptrix" or her subsequent role as "Mediatrix" implies a role of mediation by someone other than Jesus Christ, but scripture plainly states in 1 Timothy 2:5 that "there is one God and one mediator between God and men, the 'man Christ Jesus,'" and therefore no creature can rightly be a mediator.*

The definition of "mediator" (in Greek, *mesitis*— "go-between") is a person who intervenes between two other persons or parties for the goal of uniting or reconciling the parties. Applying this term to Jesus Christ, St. Paul indeed states that there is one mediator between God and humanity, namely the "man Christ Jesus." No one therefore reaches God the Father except through the one, perfect mediation of Jesus Christ.

But the question still remains, does the one perfect mediation of Jesus Christ prevent or rather provide for others to subordinately participate in the one mediation of Jesus Christ? In other words, does the one exclusive mediation of Christ prevent any creature from participating in that one essential mediation? Or does its divine and human perfection allow others to share in his one mediation in a subordinate and secondary way?

Christian Scripture offers several analogous examples where Christians are obliged to participate in something that is also "one," exclusive, and dependent entirely on the person of Jesus Christ.

The one Sonship of Jesus Christ. There is only one true son of God, Jesus Christ, who was begotten from God the Father (1 Jn. 1-4). But all Christians are called to participate in the one true sonship of Jesus Christ by becoming "adopted sons" in Christ (cf. 2 Cor. 5:17; 1 Jn. 3:1; Gal. 2:20). Filial adoption allows a true sharing in the one sonship of Christ through baptism, which allows adopted sons and daughters to also share in the inheritance of the one Son, that of everlasting life.

Living in the One Christ. All Christians are called to share in the "one life" of Jesus Christ, for *grace* is to participate in the life and the love of Jesus Christ, and through him in the life and love of the Trinity. As St. Paul teaches, "it is not I, but Christ who lives in me" (Gal. 2:20) and 2 Peter 1:4 calls Christians to become "partakers of the divine nature," to live in the one Christ, and thus in the life of the Trinity.

The one Priesthood of Jesus Christ. All Christians are also called to share in different degrees in the one priesthood of Jesus Christ. The book of Hebrews identifies Jesus Christ as the one "high priest" (cf. Heb. 3:1; 4:14; 5:10) who offers the great spiritual sacrifice of himself on Calvary. And yet Scripture calls all Christians, albeit on different levels of participation, ministerial (cf. Acts 14:22) or royal (cf.1 Pet. 2:9), to participate in the one priesthood of Jesus Christ in offering spiritual sacrifice. All Christians are instructed to "offer spiritual sacrifices acceptable to God" (1 Pet. 2:5, 2:9).

In all these cases, the New Testament calls Christians to share in that which is one and unique of Jesus Christ, the Alpha and Omega, in true though completely subordinate levels of participation. In reference, then, to Christ the one Mediator (1 Tim. 2:5), we see the same Christian imperative for others to share or participate in the one mediation of Jesus Christ, but in a secondary mediation entirely dependent upon the one perfect mediation of Jesus Christ.

The pivotal christological question must then be asked: Does such subordinate sharing in the one mediation of Christ obscure the one mediation of Christ, or rather does it manifest the glory of his one mediation? This is easily answered by imagining a contemporary world without "adopted sons and daughters in Christ," without Christians today sharing in the one life of Jesus Christ in grace, or further, without any Christians offering spiritual sacrifices in the domain of Christian priesthood. Such an absence of human participation would only result in obscuring the one Sonship, the one High Priesthood, and the very Life of grace in Jesus Christ.

The same principle holds true regarding participation in the one mediation of Jesus Christ in a dependent and subordinate way. *The principle is clear: the more humanity participates in the one mediation of Christ, the more the perfection, power, and glory of the unique and necessary mediation of Jesus Christ is manifested to the world.*

Christian Scripture moreover offers several examples of God-instituted human mediators who cooperated by divine initiative in uniting humanity with God. The great prophets of the Old Testament were God-ordained mediators between Yahweh and the people of Israel, oftentimes seeking to return the people of Israel to their fidelity to Yahweh (cf. Is. 1; Jer. 1: Ez. 2). The Old Testament patriarchs, Abraham, Isaac, Jacob, and Moses, were, at God's initiative, the human mediators of the saving covenant between Yahweh and the people of Israel (cf. Gen. 12:2; 15:18; Ex. 17:11). St. Paul identifies Moses' mediation of the law to the Israelites: "Why then the law? It was ordained by God through an intermediary" (Gal. 3:19-20). The angels, with hundreds of mediating acts spanning Old and New Testaments, are God's messengers, who mediate for reconciliation between God and the human family, both before and after the coming of Christ, the one Mediator (cf. Gen. 3:24; Lk. 1:26; Lk. 1:19).

In regards to Mary, Christian Scripture also clearly reveals the secondary and subordinate participation of the Mother of Jesus in the one mediation of Jesus Christ. At the Annunciation, Mary's free and active "yes" to the invitation of the angel mediates to the world Jesus Christ, the Redeemer of the world and the Author of all graces (cf. Lk. 1:38). For this unique participation in giving to the Redeemer his body and mediating the Source of all graces to the world, Mary can rightly be called both "Co-redemptrix" and "Mediatrix of all graces" as one who uniquely shares in the one mediation of Jesus Christ.

This unique Marian participation in Christ's mediation, specific to the Redemption of Jesus Christ, is climaxed at Calvary. At the cross, her spiritual suffering united to the redemptive sacrifice of her Son, as the New Eve with the New Adam, leads to the universal spiritual fruits of the acquisition of the graces of redemption. This, in turn, leads to the gift of spiritual motherhood from the heart of the Crucified Christ to every human heart: "Behold your mother" (Jn. 19:27). The Redeemer's gift of his own mother as spiritual mother to all humanity leads to the spiritual nourishment from the Mother to her children in the order of grace. This constitutes her role as Mediatrix of all graces, which perpetually continues her unique sharing in the one saving mediation of Jesus Christ.

John Paul II explains this unique Marian participation in the one mediation of Jesus Christ:

> Mary entered, in a way all her own, into the one mediation between God and men "which is the mediation of the man Christ Jesus...." We must say that through this fullness of grace and supernatural life, she was especially pre-disposed to cooperation with Christ, the one mediator of human salvation. And such cooperation is precisely this mediation subordinated to the mediation of Christ. In Mary's case, we have a special and exceptional mediation.[22]

And in his commentary on 1 Timothy 2:5 and Mary's maternal mediation, the Pontiff further states:

> We recall that Mary's mediation is essentially defined by her divine motherhood. Recognition of her role as mediatrix is moreover implicit in the expression "our Mother," which presents the doctrine of Marian mediation by putting the accent on her motherhood ... In proclaiming Christ the one mediator (cf. 1 Tim. 2:5-6), the text of St. Paul's Letter to

---

[22] John Paul II, *Redemptoris Mater*, 21, 39.

Timothy excludes any other parallel mediation, but not subordinate mediation. In fact, before emphasizing the one exclusive mediation of Christ, the author urges "that supplications, prayers, intercessions and thanksgivings be made for all men" (2:1). Are not prayers a form of mediation? Indeed, according to St. Paul, the unique mediation of Christ is meant to encourage other dependent, ministerial forms of mediation...In truth, what is Mary's maternal mediation if not the Father's gift to humanity?[23]

We see then Mary's participation in the one mediation of Jesus Christ as unique and unparalleled by any other human or angelic participation, and yet entirely subordinate and dependent upon the one mediation of Jesus Christ. As such, Mary's motherly mediation manifests the true glory and power of Christ's mediation like no other. The Marian titles and roles of Co-redemptrix and Mediatrix of all graces (as well as intercessory Advocate) do not in any way violate the prohibition of 1 Tim. 2:5 against any parallel, autonomous, or rival mediation, but bespeak a unique and exceptional motherly participation in that one, perfect, and saving mediation of Jesus Christ.

In the words of Anglican Oxford scholar, Dr. John Macquarrie:

The matter [of Marian mediation] cannot be settled by pointing to the danger of exaggeration and abuse, or by appealing to isolated texts of scripture as the verse quoted above from 1 Timothy 2...or by the desire not to say anything that might offend one's partners in ecumenical dialogue. Unthinking enthusiasts may have elevated Mary's position to a virtual equality with Christ, but this aberration is not a *necessary* consequence of recognizing that there may be a truth striving for expression in words like *Mediatrix* and *Co-redemptrix*.

---

[23] John Paul II, Papal Address, Rome, October 1, 1997, *L'Osservatore Romano*, 1997, 41.

All responsible theologians would agree that Mary's co-redemptive role is subordinate and auxiliary to the central role of Christ. But if she does have such a role, the more clearly we understand it, the better. And like other doctrines concerning Mary, it is not only saying something about her, but something more general about the Church as a whole, and even humanity as a whole.[24]

Objection 4: *To call Mary a co-redemptrix or to call Christians in general "co-redeemers" is to have a human being actively participate in redemption, which is a divine or, more specifically, a "theandric" activity, accomplished by Jesus Christ in his divine and human natures alone, and thus forbidden by Christianity. Such would only encourage paganism, since it places a human person, Mary, as part of a divine redemptive action which only Jesus Christ can accomplish.*

In many ways, the response to this objection can be found in the same foundational evidence from Christian Scripture that responds to the previous objection to any subordinate or human participation in the one mediation of Jesus Christ (a mediation which includes redemption). But let us examine the specific objection regarding Mary's active participation in the divine act of Redemption.

The full objection to Mary's active participation as Co-redemptrix in the redemption accomplished by Jesus Christ has been set out by some objectors as follows. Theandric activity refers to an action by Jesus Christ that is accomplished through both of his natures, divine and human. Since the act of redemption by Jesus Christ was a theandric activity, and Mary was merely human, her actions were not theandric and therefore she can-

---

[24] J. Macquarrie, "Mary Co-redemptrix and Disputes over Justification and Grace" in *Mary Co-redemptrix, Mediatrix, Advocate, Theological Foundations II*, p. 246., also in this present volume.

not actively participate in redemption. Hence, Mary cannot be properly called a "co-redemptrix," a term which means she "bought back" humanity with the Redeemer. Nor should any Christians be called "co-redeemers" since no creature can participate in theandric activity.

To best address this objection, we must return to the essential etymological meaning of the term, "co-redemptrix." The Latin prefix, *cum*, means "with" (and not "equal to"). The Latin verb, *re(d)-emere* means, "to buy back," and the suffix *-trix*, meaning "one who does something," is feminine. In its complete form then, the term co-redemptrix refers to the "woman with the redeemer," or more literally, "the woman who buys back with [the Redeemer]."

As used by the Catholic Church, the term co-redemptrix expresses Mary's active and unique participation in the divine and human activity of redemption accomplished by Jesus Christ. Again, radically dependent and subordinate to the theandric redemptive action of Jesus Christ, the very perfection of this divine and human redemption provides for, rather than prohibits, various levels of true and active human participation.

While it is legitimate to distinguish theandric actions from human actions, it runs contrary to Christian Scripture and Christian Tradition, both ancient and developed, to reject *active human participation in the theandric activity of Jesus Christ.*

To actively participate in a theandric action does not require that the participator also have a divine and human nature. Such is to misunderstand the distinction between "being" (*possessing* the essence and specific attribute as part of who you are) from "participation" (*sharing* in the essence and specific attribute as possessed by another). Thus, Mary as a human creature can actively share in the theandric redemptive action of Jesus Christ without herself possessing the essence of divinity as a specific attribute. In a similar way, all Christians share in the divine nature of Jesus Christ (cf. 2 Pet 1:4), without being gods; participate in the sonship of Jesus Christ (cf. Gal. 4:6) without being divinely begotten; share in the mediation of Christ (cf. Gal. 3:19, 1 Tim. 2:1) without being the one divine and human Mediator (1 Tim. 2:5).

As cited in the first response, Christian Scripture attests to Mary's singular active participation in the Redemption of Jesus Christ. With Mary's free and active "fiat" to the invitation of the angel Gabriel to become the mother of Jesus, "Be it done unto me according to your word" (Lk. 1:38), she uniquely cooperated with the work of redemption by giving the divine Redeemer his body, which was the very instrument of human redemption. The prophecy of Simeon reveals the unparalleled coredemptive mission of Mary in direct union with her Redeemer son in their one unified work of redemption: "And a sword shall pierce your own soul, too" (Lk. 2:34-5). And the climax of Mary's role as Co-redemptrix with and under her divine Son takes place at the foot of the Cross, where the total suffering of the mother's heart is obediently united to the suffering of the Son's heart in fulfillment of God the Father's plan of redemption: "Woman, behold your son!' Then he said to the disciple, 'behold, your mother!'" (Jn. 19:27).

And again as previously cited, the earliest Christian writers and Fathers of the Church explained Marian participation with and under Christ in "buying back" the human family from the slavery of Satan and sin in the first theological model of Mary as the "New Eve." These ancient writers attested to the unity of Redemption by Christ and coredemption by Mary by articulating that as Eve, the first "mother of the living" (Gen. 3:20) was an instrumental cause with Adam, the father of the human race in the loss of grace for all humanity, so too Mary, the "New Eve" was an instrumental cause with Jesus Christ, the "New Adam" (cf. 1 Cor. 15: 45-48, 20-25), in the restoration of grace to all humanity.

In the words of St. Irenaeus: "Just as Eve, wife of Adam, yet still a virgin, became by her disobedience the cause of death for herself and the whole human race, so Mary, too, espoused yet a virgin … became by her obedience the cause of salvation for herself and the whole human race." [25]

Explicit teachings of Mary's active participation with Jesus Christ in redeeming or "buying back" humanity from the slavery of Satan and sin are present throughout early and later Christian Tradition:

Through Mary, we "are redeemed from the tyranny of the devil" (Modestus of Jerusalem, 7th century); [26]

"Hail thou, through whom we are redeemed from the curse" (St John Damascene, 8th century); [27]

"Through her, man was redeemed" (St. Bernard of Clairvaux, 12th century); [28]

"That woman (namely Eve), drove us out of Paradise and sold us; but this one [Mary]brought us back again *and bought us*" (St. Bonaventure, 13th century); [29]

"Just as they [Adam and Eve] were the destroyers of the human race, so these [Jesus Christ and Mary] were its repairers" (St. Bonaventure); [30]

"She [Mary] also merited reconciliation for the entire human race" (St. Bonaventure); [31]

"She paid the price [of redemption] as a woman brave and

[25] St. Irenaeus of Lyons, *Adversus haeresus*, III, 22, emphasis author's.
[26] Modestus of Jerusalem, Migne PG 86; 3287.
[27] St. John Damascene, PG 86; 658.
[28] St. Bernard of Clairvaux, Ser. III, *super Salve*.
[29] St. Bonaventure, de don. Sp. 6; 14., emphasis author's.
[30] St. Bonaventure, Sermo III *de Assumptione*, Opera Omnia, v.9.
[31] St. Bonaventure, Sent. III.

loving—namely when Christ suffered on the cross to pay that price in order to purge and wash and redeem us, the Blessed Virgin was present, accepting and agreeing with the divine will" (St. Bonaventure);[32]

"To her alone was given this privilege, namely a communication in the Passion...and in order to make her a sharer in the benefit of Redemption, He willed that she be a sharer in the penalty of the Passion, in so far as she might become the mother of all through re-creation..." (St. Albert the Great [or Pseudo-Albert], 13th century);[33]

"God accepted her oblation as a pleasing sacrifice for the utility and salvation of the whole human race...He foretold to thee [Mary] all thy passion whereby he would make thee a sharer of all of his merits and afflictions, and thou would co-operate with him in the restoration of men to salvation" (John Tauler, 14th century);[34]

"...as one suffering with the Redeemer, for the captive sinner, Co-redemptrix would you be" (14th century).[35]

The Christian teaching on Co-redemptrix continues consistently from the middle ages on into the modern period,[36] as evidenced in these representative citations:

"Saints and doctors have united in calling our Blessed Lady co-redemptrix of the world. There is no question of the lawfulness of using such language, because there is overwhelm-

---

[32] St. Bonaventure, *Collatio de donis Spiritus Sancti 6*, n.16.

[33] St. Albert the Great (or Pseudo-Albert) *Mariale*, Q. 150.

[34] John Tauler, *Sermo pro festo Purificationis Beate Mariae Virginis*.

[35] Oratione, St. Peter's in Salzburg, in *Analecta hymnica medii aevi*, v. 46, p. 126.

[36] For a more comprehensive treatment of Co-redemptrix throughout Christian Tradition, cf. J.B. Carol, *De Corredemptione Beatae Virginis Mariae*, Typis Polyglottis Vaticanis, 1950, p. 125; G. Roschini, O.S.M., *Maria Santissima Nella Storia Della Salvezza*, 1969, v. II, p.171.

ing authority for it…" (Faber, 19th century);[37]

"We think of all the other extraordinary merits, by which she shared with her Son Jesus in the redemption of mankind.…She was not only present at the mysteries of the Redemption, but was also involved with them" (Pope Leo XIII, 19th century);[38]

"To such extent did she suffer and almost die with her suffering and dying Son; to such extent did she surrender her maternal rights over her Son for man's salvation, and immolated Him—insofar as she could—in order to appease the justice of God, that we may rightly say she redeemed the human race together with Christ" (Pope Benedict XV, 20th century);[39]

"From the nature of his work the Redeemer ought to have associated his Mother with his work. For this reason, we invoke her under the title of Co-redemptrix" (Pope Pius XI, 20th century);[40]

"Thus the Blessed Virgin advanced in her pilgrimage of faith, and faithfully persevered in union with her Son unto the cross, where she stood, in keeping with the divine plan, enduring with her only begotten Son the intensity of his suffering, associated herself with his sacrifice in her mother's heart, and lovingly consenting to the immolation of this victim which was born of her" (Second Vatican Council);[41]

"Crucified spiritually with her crucified Son (cf. Gal. 2:20), she contemplated with heroic love the death of her God.…her role as Co-redemptrix did not cease with the glorification of

---

[37] Fr. Fredrick Faber, *At the Foot of the Cross (Sorrows of Mary)*, Reilly Co., 370.

[38] Pope Leo XIII, *Parta humano generi*.

[39] Pope Benedict XV, *Inter Sodalicia*, 1918.

[40] Pope Pius XI, Allocution to Pilgrims of Vicenza, Nov. 30, 1933.

[41] Second Vatican Council, *Lumen Gentium*, n.58.

her Son" (Pope John Paul II, 1985);[42]

"The collaboration of Christians in salvation takes place *after* the Calvary event, whose fruits they endeavor to spread through prayer and sacrifice. Mary instead co-operated *during the event itself* and in the role as mother; thus her co-operation embraces the whole of Christ's saving work. *She alone* was associated in this way with the redemptive sacrifice that merited the salvation of mankind" (Pope John Paul II, 1997).[43]

The Christian Tradition of Mary's unique co-redemptive role continues into the third millennium with this recent papal teaching of John Paul II, where Mary's intimate participation in the death of her Son at Calvary is compared with the Old Testament sacrificial offering made by Abraham (likewise of his own son, offered in an obedience of faith to God):

The summit of this earthly pilgrimage of faith is Golgotha where Mary intimately lives the paschal mystery of her Son: moved in a certain sense as a mother in the death of her Son, and opens herself to the "resurrection" with a new maternity in relation to the Church (cf. Jn. 19:25-27). There, on Calvary, Mary experiences the night of faith, similar to that of Abraham on Mount Moriah ... March 21, 2001).[44]

Without question of the total and radical dependency of Mary's participation in redemption upon the divine work and merits of Jesus Christ, Church Fathers and doctors, along with later and contemporary Christian Tradition nonetheless, do not hesitate to teach the active participation of the woman, Mary, with Jesus Christ in the theandric "buying back" or redeeming of humanity from the slavery of Satan and sin. This Marian

---

[42] John Paul II, Papal Address at Guayaquil, January 31, 1985. (ORE, 876).

[43] John Paul II, General Audience, April 9, 1997.

[44] John Paul II, General Audience, March 21, 2001.

sharing in redemption reflects the ancient Christian teaching that as humanity was lost or "sold" by a man and a woman, so it was God's will that humanity would be redeemed or "bought back" by a Man and a woman.

In what precise way does Mary's participation as Co-redemptrix in human redemption differ from the general call of Christians to participate in the redemption of Jesus Christ?

Indeed Christian Scripture calls all Christians to "make up what is lacking in the sufferings of Christ for the sake of his body, which is the Church" (Col. 1:24). This teaching of St. Paul is not speaking of a participation of all Christians in the historical and universal redemption on Calvary where Jesus Christ acquired the graces of Redemption by his passion and death or "objective redemption." If so, this would incorrectly infer that something was "lacking" in the historic redemptive sufferings and concurring saving merits of Jesus Christ, which were, in itself infinite and inexhaustible.

Rather, St. Paul's teaching refers to the Christian imperative through free co-operation, prayer, and sacrifice to participate in the *release and distribution* of the infinite graces acquired by Jesus Christ on Calvary to the human family or "subjective redemption." Just as every human heart must actively respond in freedom to the saving grace of Jesus Christ for his own personal, subjective redemption, so too the Christian is called to actively participate in the release and distribution of the graces of redemption for others as well, and, in this way, to "make up" what St. Paul calls "lacking" in the sufferings of Christ for the sake of Christ's body. In this regard, all Christians truly participate in subjective redemption, the saving distribution of grace as "God's co-workers" (1Cor. 3:9) or "co-redeemers" (to use the expression of 20th century popes).[45]

Mary's redemptive participation differs from this general Christian call to participate in the distribution of saving graces

---

[45] For example, cf. Pius XI, Papal Allocution at Vicenza, Nov. 30, 1933.

in individual and personal subjective redemption in so far as *she alone also participated*, once again subordinately and entirely dependent upon the Redeemer, in the objective, historical and universal redemption as well, as the New Eve with and under the New Adam. This is why the title Co-redemptrix must in the first place refer exclusively to Mary. As once again articulated by John Paul II in an 1997 Address:

> The collaboration of Christians in salvation takes place *after* the Calvary event, whose fruits they endeavor to spread through prayer and sacrifice. Mary instead co-operated *during the event itself* and in the role as mother; thus her co-operation embraces the whole of Christ's saving work. *She alone* was associated in this way with the redemptive sacrifice that merited the salvation of mankind" (John Paul II, 1997).[46]

Hence, the title and truth of Mary Co-redemptrix as seen in Christian Scripture and Christian Tradition underscores the legitimacy and spiritual fruitfulness for active human participation in the theandric redemptive action of Jesus Christ. For Mary Co-redemptrix, this participation in redemption constitutes a participation in both acquisition and distribution of redemptive graces; and for all other Christians a participation in the distribution of redemptive graces as co-redeemers in Christ. As alluded to by Roman theologian, Fr. Jean Galot, S.J. in his 1997 *L'Osservatore Romano* article on "Mary Co-redemptrix:"

> The title [Co-redemptrix] is criticized because it would suggest an equality between Mary and Christ. The criticism has no foundation...Coredemption implies a subordination to the redemptive work of Christ, because it is only a cooperation and not an independent or parallel work. Hence any equality with Christ is excluded...The word "coredemption," which means "cooperation in redemption," can be applied

---

[46] John Paul II, General Audience, April 9,1997.

to every Christian and to the whole Church. St. Paul writes: "We are God's co-workers" (1 Cor. 3:9).[47]

Objection 5: *The idea of Mary as Co-redemptrix and the teaching of Marian coredemption is a pious belief held by some devotional Catholics, but is not a doctrinal teaching of the Catholic Church. It is found only in minor papal texts and is neither officially taught by the Magisterium, nor is doctrinally present in the teachings of the Second Vatican Council.*

For a member of the Catholic faith, the question of whether a given theological position constitutes an authentic doctrinal teaching of the Church or not is essentially manifested by its presence (or lack thereof) in the teachings from recognized Church authority. The official teaching authority of the Catholic Church, or "Magisterium," consists of the official teaching of the pope and bishops in union with the pope under the guidance of the Holy Spirit.[48]

Although there exists a certain hierarchy amidst the expressions of official Catholic teaching authority, (from the defined dogma of an ecumenical council or papal *ex cathedra* infallible statement, to general ecumenical council doctrinal teaching, to encyclical letters, to more general papal teachings contained in papal addresses), there at the same time remains the general directive for the Catholic faithful that is stated by the Second Vatican Council of the need for a religious assent of mind and heart to the manifest mind of the pope, even when he is not speaking infallibly.[49] And certainly all doctrinal teachings from ecumenical councils, papal encyclicals, or consistently repeated papal teachings would constitute authentic doctrinal teachings

---

[47] Galot, S.J., "*Maria Corredentrice*" in *L'Osservatore Romano*, September 15, 1997, Daily Italian Ed.

[48] Cf. Second Vatican Council, *Dei Verbum*, II, nn.9-10.

[49] Cf. Second Vatican Council, *Lumen Gentium*, n.25.

of the Catholic Church.

Let us now apply this criteria for official Catholic doctrine to the question of the doctrinal status of Marian coredemption.

From the basis of the doctrinal teachings of the Second Vatican Council *alone*, the certainty of the doctrinal status of Marian coredemption is clear. Vatican II repeatedly teaches Mary's unique participation in the redemption of Jesus Christ:

> ...She devoted herself totally, as handmaid of the Lord, to the person and work of her Son, under and with him, serving the mystery of redemption, by the grace of Almighty God. Rightly, therefore, the Fathers see Mary not merely as passively engaged by God, but as freely cooperating in the work of man's salvation through faith and obedience.[50]

And further:

> Thus the Blessed Virgin advanced in her pilgrimage of faith, and faithfully persevered in union with her Son unto the cross, where she stood, in keeping with the divine plan, enduring with her only begotten Son the intensity of his suffering, associated herself with his sacrifice in her mother's heart, and lovingly consenting to the immolation of this victim which was born of her.[51]

And further by the Council:

> She conceived, brought forth, and nourished Christ, she presented Him to the Father in the temple, shared her Son's suffering as He died on the cross. Thus, in a wholly singular way she cooperated by her obedience, faith, hope, and burning charity in the work of the Savior in restoring supernatural life to souls. For this reason she is a mother to us in the order of grace.[52]

---

[50] Second Vatican Council, *Lumen Gentium*, n. 56.

[51] *Lumen Gentium*, n. 58.

[52] *Lumen Gentium*, n. 61.

Fr. Jean Galot, confirms the official doctrinal status of Marian coredemption in light of Vatican II teaching:

> Without using the term "co-redemptrix," *the Council clearly enunciated the doctrine:* a cooperation of a unique kind, a maternal cooperation in the life and work of the Savior, which reaches its apex in the participation in the sacrifice of Calvary, and which is oriented towards the supernatural restoration of souls...[53]

And as articulated by Galot in the Vatican newspaper, *L'Osservatore Romano*: "The Second Vatican Council, which avoided employing this debated title [Co-redemptrix], nevertheless *affirmed with vigor the doctrine it implies*..."[54]

Beyond its certain doctrinal presence in Vatican II, Marian coredemption, along with the explicit use of the title coredemptrix, is a repeated papal teaching spanning the 19th to the 21st century, which further assures its authentic doctrinal status within the Church. Marian coredemption is repeatedly taught in numerous papal encyclicals and general teachings, as reflected in the following representative citations of official papal teachings:[55]

Leo XIII: "When Mary offered herself completely to God together with her Son in the temple, she was already sharing with Him the painful atonement on behalf of the human race. It is certain, therefore, that she suffered in the very depths of her soul with His most bitter sufferings and with His torments.

---

[53] Jean Galot, S.J., "Maria Corredentrice. Controversie e problemi dottrinali," *Civilta Cattolica*, 1994, III, 213-225, author's emphasis.

[54] "Maria Corredentrice," *L'Osservatore Romano*, September 15, 1995, p. 4.

[55] For a more comprehensive treatment, cf. Schug and Miravalle, "Mary Co-redemptrix in the Documents of the Papal Magisterium" *in Mary Co-redemptrix, Mediatrix, Advocate, Theological Foundations I*, Queenship Pub. 1995; Calkins, "Pope John Paul's Teaching on Marian Coredemption" in *Mary Co-redemptrix, Mediatrix, Advocate, Theological Foundations II*, pp. 113-148.

Finally, it was before the eyes of Mary that the Divine sacrifice for which she had born and nurtured the victim, was to be finished...we see that there stood by the Cross of Jesus His Mother, who in a miracle of charity, so that he might receive us as her sons, willingly offered Him up to divine justice, dying with Him in her heart, pierced with the sword of sorrow." [56]

St. Pius X: "Owing to the union of suffering and purpose existing between Christ and Mary, she merited to become most worthily the Reparatrix of the lost world, and for this reason, the dispenser of all the favors which Jesus acquired for us by His death and His blood... and because she was chosen by Christ to be His partner in the work of salvation, she merits for us *de congruo* as they say, that which Christ merits for us *de condigno*..."[57]

Benedict XV: "The fact that she was with her Son, crucified and dying, was in accord with the divine plan. To such extent did she surrender her maternal rights over her Son for man's salvation, and immolated Him—in so far as she could—in order to appease the justice of God, that we may rightly say she redeemed the human race together with Christ." [58]

Pius XI: "O Mother of love and mercy who, when thy sweetest Son was consummating the Redemption of the human race on the altar of the cross, did stand next to Him, suffering with Him as a Co-redemptrix...preserve in us, we beseech thee, and increase day by day the precious fruit of His Redemption and the compassion of His Mother." [59]

---

[56] Pope Leo XIII, Encyclical *Jucunda Semper*, 1884.
[57] Pope St. Pius X, Encyclical *Ad diem illum*, 1904.
[58] Pope Benedict XV, Apostolic Letter, *Inter Sodalicia*, 1918.
[59] Pope Pius XI, Prayer of the Solemn Closing of the Redemption Jubilee, April 28, 1933.

Pius XII: "It was she who, always most intimately united with her Son, like a New Eve, offered Him on Golgotha to the Eternal Father, together with the sacrifice of her maternal rights and love, on behalf of all the children of Adam, shamed by the latter's shameful fall." [60]

John Paul II: "In her, the many and intense sufferings were amassed in such an interconnected way that they were not only a proof of her unshakable faith, but also a contribution to the redemption of all….It was on Calvary that Mary's suffering, beside the suffering of Jesus, reached an intensity which can hardly be imagined from a human point of view, but which were mysteriously and supernaturally fruitful for the Redemption of the world. Her ascent of Calvary and her standing at the foot of the cross together with the beloved disciple were a special sort of sharing in the redeeming death of her Son." [61]

John Paul II: "Crucified spiritually with her crucified son (cf. Gal. 2:20), she contemplated with heroic love the death of her God, she 'lovingly consented to the immolation of this victim which she herself had brought forth' (Lumen Gentium, 58)…In fact at Calvary she united herself with the sacrifice of her Son which led to the foundation of the Church….In fact, Mary's role as Co-redemptrix did not cease with the glorification of her Son." [62]

We see then both from the criteria of ecumenical council teaching and from repeated papal teaching through encyclical and general instruction, the teaching of Marian coredemption essentially constitutes an authentic doctrine within the authori-

---

[60] Pope Pius XII, Encyclical *Mystici Corporis*, 1943.
[61] Pope John Paul II, Apostolic Letter, *Salvifici Doloris*, n.25.
[62] John Paul II, Papal Address at Guayaquil, Ecuador, Jan. 31, 1985.

tative teachings of the Magisterium.

It is sometimes objected that the specific title Co-redemptrix only appears in papal teachings of lesser importance, and therefore does not represent Catholic doctrinal teachings. This would be to *artificially separate the title Co-redemptrix, from the theological doctrine of coredemption*, to which the title is essentially linked and derived from. The title refers to the spiritual function which Mary performs in her unique cooperation in Redemption, and therefore to separate the title from the doctrine is to inappropriately and dangerously disconnect the title from its authoritatively taught doctrinal foundation. In sum, the doctrinal certainty of Marian coredemption guarantees the doctrinal certainty of Mary Co-redemptrix.

Moreover, the repeated papal use of the Co-redemptrix title by the present pope on six separate occasions[63] should in itself, for the faithful Catholic, immediately remove any question of the doctrinal legitimacy of the title Co-redemptrix (whether personally preferable to the individual Catholic or not). To do otherwise would be to dubiously conclude that Pope John Paul II has repeatedly used a Marian title which is *in itself doctrinally erroneous*, theologically unsound, or intrinsically without Christian doctrinal foundation. This would appear to be foreign to the religious assent of mind and will to be given to the manifest mind of the pope in non-infallible papal teachings.[64]

In sum, in light of both conciliar and repeated papal teachings, Marian Coredemption and its corresponding title, Mary Co-redemptrix, constitutes an official doctrinal teaching of the Church.

Objection 6: *On a more speculative theological level, it appears that Mary cannot participate in the acquisition of*

---

[63] Cf. For six citations and commentary, cf. Calkins, *The Mystery of Mary Co-redemptrix in the Papal Mayisterium* in this present volume.

[64] Again, cf. *Lumen Gentium*, n. 25.

the graces of redemption (or "objective redemption") as the Co-redemptrix when she herself needed to be redeemed. If she did cooperate in objective redemption, it is because without her, objective redemption has not been accomplished. But if objective redemption has indeed not been accomplished, then she herself cannot benefit from it personally. This would be to accept that at the same time objective redemption is in the act of being accomplished and has already been accomplished, which would be a contradiction.

This apparent contradiction is removed with the proper understanding of how Mary received what is called "preservative redemption" in light of the foreseen merits of Jesus Christ on the cross.

It is true that Mary needed to be "redeemed" in order to actively participate in the process of Redemption as the sinless partner, the New Eve, with and under Jesus Christ, the New Adam. To have original sin or its effects would not allow Mary to be completely united with the Redeemer and in "enmity" or complete opposition from Satan and his seed of sin and its effects (cf. Gen.3:15) in the redeeming process of "buying back" the human family from Satan and restoring grace to humanity. Any sin on Mary's part would attribute to her a "double-agency," in being in some part united both to the Redeemer and to Satan. Therefore Mary, as a daughter of Adam and Eve by virtue of her humanity, needed to be redeemed in the form of being preserved from sin and its effects in order to rightly perform the task of Co-redemptrix with the Redeemer in the process of universal objective redemption.

In the papal definition of Mary's Immaculate Conception by Bl. Pope Pius IX in 1854, it states that Mary, from the first instant of her conception was freed from original sin and all its effects "in view of the merits of Jesus Christ."[65] This refers to the higher or "more sublime manner" in which Mary was redeemed, beyond all other children of Adam and Eve. In Mary's redemption, she did not have to suffer the experience of original sin and its effects, but rather through the foreseen merits of Jesus Christ at Calvary, was preserved from any experience or effect of original sin, and is thereby redeemed in a more sublime manner (and consequently, for this reason, owes more to her saving Son's redemption than any other redeemed creature).

How then specifically is Mary's redemption in the higher form of preservation from sin enacted so as to allow her to historically participate in objective redemption? This more sublime manner of redemption takes place at Calvary in the fact that the *first intention* of the redemptive sacrifice of Jesus Christ,[66] according to the providential plan of the Father, was to redeem his own mother, (accomplished in view of the redemption and coredemption which would then ransom from Satan and sin the rest of the human family).

This first intention of the Redeemer to redeem Mary is in itself another manifestation of the higher and more sublime manner of Mary's redemption. The graces of this first intention of the Redeemer are then applied to Mary at the moment of her Immaculate Conception, allowing her then to become the sinless Co-redemptrix, the historical New Eve, in the objective historic redemption of Jesus Christ at Calvary. Jesus Christ first redeemed his own mother (applied to her at the moment of her conception, preserving her from sin) and then with her active coredemption the rest of humanity at Calvary.

Therefore there is no contradiction in the historic role of the Co-redemptrix in the objective redemption at Calvary and

---

[65] Bl. Pope Pius IX, Dogmatic Bull, *Ineffabilis Deus*, December 8, 1854.

[66] For an extended treatment, cf. J. B. Carol, "Our Lady's Co-redemption," in *Mariology*, Vol. II, Bruce, 1958; Friethoff, *A Complete Mariology*, Blackfriars Pub., London, 1985, p.182; Galot, S.J., Maria: Mediatrice o Madre Universale?," *Civilta Cattolica*, 1996, I, 232-244.

Mary's own personal need and receipt of the graces of redemption. In virtue of her Immaculate Conception (redemptive graces applied to her at conception in view of the future merits of Jesus Christ at Calvary) and as the first intention of Jesus Christ's redemptive sacrifice, Mary was then able to uniquely participate in the historic redemption of the rest of humanity with her Redeemer Son. As Fr. Galot well summarizes:

> The first intention of the redemptive sacrifice was concerned, according to the divine plan, with the ransom of Mary, accomplished in view of our ransom…Thus, while she was associated in the sacrifice of Calvary, Mary already benefited, in advance, from the fruits of the sacrifice and acted in the capacity of a ransomed creature. But she truly cooperated in the objective redemption, in the acquisition of the graces of salvation for all of mankind. Her redemption was purchased before that of other human beings. Mary was ransomed only by Christ, so that mankind could be ransomed with the collaboration of his mother… Hence there is no contradiction: coredemption implies the foreseen redemption of Mary, but not the foreseen fulfillment of the redemption of mankind; it expresses the unique situation of the mother who, while having received a singular grace from her own Son, cooperates with him in the attainment of salvation for all. [67]

Still other theological schools prefer to distinguish the general notion of redemption into the two categories of "preservation" and "ransoming." Because Mary was never technically under the slavery of Satan's bondage since she never experienced sin, then the term "ransom" is less accurate for her, as it infers returning someone from a previous slavery. Hence the term, "preservation" or preservative redemption may more accurately distinguish the uniqueness of Mary's need to be redeemed by

---

[67] Galot, S.J., "Maria Corredentrice: Controversie e problemi dottrinali", Civilta Cattolica, 1994, III, p. 218, also as contained and translated in this volume.

Christ first and as a daughter of Adam and Eve, but does not infer that she was ever under Satan's slavery of sin. It is illustrative of her higher form of preservative redemption and her subsequent participation in the true "ransoming" of the rest of humanity.[68]

Does this primordial intention of Jesus Christ to redeem his mother and then, as subsequent intention, the rest of humanity violate the "one sacrifice" of Jesus Christ offered for all as discussed in Hebrews (cf Heb. 10:10)? It does not, as the redemption remains one, although its intentions and efficacious applications are twofold. The one redemptive sacrifice of Jesus Christ at Calvary does not constitute "two redemptions," but one sublime redemption with two saving applications: the first application effecting the Immaculate Conception of Mary and thus preparing her to be the Co-redemptrix in her cooperation in objective redemption; the second application effecting the redemption of the human family accomplished with the Co-redemptrix.[69]

In his homily on the Feast of Immaculate Conception in the cathedral in Krakow, Karol Cardinal Wojtyla succinctly summarized this Marian truth: "In order to be the Co-redemptrix, she was first the Immaculate Conception."[70]

Objection 7: *While granting the legitimacy of Mary Co-redemptrix and its corresponding doctrine of coredemption, there are no substantial reasons or fruits for its papal definition at this time, and in fact such a definition would cause serious division within the Church.*

It must be stated from the outset that such a position re-

---

[68] Cf. Friethoff, *op. cit.*
[69] Cf. J.B. Carol, *op. cit.*
[70] Karol Cardinal Wojtyla, Homily on the Feast of the Immaculate Conception, December 8, 1973.

garding a potential papal definition of Mary Co-redemptrix is certainly an acceptable position by a faithful member of the Catholic Church.

Notwithstanding, let us explore, in a brief summary format, some of the numerous contemporary reasons presently being offered in support of the appropriateness and consequent positive fruits of a formal papal definition of Mary Co-redemptrix.

1. Greater theological clarity to an area of present misunderstanding.

When Bl. Pius IX raised the Church doctrine of the Immaculate Conception to the level of dogma in 1854, he stated that the fruits of such definition would be to "bring to perfection" the doctrine, adding greater clarity and light for the benefit of all:

> The Church labors hard to polish the previous teachings, to bring to perfection their formulation in such a way that these older dogmas of the heavenly doctrine receive proof, light, distinction, while keeping their fullness, their integrity, their own character...[71]

In light of the substantial contemporary confusion concerning precisely what the Catholic Church means to convey in the doctrine of Marian coredemption (as evidenced by the recent *New York Times* piece and its reaction), it would seem most beneficial to have a precise statement, scripturally formulated in light of Christian Tradition, from the highest authority of the Catholic Church, ensuring its doctrinal precision and authenticity.

---

[71] Bl. Pius IX, *Ineffabilis Deus*, December 8, 1854, DS 2802.

2. Ecumenical benefits in an authentic Catholic expression of doctrinal dialogue

Rather than its perception as being against the imperative of working for Christian unity, a precise formulation of what Catholics believe regarding Mary Co-redemptrix, and at the same time what they do not believe (i.e., equality with Jesus Christ, divinity of Mary, etc.) will only serve authentic ecumenical dialogue based on integrity and truth as to what is already a Catholic doctrinal teaching.

As previously cited, the late Cardinal John O'Connor of New York referred to this potential ecumenical fruit in his letter of endorsement for the papal definition of Mary Co-redemptrix:

"Clearly, a formal papal definition would be articulated in such precise terminology that other Christians would lose their anxiety that we do not distinguish adequately between Mary's unique association with Christ and the redemptive power exercised by Christ alone." [72]

Such a definition would help avoid the dangerous tendency to present in ecumenical dialogue only those doctrinal elements Christians share together, rather than the difficult but necessary aspect of sharing those doctrinal elements Christians do not hold in common. Such integrity in ecumenical doctrinal exchange is critically necessary in eventually arriving at any true Christian unity.

3. Proper development of Marian doctrine

The existing four Marian Dogmas, the Motherhood of God (431), the Perpetual Virginity (649), the Immaculate Conception (1854), and the Assumption (1950), all deal with the attributes or qualities of Mary's earthly life, but none directly re-

---

[72] John Cardinal O'Connor, Endorsement Letter For Papal Definition of Mary, Co-redemptrix, Mediatrix, Advocate, February 14, 1994.

fer to the Mother of Jesus *in relation to the human family*.

It is interesting to note historically that only one month following the papal definition of Mary's Assumption in November 1950, the International Mariological Congress formally petitioned Pope Pius XII for the papal definition of Mary's universal mediation as a logical progression following the definition of the Assumption.[73]

After the early life and attributes of Mary have received their respective "perfections of doctrine" in solemn dogmatic definitions, so too it would seem appropriate that Mary's heavenly prerogative as spiritual mother of all peoples in the order of grace, inclusive of and founded upon her unique coredemption, would also receive its doctrinal perfecting in the form of a dogmatic definition.

4. Affirmation of the dignity of the human person and human freedom

Personalist philosopher, Professor Dr. Josef Seifert,[74] argues that a dogma of Mary Co-redemptrix would constitute a supreme confirmation of the dignity and freedom of the human person:

> A dogma that declares Mary Co-redemptrix would give a unique witness to the full freedom of the human person as we have seen, and to God's respect for human freedom. This dogma would recognize in an ultimate way that a *free decision* of the human person of Mary, who was not even to become the Mother of God without her free *fiat*—a decision which was not exclusively caused by divine grace but was also the fruit of her own personal choice—was *necessary* for

---

[73] *Alma Socia Christi*, Proceedings of the Rome International Mariological Congress, 1950, p.234.

[74] Dr. Josef Seifert is Rector of the International Academy of Philosophy in Liechtenstein and member of the Pontifical Council For Life. His article apperars later in the present volume.

our salvation, or played an *indispensable part* in the concrete way of our redemption chosen by God.

In our age, in which a personalist philosophy was developed more deeply than ever before in the history of mankind, and in which at the same time terrible anti–personalist ideologies reign, such a dogma would rightfully be perceived as a supreme confirmation of the dignity of the human freedom.

In all of this I would see a crucial value and significance for this dogma being proclaimed in our century, one in which both a new awareness of personal dignity arose and one in which the person was also more degraded in action and denied in theory (also in many pseudo-personalistic and situational ethics theories) than ever before.[75]

5. *Re-affirmation of the dignity of woman*

In the contemporary discussion of feminism and the nature of woman, the papal proclamation of Mary Co-redemptrix would underscore what could properly be identified as God's radical love and respect for woman. According to Christian Scripture, the entire providential plan of God the Father to send his Son for the redemption of the world was contingent upon the free fiat of a woman (Cf. Lk 1:38; Gal 4:4). What "trust" God the Father has in woman in the person of Mary that He would make the coming of the Redeemer of the entire human family conditional upon this woman's free consent.

As Dr. Seifert again points out:

This new declaration of the Traditional doctrine would therefore show anew *a perpetual truth about Mary and about woman*, a truth which was always held by the Church but

---

[75] Seifert, "Mary as Co-redemptrix and Mediatrix of all Graces – Philosophical and Personalist Foundations of a Marian Doctrine," in *Mary Co-redemptrix, Mediatrix, Advocate, Theological Foundations II*, p. 166, and later in the present volume.

never clearly and indubitably stated: *the greatest deed of God's gracious love—the Redemption of mankind and our salvation—is in some real sense also the consequence of a free act of a woman and thus also the gift of a woman to humanity.*[76]

And further:

> This dogma would express the dignity of a woman's action which exceeds in activeness, sublimity and effectiveness the deeds of all pure creatures and men: of all kings and politicians, thinkers, scientists, philosophers, artists and craftsmen from the beginning of the world to the end...[77]

The papally defined revelation of the role of Mary Co-redemptrix could thereby be offered as an exemplary foundation for better understanding the unique contribution of feminism to humanity and, as such, constitute a foundational anthropological basis for authentic Christian feminism.

6. Re-emphasis of the Christian need to cooperate with God's grace for salvation

Anglican Oxford scholar, Dr. John Macquarrie, states that the role of Mary Co-redemptrix provides a concrete expression of the human necessity to freely and actively cooperate with God's grace for salvation. He moreover sees the Christian truth of Mary Co-redemptrix as a corrective for theologies that remove such dignity from the person, and in consequence, put forth an undesirable image of Christianity itself. As synthesized by Macquarrie in this extended citation:

> In some forms of this teaching, it is even believed that human beings can be saved without even knowing that sal-

---

[76] Seifert, *op. cit.*, p.168.
[77] *Ibid.*

vation is taking place. It has all taken place already through the once-for-all redeeming work of Christ. It is a fact, whether anyone recognizes it or not…For him [Barth], the [subjective] Redemption is a purely objective act, already finished "outside of us, without us, even against us"…Redemption is not, in his view, to be considered as an ongoing process in which we have some part, but as the once-for-all act of God long before we were born…

Now if one conceded Barth's point, then I think one would have to say that he is indeed treating human beings like sheep or cattle or even marionettes, not as the unique beings that they are, spiritual beings made in the image of God and entrusted with a measure of freedom and responsibility…It is understandable that Feuerbach, Marx, Nietzsche and a whole galaxy of modern thinkers came to believe that Christianity alienates them from a genuine humanity…

Let us now come back to the consideration of Mary as *Co-redemptrix*. Perhaps we do have to acknowledge that Barth and others have been correct in believing that the place given to Mary in catholic theology is a threat to the doctrine of *sola gratia*, but I think this is the case only when the doctrine of *sola gratia* is interpreted in its extreme form, when this doctrine itself becomes a threat to a genuinely personal and biblical view of the human being…a being still capable of responding to God in the work of building up creation. This hopeful view of the human race is personified and enshrined in Mary.

In the glimpses of Mary that we have in the gospels, her standing at the cross beside her Son, and her prayers and intercessions with the apostles, are particularly striking ways in which Mary shared and supported the work of Christ…it is Mary who has come to symbolize the perfect harmony between the divine will and the human response, so that it is she who gives meaning to the expression *Co-redemptrix.*[78]

---

[78] J. Macquarrie, "Mary Co-redemptrix and Disputes over Justification and Grace" in *Mary Co-redemptrix, Mediatrix, Advocate, Theological Foundations II,* p. 248, 255., and as contained in this present volume.

Mary Co-redemptrix and its new proclamation would serve to protect human freedom, dignity, and the human imperative to freely cooperate with grace for salvation.

7. *"Suffering is Redemptive" and the "Culture of Death"*

A solemn definition of Mary Co-redemptrix would be a Christian proclamation to the world that *"suffering is redemptive."* The Christian example of the Co-redemptrix manifests to the world that to accept the providentially permitted crosses of our human existence is not a valueless waste to be avoided at all costs, sometimes as manifested in the intrinsic evils of euthanasia and abortion. But rather that the patient endurance of all human hardships are of supernatural value when united with the sufferings of Jesus Christ, a participation in the distribution of the redemptive graces of Calvary, both for ourselves and for others (Cf. Col. 1:24).

The example of Mary's "yes" to unborn life, even in circumstances which could foster undue judgement and ridicule from people surrounding her, is in itself a valuable example of the co-redemptive "yes" that all men and women should give in response to the event of unborn life, regardless of the circumstance.

John Paul II describes the present "Culture of Death" as a "cultural climate which fails to perceive any meaning or value in suffering, but rather considers suffering to be the epitome of evil, to be eliminated at all cost. This is especially the case in the absence of a religious outlook which could help provide a positive understanding of the mystery of suffering."[79]

The concrete example of Mary Co-redemptrix offers to the Church and the world the positive Christian message that "suffering is redemptive" in all possible circumstances, from Christian persecution, to terminal cancer, to "unwanted" pregnancy,

---

[79] John Paul II, 1995 Encyclical, *Evangelium Vitae*, n.15

to the ordinary crosses of daily life.

8. *Unity through papal charism within the Catholic Church*

From a Catholic perspective, the charism of the Holy Spirit that is given to St. Peter and his successors, the subsequent popes (cf. Mt. 16:15-20), is a source of unity in doctrine and in life for the members of the Church. When the specific papal charism of infallibility is used in a preservation from error by the Holy Spirit on matters of faith and morals, such exercise of this papal charism safeguards and properly reinforces a Catholic unity in life based on a unity in faith, truth and doctrine. The same benefit of unity which comes with the exercise of the papal charism would also be given in the case of a solemn papal definition of Mary Co-redemptrix.

It is sometimes objected that such a definition on Marian coredemption would "cause division" within the Church. It is imperative to be clear on this point: Christian truth by its nature unites; *it is only the rejection of Christian truth that divides.* The same would hold true for a potential definition of Mary Co-redemptrix.

In the first case, Marian Coredemption is already a doctrinal teaching of the Church and thereby should already be accepted by the Catholic faithful with a religious assent of mind and will.[80] Secondly, an exercise of the papal charism of infallibility in the service of Christian truth and as guided by the Holy Spirit in itself brings with it the grace of unity of hearts based on unity of truth and faith. But as was true for Jesus Christ, the "Sign of Contradiction" (cf. Lk. 2:35), so would be true of the rejection of the truth concerning the Mother of the "Sign of Contradiction."

Any division within the Church in response to a papal infallible definition of the Co-redemptrix doctrine would not con-

---

[80] Again cf. Lumen Gentium, n. 25.

stitute a true or valid component of the papal definition itself, but only its unfortunate rejection by members choosing to be separated from Christ's Vicar of both Truth and unity.

9. Modern saints and Mary Co-redemptrix

One possible indication of the maturity of the Co-redemptrix doctrine and its potential definability is the modern testimony and teaching of this Marian truth by a great number of contemporary canonized saints and blesseds. The generous appreciation by recent saints and blesseds of Marian coredemption indicates its spiritual ripeness in the hearts of heroic sanctity within the Body of Christ today.

Those particularly vocal in their appreciation of Marian coredemption, both as a Marian doctrine and as a model of Christian spiritual life, include St. Therese of Liseux, St. Maximilian Kolbe, Pope St. Pius X, St. Francis Xavier Cabrini, St. Gemma Galgani, St. Leopold Mandic, Bl. Elizabeth of the Trinity, St. Edith Stein, Bl. Jose Maria Escriva, Blessed Padre Pio, and numerous others.[81]

Even though not as yet officially beatified, it nonetheless seems appropriate to quote the late Mother Teresa's endorsement for the papal definition of Mary Co-redemptrix: "The papal definition of Mary Co-redemptrix, Mediatrix of all graces, and Advocate will bring great graces to the Church. All for Jesus through Mary."[82]

---

[81] For a more comprehensive treatment of modern hagiography on Marian Coredemption, cf. Stefano Manelli, FFI, "Twentieth Century Hagiography on Marian Coredemption" in Mary at the Foot of the Cross, Acts of the England Symposium on Marian Co-redemption, 1999, and reprinted in this volume.

[82] Mother Teresa of Calcutta, Endorsement Letter for the Fifth Marian Dogma, August 14, 1993.

10. Initiation of the Fatima prophesied Triumph of the Immaculate Heart of Mary

A significant number of contemporary Marian authors and thinkers worldwide[83] also see in the papal proclamation of Mary Co-redemptrix, along with her subsequent spiritual roles as Mediatrix of all graces, and Advocate, what has been referred to as the definitive "initiation" or beginning of the Triumph of the Immaculate Heart of Mary, as prophesied in the 1917 Apparition of Mary at Fatima, Portugal.

The particular notion of the "Triumph of the Immaculate Heart" comes from the words of the Church approved apparitions of Mary at Fatima to the young Portuguese children seers. After prophesying such upcoming events as the rise of atheistic communism, persecutions for the Church and the Holy Father, a potential second world war, and the annihilation of various nations, the Virgin Mary, under the title of "the Lady of the Rosary" then stated to the children, "In the end, my Immaculate Heart will triumph...and a period of peace will be granted to the world."[84]

The Triumph of the Immaculate Heart of Mary is hence foreseen as a dramatic influx of supernatural grace upon the world, mediated to the world by the Co-redemptrix, Mediatrix, and Advocate, and leading to a period of spiritual peace for humanity.

The role of the papal proclamation of Mary Co-redemptrix in the prophesied Triumph of the Immaculate Heart would be seen by some contemporaries as the official recognition by the pope, as the highest Church authority, in exercising the required

---

[83] For a sample of such thought, cf. In Miravalle, ed., *Contemporary Insights on a Fifth Marian Dogma, Theological Foundations III*, Queenship, 2000, the following essays: Ambassador Howard Dee, "Our Lady's Ambassador, John Paul II, Fatima, and the Fifth Marian Dogma;" Dr. Bartholomew, "A Scientist Explores Mary, Co-redemptrix;" Calkins, "The Messages of the Lady of All Nations."

[84] Memoirs of Sr. Lucia of Fatima, July 13, 1917.

freedom on the part of humanity to allow the full mediational and intercessory power of Mary Co-redemptrix, Mediatrix, and Advocate to be released in distributing the redemptive graces of Calvary to the contemporary world.

God does not force his grace upon us, but awaits the free consent of humanity. With the official papal definition of Mary Co-redemptrix, Mediatrix, and Advocate by the highest human authority's exercise of free will on behalf of humanity, this free act would "release" the Co-redemptrix to most fully distribute the graces of redemption in a new outpouring of the Holy Spirit for the world. As explained by former Vatican Ambassador Howard Dee of the Philippines:

> Two thousand years ago, during the First Advent, the Holy Spirit came upon Mary, and when the power of the Most High overshadowed her, she conceived Jesus, Son of God. Now, during this New Advent, it is the Mother of All Peoples, Co-redemptrix, Mediatrix of all graces, and Advocate, who will accompany her Spouse to descend into our hearts and our souls and recreate in each of us—if we give our fiat—into the likeness of Jesus…The proclamation of the Fifth Dogma is no longer our prerogative; it is our duty.[85]

As such, the papal proclamation of Mary Co-redemptrix would effect a historic release of spiritual grace upon the world by the full exercise of the spiritual mother of all peoples in her most generous and complete exercise of her roles as Co-redemptrix, Mediatrix of all grace and Advocate.[86]

---

[85] Ambassador Howard Dee, "Our Lady's Ambassador, John Paul II, Fatima, and the Fifth Marian Dogma," in *Contemporary Insights on a Fifth Marian Dogma*, Queenship, 2000, p. 12-13.

[86] For an extended treatment, cf. Miravalle, *The Dogma and the Triumph*, Queenship, 1998.

Conclusion

It is to be hoped that some light has been shed upon the principal questions concerning the present discussion of the issue of Mary Co-redemptrix in itself and, at least by way of introduction, in discussing the specific aspect of a potential papal definition of the Co-redemptrix doctrine.

In regards to any future potential definition of Co-redemptrix from a Catholic perspective, peace and trust in the guidance of the Church by the pontiff in matters of faith and morals should ultimately reign supreme in the Catholic faithful's mind and heart, regardless of present legitimate personal opinions of diversity on the issue.

From the general Christian perspective regarding the doctrine of Mary Co-redemptrix and other doctrines which presently divide us, let us keep faith in the eventual fulfillment of the prayer of Jesus Christ for Christian unity at the Last Supper that "... they may all be one, even as thou, Father art in me, and I in thee, that they also may be in us, so that the world may believe that thou has sent me" (Jn. 17:21). Apart from temporary historical advances or setbacks, Christians must have faith in an ultimate historic unity of Christian hearts, which will then blossom into a Christian unity of mind, truth, faith and Body, based on the one Jesus Christ, who is "the Way, the Truth, the Life" (Jn. 14:6).

Mary Co-redemptrix and Disputes Over Justification and Grace: An Anglican View

Dr. John Macquarrie

Professor John Macquarrie, Anglican Philosopher and Theologian, has served as Lady Margaret Professor of Divinity and Canon of Christ Church, Oxford. He is a distinguished author of numerous important works on Philosophy, Theology and Mariology, and a contributor to the Ecumenical Society of the Blessed Virgin Mary. *

There have been times in the history of Christianity when Christ himself has become such a divine, exalted, numinous figure that the worshippers found him so distant that they needed a new mediator or *mediatrix* closer to their own humanity to fill the space that had opened between themselves and the original mediator. No doubt this is something that should never have happened, and the New Testament itself teaches clearly, "There is one God, and there is one mediator between God and men, the man Christ Jesus" (1 Tim. 2:5). Not only should it not have happened, I think we can say that in fact it is not happening at the present time, because for several generations theologians have been stressing the humanity of Christ. The

---

* Originally printed in *Mary Co-redemptrix, Mediatrix, Advocate: Theological Foundations II, Papal, Pneumatological, Ecumenical*, Queenship, 1996.

Christ of post-Enlightenment theology is not a distant and exalted Christ in glory but more commonly a Christ reduced to all-too-human proportions. So the need for a *mediatrix* is not likely to be felt today with the intensity that was sometimes known in the past.

However, the matter cannot be settled by pointing to the dangers of exaggeration and abuse, or by appealing to isolated texts of scripture such as the verse quoted above from 1 Timothy, or by the changing fashions in theology and spirituality, or by the desire not to say anything that might offend one's partners in ecumenical dialogue. Unthinking enthusiasts may have elevated Mary to a position of virtual equality with Christ, but this aberration is not a *necessary* consequence of recognizing that there may be a truth striving for expression in words like *Mediatrix* and *Co-redemptrix*. All responsible theologians would agree that Mary's co-redemptive role is subordinate and auxiliary to the central role of Christ. But if she does have such a role, the more clearly we understand it, the better. It is a matter for theological investigation. And, like other doctrines concerning Mary, it is not only saying something about her, but something more general concerning the Church as a whole or even humanity as a whole. At this point as at others, mariology impinges on anthropology.

The general question which, as it seems to me, is raised by the specifically mariological question about the co-redemptive role of the Virgin, is that of the human role in any adequate theology of salvation. Is this human role purely a *passive* one, or is it, as Vatican II asserted about Mary, a role that is also *active*? This is where mariology threatens to revive old controversies. With Martin Luther, the principle *sola gratia*, "by grace alone," was fundamental. Although Pelagianism, the view that the human being has in himself the resources to find the path of salvation and to progress along it, has made great inroads into all the churches in the past two hundred years, the principle "by grace alone" has remained a shibboleth of orthodox Protestant theology. It is prominent, for instance, in the work of Karl Barth. On this view, fallen man is so disabled by sin that he is totally unable to help himself. Grace alone can redeem him, and he can contribute nothing.

In some forms of this teaching, it is even believed that human beings can be saved without even knowing that salvation is taking place. It has all taken place already through the once-for-all redeeming work of Christ. It is a fact, whether anyone recognizes it or not. Karl Barth speaks in this way, though admittedly there are some ambiguities in what he says. But it is his belief that from all eternity the whole human race has been elected or predestined to salvation in Jesus Christ. This event has taken place outside of humanity, without it and even against it.[1] He says also, "If the good shepherd (Jn. 10:11ff.) gives his life for the sheep, he does so to save the life of the sheep, but without any co-operation on their part."[2] We may agree that the sheep do not need to cooperate or to be aware that there is any danger—the threat is an external one (perhaps a pack of wolves in the neighborhood) and they need never know that these wolves had been around. But though this may be true of sheep and an adequate account of how sheep may be saved from physical dangers, it is not true of human beings and is a woefully inadequate view of what is required for human salvation. The salvation or redemption offered by Christianity is not from some enemy "out there," but from the enemy within, namely, sin. It is not a physical rescue that is required—that might not demand any co-operation and the person rescued might not even be conscious of what was going on—but salvation, in the Christian sense, is very different. In this case, salvation has to be appropriated inwardly by an act of penitence (turning) and faith on the part of the person saved.

---

[1] Karl Barth, *Rudolf Bultmann—ein Versuch ihn zu verstehen* (Zurich, 1952), p. 19.
[2] Barth, *Church Dogmatics* IV/1, p. 231.

The whole question was argued thoroughly a generation ago between Barth and Bultmann, but people have short memories. Bultmann had laid stress in his writings on the "decision of faith." This decision is also expressed by Bultmann as "making Christ's cross one's own," that is to say, by taking up the cross through an act of inward acceptance and appropriation. Barth strongly denied this. For him, the redemption is a purely objective act, already finished "outside of us, without us, even against us," to recall his words already quoted and used by him in his polemic against Bultmann. Redemption is not, in his view, to be considered as an ongoing process in which we have some part, but as the once-for-all act of God long before we were born—though it is hard to know whether this act in the past is the death of Christ on Calvary or the eternal predestinating decree of God in the very beginning. But it is all complete already without us.

Now, if one conceded Barth's point, then I think one would have to say that he is indeed treating human beings like sheep or cattle or even marionettes, not as the unique beings that they are, spiritual beings made in the image of God and entrusted with a measure of freedom and responsibility. This fundamental human constitution remains, even though ravaged by sin. Human beings are still human, not mere things or animals. If Barth were correct in what he says on these matters, it would make nonsense of the struggles of history, of the training and preparation of Israel, of the very incarnation of the Word, of the redemptive mission of the Church, of the preaching of the gospel and the ministration of the sacraments. These events in time could have no real significance, for everything has been settled in advance. Human beings, on such a view, have no freedom and no responsibility. They are not beings made in the image of God with some small share in the divine creativity and rationality, they are things to be passively manipulated and pushed around. Fortunately for us—or so we are assured—we are manipulated by grace rather than by a malignant fate or blind chance, nevertheless, we are manipulated. This seems to me a degradation of the concept of humanity implicit in the biblical accounts of creation. Feuerbach's words about Luther remain, alas, true of much of the theology that stems from him and from other leading Reformers: "The doctrine is divine but inhuman, a hymn to God but a lampoon of man."[3] It is understandable that Feuerbach, Marx, Nietzsche and a whole galaxy of modern thinkers came to believe that Christianity alienates them from a genuine humanity.

I was careful to say that there are ambiguities in what Barth says about salvation and the human beings' part (or lack of part) in it. Though salvation is, in his view, an objective act accomplished by God, he does believe that it is important for human beings to become aware of God's redemptive work and to appropriate it in their lives—he can even at one point introduce the controversial word "synergism" or "co-working," though he envisages this as something which does not belong to redemption itself but is subsequent to it. I do not think, however, that his occasional modifications are sufficiently clear or that they are fully integrated into his main argument. Certainly, he never concedes what is for me a vital point—that from the very first moment when the divine grace impinges on a human life, it needs for its fruition a response, however feeble, of penitence and faith. Not for a moment is it being suggested that the human being initiates the work—the initiative belongs to God. But if it is merely outside of us, without us and even against us, then nothing worthy to be called "salvation" can take place. There has got to be something corresponding to Mary's reported words to Gabriel: "Behold I am the handmaid of the Lord; let it be to me according to your word" (Lk. 1:38).

The questions to which we have come are highly controversial, and yet they are so central to the place and significance of

---

[3] L. Feuerbach, *The Essence of Faith according to Luther* (Harper & Row, 1967), p. 41.

Mary that we must pursue them further. Although we are try-ing to see Mary as a reconciling influence for different Chris-tian traditions, it would be wrong to ignore the fact that she also raises issues that have been divisive, for these must be faced if any true reconciliation is ever to be achieved. In particular, we must examine more carefully the conflict that arises from the teaching about the moral and spiritual helplessness of hu-man beings and the doctrine of justification by grace alone to which that teaching has given rise. There have been strenuous efforts in recent years to bridge the gulf that opened at the Ref-ormation on these matters—one thinks, for instance, of Hans Küng's excellent early book, *Justification*, in which he tried to show that the teaching of the Council of Trent and that of Karl Barth on this question are not so totally opposed to each other as had been assumed: or to the Anglican-Roman Catholic In-ternational Commission's document on justification, which was another praiseworthy attempt to narrow the gap between the opposing points of view. There have also been important New Testament researches into the topics of faith, justification, grace and works.

Luther himself believed that the doctrine of *sola gratia* can be clearly derived from the New Testament, especially from the writings of Paul which had become for him a kind of canon within the canon. He was especially impressed by Paul's ac-count in Romans of his unavailing struggles to fulfill the law, and likewise with Paul's strong opposition, expressed in Galatians, to those Judaizing elements who wished to impose some residual elements of the law of Moses on Gentile converts to Christianity. Luther saw these oppositions in extreme terms: on the one side, a harshly legalistic Judaism in which salvation was to be gained through good works performed in obedience to the law, and on the other side, Christianity as a religion of grace in which redemption has been gained for us by the cross and salvation is offered to us as a free gift, without regard to our merit or lack of merit. The recent work of such New Testament scholars as W. D. Davies and E. P. Sanders has called into question this simplistic but highly influential exegesis inherited from Luther. Davies puts the point quite mildly when he warns us that "it is possible to make too much of the contrast between Pauline Christianity as a religion of liberty and Judaism as a religion of obedience," and he expresses the opinion that "justification by faith" is not the dominant factor in Paul's thought."[4] These remarks have been greatly strengthened by the important studies of Sanders, who shows that in the Palestinian Judaism of Paul's time there was a stress on grace as well as works, and that Paul's own position was not so very different from that of his Jewish teachers. Sanders claims that "the Rabbis kept the indicative and the imperative (i.e., grace and works) well balanced and in the right order."[5]

Luther's exegesis of Romans was developed by him into a polemic against the Roman Catholic church, which he equated with legalistic Judaism and contrasted with the Reformation religion of grace. But now that the New Testament basis of his contrast between first-century Judaism and early Christianity has been placed in doubt, his application of this model to the relation between Roman Catholic and Protestant versions of Christianity must also be doubtful. It is interesting to note that Barth, in spite of his championship of grace versus good works, is careful to distance himself from Luther's misuse of Galatians, still uncritically accepted by many Protestant writers. Barth says:

> Certainly in Galatians there were and are many more things to be discovered than what Luther discovered then. Certainly there was and is much more to be said of the Roman church and Roman theology both then and since, than what the Reformers said then within the schema of Galatians. We

---

[4] W.D. Davies, *Paul and Rabbinic Judaism* (SPCK. 1960), pp. 145, 222.

[5] E. P. Sanders, *Paul and Palestinian Judaism* (SCM Press. 1977), p. 97.

do not need to consider ourselves bound either in the one respect or in the other by their attitude.[6]

In theology and probably in many other subjects as well, highly one-sided solutions to problems are rarely satisfactory. As far as our present problem is concerned, I believe that in any adequate theology there must be a place both for divine grace and for human effort, for divine initiative and for the human acceptance and active response. When Sanders speaks of getting these things in the right order and well balanced, I take him to mean that God's grace comes first, and presumably it is grace that evokes and enables the human response, but the priority of grace does not for a moment render the human response superfluous, or suggest that the person who is the recipient of grace is in any way delivered from the imperative to bring forth "fruits worthy of repentance" (Lk. 3:8). It is the combination of divine grace and human response that is so admirably exemplified in Mary. She is "highly favoured" of God (or "full of grace" in the familiar Vulgate rendering), but she is also, in words which I quoted from W. P. DuBose, the one who "represents the highest reach, the focusing upwards, as it were, of the world's susceptibility for God."[7] If we accept that the human being has been created by God, endowed with freedom, and made responsible for his or her own life, and even if we accept in addition that there are limits to freedom and responsibility, and especially that through the weakness of sin no human being can attain wholeness of life through effort that is unaided by divine grace—even Kant in spite of his insistence on autonomy conceded as much—yet we are still bound to say that there must be some human contribution to the work of redemption, even if it is no more than responsive and never of equal weight with the grace of God.

---

[6] Barth, *Church Dogmatics* IV/I, p. 623.

[7] W. P. DuBose, *The Soteriology of the New Testament*, p. 176.

While the champions of *sola gratia* have concentrated their attention on some passages of scripture and have probably interpreted even these in a one-sided way, there are other passages, even in the writings of Paul, where the element of co-operation in the work of salvation seems to be clearly recognized. It is Paul who, after the magnificent hymn in praise of Christ's redeeming work, in his letter to the Philippians, goes on immediately to say to the Christian believers: "Work out your own salvation with fear and trembling; for God is at work in you" (Phil. 2:12). The thought here seems clearly to be that God's work and man's work go on side by side in the realization of salvation. In another epistle, he writes: "Working together with him, then, we entreat you not to accept the grace of God in vain" (2 Cor. 6:1). A straightforward interpretation of these words seems quite incompatible with any rigorous doctrine of *sola gratia*. For what does it mean "to accept the grace of God in vain" but to fail to make any response to this grace, to refrain from any answering work? The expression "working together with him," which has also been translated "as co-workers with him," is in Greek *synergountes*, from which we derive the English word "synergism," cited at an earlier stage in the discussion. This word "synergism" is the usual theological term for the point of view I have been commending, namely, that human salvation is accomplished neither by man's own unaided efforts nor by an act of God entirely outside of man, but by a synergism or co-working, in which, of course, the initiative and weight lie on the side of God, but the human contribution is also necessary and cannot be left out of account.

Before we leave the New Testament on these questions, let us call to mind in addition to the Pauline material the letter of James. Luther was so unhappy with this letter that he questioned whether it should ever have been included in the canon of the New Testament. It seems inconsistent with Paul's insistence that we are justified by faith, not by works, or perhaps we should say, with Paul's view of these matters as interpreted by Luther. But one could say that the apparent tension between James and Paul should not be taken to mean that James should have been excluded from the canon, but rather that the inclusion of his letter is a much needed corrective to some of the more one-sided Pauline pronouncements as they have been commonly understood. "What does it profit, my brethren," asks James, "if a man says he has faith but has not works? Can his faith save him? If a brother or sister is ill-clad and in lack of daily food, and one of you say to them, 'Go in peace, be warmed and filled,' without giving them the things needed for the body, what does it profit? So faith, by itself, if it has no works, is dead" (Jas. 2:14-17). Or perhaps one should say that faith, as decision, is itself the beginning of the work.

We have already noted how Luther contrasted Jewish legalism with Christian freedom, and how he sought to find a parallel contrast in the opposition between Roman Catholicism and Protestantism. Calvin in the meantime developed a doctrine of double predestination no less rigorous than that of Augustine. But we do find a dissenting voice among the Reformers. Luther's friend and associate, Philip Melanchthon, was the principal theologian of the Lutheran Reformation. It is often claimed that he taught a doctrine of synergism, though some Lutherans have tried to play down this side of his teaching. But others have accused him of betraying the Lutheran cause and of subverting even the key doctrine of justification by grace alone. The truth is that Melanchthon retained a strong humanistic bias through the passionate controversial years following the Reformation, and therefore he could never feel at ease with doctrines which seemed to him to threaten such essential human characteristics as rationality, freedom and responsibility. So he was obviously unhappy with such notions as predestination and irresistible grace. He could not accept that, as he put it, "God snatches you by some violent rapture, so that you must believe, whether you will or not."[8]   Again, he protested that the Holy Spirit does not work on a human being as on a statue, a piece of wood or a stone. The human will has its part to play in redemption, as well as the Word of God and the Spirit of God. Such teaching might seem to us to be just common sense, but in the highly charged atmosphere of Melanchthon's time, it needed courage to say such things, and it brought angry rejoinders from other Lutherans. But Melanchthon shows that even at the heart of Lutheran theology an effort was being made to find an acceptable place for synergism or co-working between God and man in the work of salvation.

Let us now come back to the consideration of Mary as *Coredemptrix*. Perhaps we do have to acknowledge that Barth and others have been correct in believing that the place given to Mary in catholic theology is a threat to the doctrine of *sola gratia*, but I think this is the case only when the doctrine of *sola gratia* is interpreted in an extreme form, when this doctrine itself becomes a threat to a genuinely personal and biblical view of the human being as made in the image of God and destined for God, a being still capable of responding to God and of serving God in the work of building up creation. This hopeful view of the human race is personified and enshrined in Mary.

First, we have to consider Mary in the context of the Church in which she is judged to be its preeminent and paradigmatic member. Because Mary personifies and sums up in herself the being of the Church, she also exhibits in an exemplary way the redemptive role that belongs to the whole Church. In the glimpses of Mary that we have in the gospels, her standing at the cross beside her Son, and her prayers and intercessions with the apostles, are particularly striking ways in which Mary shared and supported the work of Christ—and even these are ways in which the Church as a whole can have a share in coredemption. But it is Mary who has come to symbolize the perfect harmony

---

[8] P. Melanchthon, *Loci Communes* (OUP, 1965), p. xiii.

between the divine will and the human response, so that it is she who gives meaning to the expression *Co-redemptrix*.

But secondly, there is the further context in which Mary has to be considered, the context of the incarnation of the Word. In this context, the language of coredemption is also appropriate, but in a different way, for in this regard her contribution was unique and by its very nature could not be literally shared with anyone else. We are thinking of her now not just as representative or pre-eminent member of the Church, but as *Theotokos* or Mother of God. Mary's willing acceptance of her indispensable role in that chain of events which constituted the incarnation and the redemption which it brought about, was necessary for the nurture of the Lord and for the creation of the Church itself. So Mary is not only in the Church and of the Church, she is also prior to the Church, as is implied in her title, Mother of the Church.

Mary Co-redemptrix: Philosophical and Personalist Foundations

Dr. Josef Seifert

Prof. Dr. Josef Seifert is Rector of the International Academy of Philosophy in Liechtenstein, and an internationally acclaimed Personalist Philosopher. He is also a member of the Pontifical Academy for Life. *

My Initial Doubts concerning the Advisability of a Dogma of Mary as Co-redemptrix and Mediatrix[1]

When Professor Mark Miravalle shared information with me concerning the efforts and prayers of many Catholics to obtain a new dogma that would declare that Mary—in cooperation with, and in radical creaturely subordination to, her divine Son—is Co-redemptrix and Mediatrix of all graces,[2] I was at first hesitant whether I should declare support for the declaration of such a double (or triple) Marian dogma. For to call Mary Mediatrix of *all* graces seems to be an exaggeration

---

[1] Paper delivered on June 1, 1996, held at the Domus Mariae in Rome, Italy at the *Vox Populi Mariae Mediatrici* Leaders Conference.

[2] As well as *Advocate* for the People of God in the domain of Marian Mediation.

* Originally printed in *Mary Co-redemptrix, Mediatrix, Advocate: Theological Foundation II, Papal, Pneumatological, Ecumenical,* Queenship, 1996.

and almost contradictory: how could she be the Mediatrix of the graces Adam and Eve received, or Abraham, or her own ancestors, or of those graces which she herself received such as her Immaculate Conception? On the other hand, to give Mary the title Co-redemptrix seemed to me at first to touch a merely marginally Catholic belief and one that is open to many misunderstandings, given the fact that there is only one Saviour and one Redeemer, Jesus Christ.[3] I thought that a dogmatic declaration of this truth, though I firmly believed it, would be unnecessary and even undesirable for various reasons: it would bind all faithful to accept a truth which (1) neither appears inseparable from the deposit of faith nor (2) free of being prone to an enormous misunderstanding that would efface the difference between God and man and turn Mary into some kind of fourth divine person. (3) Besides, this doctrine did not seem to me central enough to justify a dogmatic formulation. For a dogma does not only assert the objective and indubitable reality of a supernaturally revealed truth or a doctrine presupposed by the faith (such as the ability of man to know the existence and some attributes of God by means of his reason, a philosophical content defined by Vatican I). Much more than that, a dogma binds all faithful to accept it, and it involves, and in some cases even creates, the moral obligation of all the faithful to consent to the dogmatically declared truth of the Catholic faith, as a condition of achieving eternal salvation. Thus a dogma is a very serious thing not to be demanded lightly.

Some dogmas, such as that of the divinity of Christ, formulate such clear contents of Scripture and of Christian faith that a faithful acceptance of them was binding for Christians long

---

[3] See on this the Pauline text on the *one mediator* 1 Tim 2:5-6: (5) For there is one God, and one mediator between God and men, the man Christ Jesus; (6) Who gave himself as a ransom for all, the testimony to which was borne at the proper time.(7) See also 1 Cor 1:30; Eph 1:7; 1, 17; Col 1:14, and many other texts.

before their dogmatic declaration.[4]

Other dogmas, however, could well be rejected by good and holy Christians before they were declared dogmatically, but from the time on when they have been declared, they bind all Catholics to accept them as part of the infallibly revealed *depositum fidei*. To this second category of dogmas one can reckon the Marian dogma on the Immaculate Conception which, while it was held, prior to its declaration, by many great theologians, Saints and Blessed, for example by Duns Scotus, was rejected by others, for example by Saint Thomas Aquinas who offered strong arguments against this teaching. Since the declaration of the Immaculate Conception as a dogma, however, no Catholic is free any longer to doubt or to reject it without contradicting the Catholic faith and betraying it. By binding, through a dogma, every faithful to give his consent to the doctrine of Mary as Co-redemptrix and Mediatrix, the Church would seem to give to this marginally significant truth an exaggerated weight, making its acceptance necessary for salvation. It certainly appears difficult to *demand* the consent of all the faithful to such a particular and incomprehensible aspect of Mary's role and activity, especially at a time when the most basic contents of the Creed are unknown and denied by many.

(4) Additionally, such a dogmatic declaration of which I was skeptical for a long time, appeared not especially timely to me (given the fact that the Church today is shaken to its foundations by other greater issues, rather than this one, and Catholic doctrines of much greater weight are in peril, such as the true divinity of Christ, the possibility of knowing God's existence and some divine attributes, the existence of the soul, the immortal and eternal life, the bodily virginity of Mary, the exist-

---

[4] Though of course the true divinity of Christ was and still is often denied by heresies (such as the Arian heresy), by a considerable number of contemporary theologians and by other religions such as Jehovah's Witnesses.

ence of intrinsically evil acts,[5] etc.).[6]

(5) Moreover, such a Marian dogma, because it would seemingly not possess any biblical roots, would appear to be based purely on oral sacred Tradition and hence put new obstacles in the way of Jews or of exclusively Scripture-oriented Protestants accepting the Catholic Church, and possibly also divide the Catholic Church itself anew over a non-necessary issue (because a "dogma" on Mary as Co-redemptrix would undoubtedly seem even to many well-intentioned and orthodox Catholics to be an exaggerated and problematic teaching). In fact, most Catholics and theologians today are rather ashamed by the very claim of the Catholic Church to have the authority from the Holy Spirit to formulate infallibly true propositions or to possess, prior to any dogmatic declarations, the general infallibility of the *sensus fidelium* with respect to all essential dogmatic and moral teachings of the Church.

First Resolution of My Initial Doubts Concerning the Advisability of a Dogma of Mary as Co-redemptrix-Mediatrix

While these objections left for a long time some serious

---

[5] Which are denied by many moral theologians today who reject many central parts of the moral teachings of the Church. See the encyclical of Pope John Paul II, *Veritatis Splendor*, ch. 2.

[6] Some have suggested that the negation of the "bodily" or "biological virginity" of Mary, widespread among contemporary theologians (analogous to the way in which some theologians affirm the "spiritual event of the resurrection" while denying the "bodily resurrection" of Christ) constitutes today an issue of extremely relevant significance. They believe that the actual theological debate with enormously negative pastoral effects would make it even more desirable to reiterate at this time the perpetual bodily (physical) and spiritual virginity of Mary as dogma. Those who believe this hold that to react to this powerful heresy (a heresy which attacks the foundations of our faith) by declaring a definition of the "bodily virginity" of Mary is more important today than defining her role as Co-redemptrix. I fully endorse the suggestion that this doctrine should be solemnly reiterated. Yet, given the already existing firm doctrinal teaching of the Church on Mary's perpetual virginity, it might be sufficient to *include* in a new dogmatic declaration on Mary as *Co-redemptrix* an *explicit* reference to her "perpetual physical and spiritual virginity."

doubts in my mind as to whether the declaration of such a dogma would be justified, and while not any trace of these doubts has been removed until now, upon more serious reflection and prayer I reached the conclusion that none of these arguments are decisive ones against the dogma *Vox Populi Mariae Mediatrici* seeks to obtain. More and more, the very contrary of what these objections stated seemed to be true to me. Here I wish to mention only briefly the main stages of the way in which I reached this conclusion, which the rest of this lecture aims at clarifying more deeply:

(Ad 1) It appeared to me more and more evident that this doctrine of Mary as Co-redemptrix is not marginal but essentially connected with other Catholic dogmas, especially with that of the justification through grace *but not without* freely performed works, so much so that the dogma of Mary Co-redemptrix might be regarded as a mere logical conclusion from the already existing dogmas. Moreover, the belief itself that Mary is Co-redemptrix did not seem to be marginal to me any longer, no more than the preceding Marian dogmas. Of course, this is rather obvious for the first two Marian dogmas. There is no doubt in my mind that the dogmatic declaration of the Council of Ephesus, which pronounced Mary to be truly the Mother of God, and the dogmatic declaration of her Perpetual Virginity, especially before the birth of Jesus, are quite centrally connected with the divinity of Jesus and with the truth of his Incarnation, and thus with the center of our faith, in my opinion even much more so than the doctrine of Mary as Co-redemptrix. Therefore the dogma of Mary's motherhood of God was already defined in the early centuries of the Church and played a crucial role in the times of Arianism and throughout the history of the Church. Also the teaching of her virginity when conceiving Christ was defined long before the other two Marian dogmas and is a strong confirmation of the true mystery of the Incarnation of God in Jesus which is at the core of our faith. The later two Marian dogmas cannot be put in the same level with respect to their essential connection with the Christian faith. Even within the dogmatic declaration of Mary's *Perpetual* Virginity (before, during and after Christ's birth) we find a gradation of the significance of these three truths, and while some parts of this dogma are of more central significance to the Catholic faith, others could be perceived as less significant. The truth of Mary's virginity before the birth of Jesus could be seen as more essential to our faith than the declaration of her sacred virginity after Jesus' birth—however beautiful and fitting this is. Even more clearly, her virginity before and after birth in the sense of not having had sexual relations with Joseph or other men, is more important for our faith than the declaration of—the miracle of—her purely biological virginity *during* birth which to include in a dogma even might seem odd to us, so much so that some have doubted its dogmatic character with serious arguments.

The teaching on Mary as Co-redemptrix, however, is possibly much more central to the Catholic faith than the previously defined Marian dogma of Mary's Immaculate Conception (a teaching which even the universal and angelic Doctor Saint Thomas had rejected before it had been defined). Before this dogma of her freedom from the stain of original sin prior to Christ's death and of her freedom from all personal sins, which does not appear to be inseparably linked with any Christological dogmas, had been declared, it was not binding in the same manner for all Catholics to believe. For it is not, in the perception of some, clearly connected with the center of the Catholic faith and appeared to Saint Thomas to even contradict the faith that all redemption and all cleansing from original sin and personal sins comes to us only through Jesus Christ's crucifixion and resurrection. And still this teaching was declared as dogma, though being less central to our faith. The dogma of the bodily assumption of Mary into heaven appears still less essentially connected with the center of the Catholic faith than Mary's Immaculate Conception or her role as Co-redemptrix and yet this glorious truth about Mary was also declared as dogma by the Catholic Church, through Pope Pius XII. This dogma that is connected with the highest feast of Mary does not, in any way, have a more direct bearing on our faith than Mary's role as Co-redemptrix. On the contrary, the doctrine of Mary as Co-redemptrix is more essentially interwoven with the Catholic teaching of justification and thus more profoundly linked with the center of our faith, than even the teaching about the bodily assumption of Mary into heaven. Therefore one cannot argue against the new dogma from the point of view that it is not essential to the core of our faith. In fact, from this point of view the proposed new dogma deserves fuller support even than some of those Marian dogmas which have already been defined before and which the believing Catholic firmly embraces as gifts of participation in the infallible truth of Mary's special privileges, in whose light also the glory of Christ, the cause of all Marian privileges of grace, shines forth more fully.

(Ad 2) In view of the essential logical connection between the dogmas regarding justification and free cooperation with grace and the proposed dogma of Mary Co-redemptrix, a declaration of the latter truth would not impose new burdens of "having to believe" on the faithful (what a sad way of seeing the gloriously liberating force of the infallible revelation of truth!). Rather, it is already (prior to its desired solemn declaration) a truth to be accepted by every Catholic because it is a direct logical consequence of the need for free cooperation with grace and of Mary's being the mother of God, as we shall see further.

(Ad 3) The mere possibility of misunderstandings cannot suffice to prevent the Church from the declaration of an important religious truth as dogma. The possibility of such misunderstandings only requires that the dogma be clearly and unambiguously defined so as to exclude any such misunderstanding.

(Ad 4) I came to conclude also that the pronouncement of this dogma was eminently timely in spite of the fact that Mary's role of Co-redemptrix is not a hotly debated theological issue now as the motherhood of God had been prior to its declaration.[7] For this proposed and most personalistic Marian dogma would address crucial positive concerns of the best of personalist philosophy and theology in our century. It would simultaneously help to overcome the great theoretical and practical crisis in the understanding of the dignity of persons which we likewise find in our century: in evolutionism and other theories, in Nazism or in Communism both in theory and praxis, as well as in the almost universal practical atrocities of abortion and euthanasia, just to mention a few of the most shocking forms of antipersonalism. On the free decision of a person, Mary, the greatest of goods— even our salvation—depended. Would we still kill a baby or the elderly if we believed that they possessed that same profound dignity as persons? From a religious, but especially from a philosophical standpoint, I found this proposed Marian dogma the greatest antidote against the haunting specter of antipersonalism, because it is the most personalistic Marian dogma, one that underlines the *salvific* dimension of the decision of a created person. No living being below the person would be capable of a coredemptive role. Precisely because of its personalistic dimension I found this potential dogma particularly opportune at a time of both great personalist philoso-

---

[7] Incidentally, not all dogmas were declared for this important reason. For example, the dogma of Mary's bodily assumption into heaven does not seem to have been necessary for putting an end to a hot theological debate or disagreement among the faithful but was inspired simply by the wish to hold out to the faithful a beautiful truth that inspired their spiritual lives.

phies in our century,[8] which would find a certain "supernatural coronation" through this dogma, and in the face of an absolute oppression of persons in our time which demands that the Church declare more and more fully the immense dignity of the person. The timeliness of such a dogma appears even clearer when thinking of feminism and of the opposition to the Vatican position against women's admission to the holy orders, a point to which I shall return.

(Ad 5) Moreover, the lack of biblical foundation is least true for this proposed dogma. I found a very striking and direct biblical foundation for this teaching to be explained below. Apart from the sacred tradition of the Church the Bible itself also guarantees, I came to conclude, the infallible truth of this doctrine. To the firm biblical foundation of this teaching already in the Old Testament and to its great ecumenical significance in relation to the Jews I will return. And most paradoxically, I discovered an extraordinary ecumenical significance of this teaching—not only in the dialogue with the modernist defenders of priesthood for women and feminists, but also, and on a much firmer foundation, with orthodox Jews and Protestants.[9] Hence

---

[8] Great personalist philosophies were developed by Max Scheler, Gabriel Marcel, Karol Wojtyìa, Tadeusz Styczeî, Dietrich von Hildebrand, and many others. See for example Max Scheler, *Formalism in Ethics and Non-Formal Ethics of Values,* transl. Manfred S. Frings and Roger L. Funk (Evanston: Northwestern University Press, 1973); Karol Wojtyìa, *The Acting Person* (Boston: Reidel, 1979); cf. also the corrected text, authorized by the author (unpublished), Library of the International Academy of Philosophy in the Principality of Liechtenstein, Schaan; see also Dietrich von Hildebrand, *Ethics,* 2nd edn (Chicago: Franciscan Herald Press, 1978); the same author, *Metaphysik der Gemeinschaft. Untersuchungen über Wesen und Wert der Gemsinschaft,* 3., vom Verf. durchgesehene Aufl., Dietrich von Hildebrand, *Gesammelte Werke* IV (Regensburg: J. Habbel, 1975); or my *Essere e persona. Verso una fondazione fenomenologica di una metafisica classica e personalistica.* (Milano: Vita e Pensiero, 1989).

[9] On the ecumenical significance of this teaching in the dialogue with the Eastern Church see also Michael O'Carroll, "Mary Coredemptress, Mediatress, Advocate: Instrument of Catholic-Orthodox Unity," in: Mark I. Miravalle, (Ed.), *Mary: Co-redemptrix, Mediatrix, Advocate. Theological Foundations Towards a Papal Definition?* (Santa Barbara: Queenship Publishing, 1995), pp. 119 ff.

I came to the conviction that a declaration of this dogma, far from creating obstacles to authentic ecumenism, would possess a deep ecumenical and timely significance.

To the extraordinarily timely significance of this most personalistic teaching on Mary as Co-redemptrix and to the culmination of the unfolding of the Catholic faith regarding the universal priesthood of all baptized Christians through such a new dogma, I will likewise return.

For these reasons, which I am going to explain more in detail, I came to endorse such a dogma fully. Nevertheless, I am unable to form a categorical judgment on all the diverse and complex pastoral aspects of such a new dogmatic declaration, and am sure that it would arouse much opposition. Although I am convinced, however, that such a dogma could easily constitute a stumbling block for some potential converts and might give rise to new misunderstandings and criticisms of the Catholic Church by some Protestants, I have nevertheless come to share with many other members of the *Vox Populi Mariae Mediatrici* movement their deep estimation of the beauty and objective desirability of the "completion" of the four existing Marian Dogmas of the Church through such a fifth Marian dogma which, apart from its positive ecumenical aspects, would have a very unique and personalistic meaning which I shall seek to explain in the following.

Besides explaining the mentioned points further and besides indicating some of the specifically religious and Scriptural reasons for such a dogma (which were much better explained than I am able or competent to do by a number of theologians),[10] I would like to add to the discussion of this dogma, both as a philosopher and as a Catholic, several reasons which seem to me to speak in favor of such a new Marian dogma, some of

---

[10] Among them such renowned scholars and thinkers as Bertrand de Margerie and Ignace de la Potterie. See Mark I. Miravalle, (Ed.), *Mary: Co-redemptrix, Mediatrix, Advocate. Theological Foundations Towards a Papal Definition?* (Santa Barbara: Queenship Publishing, 1995).

which may not have been pointed out by others.

1) Mary as Co-redemptrix is a Logical and Necessary Consequence of the Biblical and Catholic Teaching on the Necessity of Free Cooperation with Grace

It is clear that few teachings distinguish Catholicism more from the various Protestant confessions than the Catholic Church's insistence, according to the letter of St. James and on many other biblical texts, that not faith alone (*sola fides*) and not grace alone (*sola gratia*) but only a faith formed by love, a *fides caritate formata* and free works suffice for our justification. In a word, the need for our free cooperation with grace as a necessary condition of our salvation is a central content of the Catholic faith.[11] With Saint Augustine, the Church believes: "Qui creavit te sine te, non justificat te sine te" (He who created you without you, does not justify you without you).

In the light of this teaching, it follows as a necessary logical consequence that Mary, too, had to cooperate freely with grace, and hence also with the singular grace given to her of becoming the mother of God. Her answer to the angel Gabriel was, according to the Bible and as logical consequence of the dogmas regarding justification, clearly free and requested by God in order to make her the mother of God. A dogma on Mary's coredemptive role would thus flow necessarily from the preceding dogmas on the need for free cooperation with grace and at the same time confirm solemnly and anew the classical Catholic teaching on justification.

---

[11] The central significance of this teaching for the entire harmonious edifice of Catholic teaching was emphasized by J.A. Möhler in his classical work *Symbolik oder Darstellung der dogmatiscen Gegensätze der Katholiken und Protestanten nach ihren öffentlichen Bekenntnisschriften* (1835), herausgegeben, eingeleitet und kommentiert von J. R. Geiselmann (Köln und Olten: J. Hegner, 1960); recently by Scott and Kimberly Hahn in their conversion story, *Rome, Sweet Home* (San Francisco: Ignatius Press, 1993).

In the light of clear Catholic doctrine, a dogma on Mary's coredemptive role would only confirm the perennial Catholic teaching on justification according to which personal freedom is indispensable and according to which there is the necessity of man's *free cooperation* with divine grace. Nevertheless, the role of Mary's free cooperation with grace, which is not restricted to her first free *fiat* but encompasses her whole life, since her freedom from all personal sin (which is part of the dogma of the Immaculate Conception at least by extension) also encompasses her free cooperation throughout her life, differs in its sublimity and in its effect from that of all other creatures.[12] This free cooperation, which possesses a unique coredemptive significance, culminates in Mary's co-passion and co-crucifixion on Calvary, where she lived through her Son's passion by participating in it, as Simeon had prophesied.[13] For she had not only to cooperate with her own justification and with that of others but also with the redemption of the whole world. And this unique free cooperation with redemption (which follows from her unique role as mother of God and from the universal need for free cooperation with grace) distinguishes Mary's co-redemptive role from

---

[12] This beautiful thought I owe to my wife Mary Katherine who pointed out to me that the dogma of Mary as Immaculate Conception, at least by extension, also includes the fact that she was free from all personal sin, not only from the stain of original sin. And since she was undoubtedly tempted, and her freedom from personal sin consequently also was a result not only of God's grace but also of her own free acts, her free cooperation enveloped her whole life of free commitment to God, and if God became man only in a sinless mother, all of Mary's free acts became part of Mary's cooperative and coredemptive role.

[13] See the extraordinarily beautiful texts on this aspect of Mary's coredemptive role in Saint Bernard of Clairvaux, St. Bonaventure, Saint Albert the Great, John Tauler, as well as in a beautiful Marian hymn from an old liturgical book found in St. Peter's in Salzburg, and in some Vatican II texts in Mark I. Miravalle, *Mary: Co-redemptrix, Mediatrix, Advocate,* Queenship Publishing, Santa Barbara, CA, 1993, pp. 13ff. On Papal documents, see ibid., pp. 12-24. See also the exposition of the magnificent discussion of the theme of the Co-redemptrix by the Fathers in Bertrand de Margerie, "Mary Co-redemptrix in the Light of Patristics," in: Mark I. Miravalle, (Ed.), *Mary: Co-redemptrix, Mediatrix, Advocate. Theological Foundations Towards a Papal Definition?* (Santa Barbara: Queenship Publishing, 1995), pp. 3-44.

the more general free cooperative role demanded of all of us. Mary's coredemptive role is also far more significant than the similar role of Christ's ancestors and the patriarchs. Therefore, the dogma on Mary as Co-redemptrix would also emphasize a uniquely *active* effect (although only possible through supernatural grace) and a truly creative aspect of Mary's free action,[14] of her free *fiat* (in union with, and radical creaturely subordination to, Christ's redemptive act). The active and uniquely coredemptive character of her free *fiat* goes far beyond the free acceptance of grace called for from all other Christians as well.

2) God's Infallible Declaration of the Dogma of Coredemption: The Firm Biblical Foundations of the Proposed Dogma of Mary as Co-redemptrix, the Unique Role of the Jews and that of Mary (Women) for Our Salvation

We see now why the proposed new dogma follows logically from Catholic teaching on justification. But does it also correspond to the Bible?

---

[14] For a philosophy of the creative and self-creative dimension of freedom see Karol Wojtyìa, *The Acting Person* (Boston: Reidel, 1979); cf. also the corrected text, authorized by the author (unpublished), Library of the International Academy of Philosophy in the Principality of Liechtenstein, Schaan.

There are quite a few texts from Scripture which can be cited in direct support of Mary's role of Co-redemptrix.[15] In fact, the Gospel clearly speaks of the respect for human freedom when the angel of God waits for her response to his announcements, answers her questions, and awaits her free *fiat*

---

[15] The most important ones are: Gen. 3:15: (14) The Lord God said to the serpent, "Because you have done this, cursed are you above all cattle, and above all wild animals; upon your belly you shall go, and dust you shall eat all the days of your life. (15) I will put enmity between you and the woman, and between your seed and her seed; he shall bruise your head, and you shall bruise his heel." Isaiah 7:14: (14) Therefore the Lord himself will give you a sign. Behold, a virgin shall conceive and bear a son, and shall call his name Immanuel.

Luke 1:38; Luke 2: 25-37: (34) and Simeon blessed them and said to Mary his mother, "Behold, this child is set for the fall and rising of many in Israel and for a sign that is spoken against (35) (and a sword will pierce through your own soul also), that thoughts out of many hearts may be revealed." John 19:25-28; 30: (25) ... But standing by the cross of Jesus were his mother, and his mother's sister, Mary the wife of Clopas, and Mary Magdalene. (26) When Jesus saw his mother, and the disciple whom he loved standing near, he said to his mother, "Woman, behold your son!" (27) Then he said to the disciple, "Behold, your mother!" And from that hour that disciple took her to his own home. (28) After this Jesus knowing that all was now finished, said (to fulfil the scripture), "I thirst." (29) A bowl full of vinegar stood there; so they put a sponge full of the vinegar on hyssop, and held it to his mouth. (30) When Jesus had received the vinegar, he said, "It is finished"; and he bowed his head and gave up his spirit. Apoc. 12. See also William G. Most, "Mary Co-redemptrix in Scripture: Cooperation in Redemption," in: Mark I. Miravalle, (Ed.), *Mary: Co-redemptrix, Mediatrix, Advocate. Theological Foundations: Towards a Papal Definition?* (Santa Barbara: Queenship Publishing, 1995), pp. 147-171, and other contributions, *ibid.,* pp. 147 ff., especially Ignace de la Potterie, "The Mediation of the Mother of Jesus at the Incarnation: An Exegetical Study," pp. 173-190; cf. Stefano Manelli, "Mary Co-redemptrix In Sacred Scripture," as found in this anthology.

before leaving her. [16]

The Old Testament describes her coredemptive role possibly even more strongly by saying that God will put enmity between the devil (the serpent) and the woman, even before attributing to her seed (Christ) the "crushing the head of the serpent," and possibly even by attributing to Mary herself this act of crushing Satan's head, an assertion that would imply even a more direct biblical statement of her mediating and coredemptive role. [17]

Thus there are clear biblical references to Mary's coredemptive role, but I think that the clearest and most direct biblical proof of the truth of this proposed dogma comes from the Old Testament, where it does not speak of Mary herself but allows us to extrapolate what is said about another person and

---

[16] *Luke 1: 26* ff (26): In the sixth month the angel Gabriel was sent from God to a city of Galilee named Nazareth, (27) to a virgin betrothed to a man whose name was Joseph, of the house of David; and the virgin's name was Mary. (28) And he came to her and said, "Hail, full of grace, the Lord is with you!" (29) But she was greatly troubled at the saying, and considered in her mind what sort of greeting this might be. (30) And the angel said to her, "Do not be afraid, Mary, for you have found favor with God. (31) And behold, you will conceive in your womb and bear a son, and you shall call his name Jesus. (32) He will be great, and will be called the Son of the Most High; and the Lord God will give to him the throne of his father David, (33) and he will reign over the house of Jacob for ever; and of his kingdom there will be no end." (34) And Mary said to the angel, "How can this be, since I have no husband?" (35) And the angel said to her, "The Holy Spirit will come upon you, and the power of the Most High will overshadow you; therefore the child to be born will be called holy, the Son of God. (36) And behold, your kinswoman Elizabeth in her old age has also conceived a son; and this is the sixth month with her who was called barren. (37) For with God nothing will be impossible." (38) And Mary said, "Behold, I am the handmaid of the Lord; let it be to me according to your word." And the angel departed from her.

[17] *Gen.* 3:15. In the King James Version the much disputed pronoun reads as "it" (referring to seed): (15) And I will put enmity between thee and the woman, and between thy seed and her seed; it shall bruise thy head, and thou shalt bruise his heel. In the American Standard Translation of 1901, and in most modern German translations, it is translated as "he" (Christ). Saint Jerome translates it instead as "she" referring it to the woman (Mary). According to the Scripture scholar Stefano Manelli, who defends this translation, Saint Jerome might have known other sources which made this translation more plausible.

apply it to Mary, to whom the application is far more perfect. If coredemption is taken in a wider sense, it clearly can be attributed also to other persons besides Mary. And even in this weaker sense the proposed dogma (which in reference to Mary finds a much stronger justification) finds a splendid and extremely strong biblical confirmation. In fact, it is in his words to Abraham that God himself declares Abraham's coredemptive role as a partial cause of redemption, saying directly, and in the strongest possible words, that *because* Abraham did not spare his son, his only son, *also God will bless all nations in him,* a promise God fulfilled when he sent his own only-begotten Son, whom he did not spare from death, as he had spared Isaac, in order that his own and only-begotten Son might redeem the world. Consider these incredible words of God to Abraham after he had prevented the sacrifice of Isaac which he had first demanded:

> "By myself I have sworn, says the LORD, because you have done this, and have not withheld your son, your only son, I will indeed bless you ... and by your descendants shall all the nations of the earth bless themselves, because you have obeyed my voice." (Gen. 22:16-18)[18]

By saying, and repeating, that such an immense thing as

---

[18] Emphasis mine. Compare the full text: (11) But the angel of the Lord called to him from heaven, and said, "Abraham, Abraham!" And he said, "Here am I." (12) He said, "Do not lay your hand on the lad or do anything to him; for now I know that you fear God, seeing you have not withheld your son, your only son, from me." (13) And Abraham lifted up his eyes and looked, and behold, behind him was a ram, caught in a thicket by his horns; and Abraham went and took the ram, and offered it up as a burnt offering instead of his son. (14) So Abraham called the name of that place The Lord will provide; as it is said to this day, "On the mount of the Lord it shall be provided." (15) And the angel of the Lord called to Abraham a second time from heaven, (16) and said, "By myself I have sworn, says the Lord, because you have done this, and have not withheld your son, your only son, (17) I will indeed bless you, and I will multiply your descendants as the stars of heaven and as the sand which is on the seashore. And your descendants shall possess the gate of their enemies, (18) and by your descendants shall all the nations of the earth bless themselves, because you have obeyed my voice." (Gen. 22:11-18).

God's own redemptive act of blessing all nations through Abraham's offspring was done *because of Abraham's act,* God himself clearly attributes a coredemptive role to Abraham to whose free sacrificial act God responds by redeeming us.[19] Thus God himself can be said to have declared and defined unambiguously in the Bible the coredemptive role of free human acts as co-causes of redemption. The Church, in solemnly declaring Mary Co-redemptrix, would hence only confirm the divine declaration of this truth and apply to Mary in a singular way what God himself has pronounced quite clearly of Abraham: that *because of Mary's (co-redemptive) free fiat the whole world was redeemed.* Because Mary spoke her "behold, I am the handmaid of the Lord," and did not withhold her will, or her womb, or her whole being, nor her only son, from God and his loving plan, all of us have been redeemed. In this true and yet utterly mysterious dependence of God's redemptive act on Mary's free human decision the whole unspeakable dignity and mission of the human person emerges clearly before our minds.[20]

The dogma of Mary as Co-redemptrix, if declared, would also emphasize the universal role and mission of all human beings who cooperate with God's grace and thereby with the completion of the redemptive work of Christ.

This dogma would also especially emphasize the co-redemptive role of the Jews which they share to some extent with Mary,

---

[19] Therefore also, considered in terms of their dependence on the Jews, the Christians are only the younger brothers and heirs of the Jews, as the documents on ecumenism and the Jews of the Vatican Council II and later Papal documents emphasized. Dietrich von Hildebrand calls Israel for the explained reasons already in 1937 the *Menschheitsvolk,* the nation of and for all humanity. See Dietrich von Hildebrand, *Die Juden und das christliche Abendland,* in: Die Erfüllung. Wien. 3. Jg. 1937. Nr. 1/2. S. 9-32; see also Dietrich von Hildebrand, *Memoiren und Aufsätze gegen den Nationalsozialismus 1933-1938.* Veröffentlichungen der Kommission für Zeitgeschichte, mit Alice von Hildebrand und Rudolf Ebneth hrsg. v. Ernst Wenisch (Mainz: Matthias Gründewald Verlag, 1994).

[20] On an expansion of the idea of Coredemptrix to other Christians according to Saint Ambrose, Saint Augustine, and other Fathers see B. de Margerie, *ibid.,* pp. 5 ff., pp. 37 ff.

as the *chosen people of God*. There is a specific Christian reason why the Jews are *the* nation among all other nations: God has sent his Son to all of mankind—but he did this not through the exclusive action of his own merciful and omnipotent will, but also in demanding and presupposing the free cooperation of certain human persons, a free cooperation to which he calls each human being but quite uniquely those without whose free co-operation the Incarnation and Redemption of the world would not have taken place. And this free cooperation can even be regarded as a mediation of salvation through human freedom. And precisely this mediation—though it concerns in a wider sense all human persons—must be primarily attributed to the Jews, mostly to the Jewish virgin mother of God, Mary, who mediated our salvation through her free *fiat* and thus became Co-redemptrix.

Yet the unique mediating role of Mary, as mother of all graces, also applies in a wider sense to *all* those Jews from Noah and Abraham on to Mary, who played some mediating role for our redemption, especially to Abraham, whose coredemptive role God himself asserts most directly and most touchingly. Thus the salvation of all mankind—while being the undeserved and free fruit of the redemptive will and graceful deed of God—depended not only on Mary's free *fiat* but also on the free accep-tance of God's will by many other great Jewish patriarchs and ancestors of Christ. In this sense, all of those Jews who partici-pated in the mystery of the Incarnation of God could receive the title—though on a far more limited level—given by the Church to Mary: As she is co-redeemer (Co-redemptrix), the Jews who, like Abraham, cooperated with God's will, are co-redeemers as well. Thus the pronouncement of this dogma would also em-phasize, in Mary, the unique role of the Jews and most properly of a Jewish woman, the virgin-mother of God, in bringing hu-manity salvation—not only as objects of divine love or as passive vessels of his grace, but also as free and cooperating agents.

3) "Mary as Co-redemptrix" Would Be the Most Explicitly "Personalistic Dogma" about Mary and Therefore Very Timely

A dogma that declares Mary Co-redemptrix would give a unique witness to the full freedom of the human person, as we have seen, and to God's respect for human freedom. This dogma would recognize in an ultimate way that a *free decision* of the human person of Mary, who was not even to become the Mother of God without her free *fiat*—a decision which was not exclusively caused by divine grace but was also the fruit of her own personal choice—was *necessary* for our salvation, or played at least an *indispensable part* in the concrete way of our redemption chosen by God.

In our age, in which personalistic philosophy was developed more deeply than ever before in the history of mankind, and in which at the same time terrible anti-personalistic ideologies reign, such a dogma would rightfully be perceived as a supreme confirmation of the dignity of human freedom.

In all of this I would see a crucial value and significance for this dogma being proclaimed in our century, one in which both a new awareness of personal dignity arose and one in which the person was also more degraded in action and denied in theory (also in many pseudo-personalistic and situational ethics theories) than ever before.

4) Mary Co-redemptrix as a Marian Dogma Which Implies a Universal Truth for all Christians

Yet at the same time, the dogma on Mary's coredemptive role would not concern only a unique prerogative of Mary (such as her Immaculate Conception, i.e., her freedom from any stain of original sin through a singular anticipatory effect of Christ's redemptive act), but a quality which analogously all Christians and truly religious persons share with Mary to a smaller extent:

to take an active part in the redemptive event and in the dispensation of the grace of redemption. This applies to the Pope, the bishops, every priest and religious, and to all of us. And no creature took a more active and a more sublime part in this redemptive work of Christ than a woman and mother: Mary!

5) Mary as Co-redemptrix—a Victory for Authentic Catholic Feminism and a Timely Response to Wrong Forms of Feminism

Such a dogma would also seem to be most opportune today as an expression of "Catholic feminism" or better as a Catholic response to feminist theology. For this dogma would not only show, as previous Marian dogmas, that our Lady—as a woman—was raised by God in dignity above all created men and angels and is second only to Christ who is "God-made-man" himself. For this fact is sufficiently shown through the four existing Marian dogmas. This new dogma of Mary's role as Co-redemptrix—even more than the declaration of Mary as Mother of God—would also express the truth of a uniquely active and effective participating role of Mary in the mystery of redemption. It would counteract the idea that human beings in general, and particularly women, are mere passive vessels of divine grace and that the Virgin Mary was made Mother of God, freed from all sin, and extolled above all creatures, *solely* by the grace and election of God, *without any* great need for her own free choice. Now, the need for Mary's own free choice for our salvation is only implied but not explicitly stated in any of the previous Marian dogmas. This new declaration of the traditional doctrine would therefore show anew *a perpetual truth about Mary and about woman*, a truth which was always held by the Church but never clearly and indubitably stated: *the greatest deed of God's gracious love—the redemption of mankind and our salvation—is in some real sense also the consequence of the free act of a woman and thus also the gift of a woman to humanity.* And while the fact of a co-redemptive role is in some general sense true for all of our free participation in the dispensation of the grace of God among the members of the Church, it is still true in a uniquely excellent sense *only of Mary* and thus *only of a woman.*

The grandeur of this teaching that a woman was not only mother of God and a vessel of God's gracious choice but that through her own free and unforced *fiat* and her deeds (which involved also her freely accepted sacrifice of her only son, as in Abraham) she became—an admittedly purely human—*co-cause of our salvation,* would be the greatest possible witness to the dignity of woman and thus complement the Marian dogmas and the Apostolic Letter *On the Dignity of Woman.* Indeed, the most radical feminist dreams about women's dignity and their equality to men, or even the call to recognize a superior status for women in comparison to men (with the exception of Christ) in the Church, could not even approach the dignity of a woman expressed in this new dogma. *This dogma would express the dignity of a woman's action which exceeds in activeness, sublimity and effectiveness the deeds of all pure creatures and men: of all kings and politicians, thinkers, scientists, philosophers, artists and craftsmen from the beginning of the world to the end of doom, and in a certain manner even of all priests except Christ. For all other priestly actions render only present Christ's redemptive grace and action but Mary's act rendered our redemption itself possible and thus mediated for mankind the most high gift of our divine Savior himself.*

It follows undoubtedly from all of these evidences that Mary, more perfectly than Abraham, whose action God himself declared to be a co-cause of redemption, must be confessed to be Co-redemptrix for all of us.

6) The Timeliness of a Dogma on Mary as Co-redemptrix as a Formulation of the Dignity of Women and of the Unique Way in Which Mary as Woman Participated in the General Priesthood Bestowed Upon all Christians in Baptism

This dogma would then also complement in an important manner the irreversible verdict of the Catholic Church against ordained priestesses. This "No" of the Church to women priests has to be seen in light of the fact that the special representation of Christ through the priest, who offers the sacrifice of the Mass, thereby renewing in an unbloody manner Christ's sacrifice on the Cross, was reserved by the will of God to men alone. But the proposed dogma of Mary as Co-redemptrix would give a magnificent defense both of the general priesthood of all Christians and of a uniquely sublime "feminine priesthood of Mary" (and of other mothers and women in a less perfect form).[21] We have to remind ourselves: *Every Christian, all men and all women, receive in baptism the general priesthood, together with the kingly and prophetic dignity and vocation.* Hence the proposed new dogma would express *the true character of Mary as a unique Mediatrix of grace and thus* constitute an important complementary truth to the Church's insistence on the impossibility of women receiving holy orders and that special ordained priesthood which Christ has reserved for men alone. At least if one of the essential elements of priesthood is a "mediation" between God and man and a "mediation of grace," Mary would by this dogma also be declared to be the most sublime *Mediatrix of God who draws upon us through her free act divine graces and the salvation itself of all mankind.* Her action does *not only render present* Christ's sacrifice and grace *after his redemptive deed, as the priest's, but in a certain way, through her antecedent "fiat,"*

---

[21] This special motherly cooperation was brought out beautifully in *Redemptoris Mater* by Pope John Paul II. See on this also Michael O'Carroll, cit., pp. 129 ff. Cardinal Mindszenty has said in his *Memoirs* that in a sense the priesthood and role of mothers, from whom Christ and all priests come, exceeds that of all other human persons. And a Swiss priest in a sermon held in Rankweil, Austria, recently said the same thing in even stronger terms, reporting on the heroic life of faith of his great-great-grandmother.

rendered possible the redemptive deed of God himself.[22] And something analogous is true for any mother who can mediate, in a certain sense, all graces for her children and can thus also become co-cause of all their temporal and eternal goods, including their redemption.

The freely chosen dependence of the divine redemptive action on Mary's fiat is just the most sublime manifestation of a more universal phenomenon which elucidates the essence and dignity of persons. God often binds, for example in human procreation, in the priestly acts of celebrating the Mass, and even in the redemption itself, his divine activity to human freedom.

7) On the Ethical and Bioethical Significance of the Proposed New Marian Dogma: Mary as Co-redemptrix and Church Teaching on the Transmission of Human Life

A new dogma of Mary as Co-redemptrix would also throw new light on the role of the family in the Church and on the metaphysical and theological sides of procreation. For, analogously to Mary's coredemptive deed, human procreation is primarily a service to, and a cooperation with, an essentially divine act of creation through which alone a human soul and the person of the embryo can be created from nothingness. And yet, in the order of nature and of creation (in spite of the fact that "God is able of these stones to raise up children unto Abraham," as Saint John the Baptist says)[23] the divine creation of human persons is mediated by free human action and cooperation. This constitutes one of the chief reasons for the immorality of con-

---

[22] In another respect it remains true that even Mary does not possess the dignity of the ordained priest and the dignity of holy orders which permit the priest to represent Christ on the altar.

[23] See Matt 3:9 and Luke 3:8: (9) and do not presume to say to yourselves, "We have Abraham as our father;" for I tell you, God is able from these stones to raise up children to Abraham.; (8) Bear fruits that befit repentance, and do not begin to say to yourselves, "We have Abraham as our father;" for I tell you, God is able from these stones to raise up children to Abraham.

traception.[24] In this respect, the pronouncing of the new dogma of Mary as Co-redemptrix by the Holy Father would constitute a beautiful continuation of the present Pope's special mission of expounding the inner reasons and metaphysical foundations of the Church's teaching on the transmission of human life, which is in a sense a co-creation—a ministry to, and co-cause of, divine creation. In a supernatural but truly analogous way, Mary's *fiat* and whole life and spiritual passion under the Cross is a service to, and a co-cause of, our redemption.

In fact, the New Covenant theology could elucidate the connection which exists here between Mary's union with God, and the human couple and the family's union with God. For also in the creation of each new human person God respects human freedom and allows free human acts of parents to become co-cause of the creation from nothing of their children. In a similar way, the free act of Mary became the co-cause of our redemption. At the same time, as the parents can in no way themselves create a new human soul but only God, so Mary cannot redeem the world, but only Christ. Therefore the new proposed dogma would in no way efface the abyss of distinction between God and the created person of Mary nor would Mary's part in redemption resemble, let alone equal, God's redemptive act.

[24] See my articles in different languages: Josef Seifert, "The Problem of the Moral Significance of Human Fertility and Birth Control Methods. Philosophical Arguments against Contraception?" in *Humanae Vitae: 20 Anni Dopo*, Acts of the Second International Congress of Moral Theology, Rome, 1988, pp. 661-672; "The Moral Distinction between Natural and Artificial Birth Control" in *The Torch of Truth, The Contemporary Catholic Renaissance* (1985); "Der sittliche Unterschied zwischen Empfängnisregelung und Kontrazeption," in *Menschenwürde und Elternschaft* (Hg. Ernst Wenisch), (Valendar: Veritas-Verlag, 1983); "Il Dono dell' Amore e Il Dono di Una Nuova Vita. Verso una visione più personalistica dell' Matrimonio. Humanae Vitae - Familiaris Consortio. 1968-1988," in: *Per una transmissione responsabile della vita umana*, a cura di Anna Cappella. IVo Congresso internazionale per la famiglia d'Africa e d'Europa (Rom: Università dell' Sacro Cuore, 1989); "Problem moralnego zcaczenia ludzkiej plodnosci i metod kontroli pocze'c," transl. J. Merecki SDS and P. Mikulska, in: Bp K. Majda'nski/T. Styczen, *Dar ludzkiego Zycia Humanae Vitae Donum. W swudziesta rocznice ogloszenia encykliki Humanae Vitae* (Lublin: KUL-Verlag, 1991), 247-259.

8) Mary as Co-redemptrix and the Completion of the Four Marian Dogmas

This dogma would also throw new light on the other Marian dogmas and in particular better explain the dogma of the Immaculate Conception and the reason why the Co-redemptrix was, due to a unique privilege of God, preserved from all stain of original and personal sin. For this appears most fitting for her role of mediating salvation as the second Eve. The same is true of her bodily assumption into heaven which befits the dignity of her, who was not only a vessel of God's grace, but through her free cooperation, Co-redemptrix. Even the first and foremost Marian dogma, that she is truly the Mother of God, receives a new meaning when one contemplates this active cooperative role she played for our salvation and redemption and which was required for her becoming the mother of God. The new dogma, as a culmination of the preceding Marian dogmas, would complement and complete them by explaining why we do not only adore and worship God who has created and used Mary as a singular vessel of his grace, but why we also venerate (and of course never adore) Mary herself as the Mother of God which she did become through the grace of God, but not without her free and heroic participation, from the belief in the angel's word and from the conception of Jesus and the acceptance of Simeon's prophecies, on until Calvary.

9) Cautions To Be Strictly Observed in Any Dogmatic Formulation of Mary as Co-redemptrix

It is clear that any dogma on Mary as Co-redemptrix would have to exclude absolutely any blurring of the distinction between Christ's redemptive deed and Mary's purely *human* way of participating in redemption and of becoming Co-redemptrix. Mary on her own is no more able to redeem the world as parents are to create their child's soul from nothing. In this sense, Mary is not Co-redemptrix and can never be our redeemer. Nevertheless and at the same time, such a dogma also should emphasize the *unique character* of the link between the God-man's redemptive act and *Mary's* freedom in becoming a co-cause of Redemption—in union with, and through the force of, Christ's Redemption. Certainly, as mentioned above, also the free acts of the ancestors of Christ, especially the faith and sacrifice of Abraham, became in a more remote way "co-redemptive" acts, foreshadowing the unique mode of direct participation in the divine cause of redemption entrusted to Mary.

It would seem to me particularly fitting that our present Holy Father, dearly beloved and so deeply Marian, who, like no other Pope, has unfolded a vision of the dignity of each human person and has entrusted the entire human race so often to Mary, could, in the act of declaring this dogma, complete his action of dedicating all humanity to the intercession of Mary, our Mother and the great *Advocate* of the whole Church before God, to Mary, who is also the *Mediatrix* of all the graces of which our fallen world, our famine- and war-ridden and sinful human race today is in such desperate need and which alone can pull mankind out of the abyss of our sins and sufferings, which again cannot happen without our free cooperation.

Wishing the Holy Father God's holy strength and light to see whether or not it is God's will to announce solemnly to the world those great truths about Mary, and through announcing them about her, announcing also more fully the truth about the human person as such, I conclude my remarks by entrusting this great cause to the incomprehensible and infinite wisdom and love of Christ and to the wisdom and love of Mary, the Mother of God, our heavenly *Co-redemptrix, Mediatrix* and *Advocate*.

The Marian Theology of Von Balthasar and the Proposed Definition of Mary Co-redemptrix

By Sr. Thomas Mary McBride, O.P.

Sr. Thomas Mary McBride is a member of the Mariological Society of America and specializes in the Theology and Mariology of Hans Urs von Balthasar.

It has been predicted in theological circles that the Swiss theologian Hans Urs von Balthasar (1905-1988) will emerge as the most important theologian of the twentieth century.[1] A striking characteristic of Balthasar's massive output is its contemplative orientation which he himself has described as "theology on one's knees."[2] Indeed, his own theological vocation was perceived and understood in prayer, in a precise moment of grace during a retreat in the Black Forest near Basle; a grace which he

---

[1] Augustine DiNoia, O.P., Professor of Theology, Dominican House of Studies, Washington D.C., Editor *The Thomist*, formerly Doctrinal advisor to U.S. Bishop's Conference, member of the International Theological Commission of John Paul II, currently Director Intracultural Forum of the John Paul II Cultural Center, Washington, D.C.; Conference given at Dominican Monastery of Our Lady of Grace, No. Guilford, Ct., 1994.

[2] Hans Urs von Balthasar, *Explorations in Theology I: The Word Made Flesh* (San Francisco: Ignatius Press, 1989), 206.

would later recount with precision.[3]

The receptive prayerful attitude that one perceives in von Balthasar's work can be best understood by means of the Marian *fiat* indicating that theology begins in the response of the creature to God's self-manifestation. According to von Balthasar, Mary made to God, through the gift of grace, the perfect nuptial response of faith, and thus the Marian *fiat* has become the archetype, principle and exemplar of the faith response of the entire Church.[4] This paper, therefore, will attempt to present a limited summary of von Balthasar's Marian theology developed around the *leitmotiv* of the nuptial *fiat*, which explicitly or implicitly, penetrates his entire theological *corpus*.

Since von Balthasar, in the tradition of the early Fathers, sees Mary as the archetypal image of the Church, it follows that his conception of the Church is Marian, feminine, and bridal. He sees the Church as person, as body, as structure, and ultimately, as bride. First and foremost, of course, the Church is Christ; but when considered as Head and body, the Church is also a response to Christ, that is, a bridal self-surrender to Christ in faith. It is by means of the Church's response in faith, her personal *fiat* to the Divine Word, that the Church bears in her own flesh and spirit the fruit of Christ. Although she is made up of many subjects, the Church is not a mere collectivity of persons: a sociological reality. Her many members participate through infused grace in a single normative subject and its con-

---

[3] Angelo Scola, *Hans Urs von Balthasar: a Theological Style* (Grand Rapids: Eerdsman, 1995), 9: "Even today, thirty years later, I could retrace my steps back to that remote path in the Black Forest, not too far from Basle, and rediscover the tree under which I was struck, as if by lightning . . . and what suddenly entered my mind then was neither theology, nor the priesthood. It was simply this: you do not have to choose anything, you have been called! You will not serve, you will be taken into service. You do not have to make plans of any sort, you are only a pebble in a mosaic prepared long before. All that I had to do was simply to leave everything behind and follow, without making any plans, without desires or particular intuitions. I had only to remain there to see how I could be useful."

[4] Von Balthasar, *Explorations in Theology II: Spouse of the Word*, essay: "Who is the Church?", trans. A.V. Littledale (San Francisco: Ignatius Press, 1991), 161.

sciousness. Her inchoateness is fulfilled in the mystery of the Holy Spirit within her inmost ground, who alone can constitute her as subject and bride.[5] By means of her sacramental structure, Christ's most intimate divine life is communicated to the real persons who form the Church in a bond of love like unto marriage. For von Balthasar this reality of Church that revelation calls the bride of Christ is a mystery of faith.[6]

In the third volume of his *Theo-Drama: Persons in Christ*, von Balthasar outlines the archetypal figure of the Virgin Mary whom he considers "the *Realsymbol*" of the Church.[7] Drawing on the Fathers and Tradition, von Balthasar presents the Virgin of Nazareth as the individual woman who personifies and is the very epitome of the Church in her essential bridal self-surrender to God. The whole life of Mary is embodied, he says, in her *fiat*, the perfect consent that "allows all," and by thus allowing God's Word to take complete possession of her body and spirit, she "becomes womb and bride and mother of the incarnating God."[8]

According to von Balthasar, Mary's consent is, in the first place, a virginal consent which only subsequently becomes a maternal and finally a bridal consent. Her virginal consent finds its source in the grace of the Immaculate Conception, source of her spotless virginity.[9] Mary was graced with perfect finite freedom: the capability for full self-realization[10] as a being totally

---

[5] Ibid., 191.

[6] Ibid., 186.

[7] Hans Urs von Balthasar, *Theo Drama*, vol. 3: *Dramatis Personae: Persons in Christ*, trans. Graham Harrison (San Francisco: Ignatius Press, 1992), 333.

[8] Hans Urs von Balthasar, *Das Katholische an der Kirche* (= *Kolner Beitrage 10*; Cologne: Wienand, 1972), 10-11 quoted in *The von Balthasar Reader*, trans. Robert J. Daly and Fred Lawrence, ed. Medard Kehl and Werner Loser with an Introduction by Medard Kehl (Edinburgh T. & T. Clark, 1985), 214.

[9] For von Balthasar's discussion of the development of the dogma of the Immaculate Conception see Hans Urs von Balthasar, *Theo-Drama*, vol. 3: *Dramatis Personae: Persons in Christ*, 296-297; 319-323.

[10] Hans Urs von Balthasar, *The Threefold Garland*, trans. Erasmo Leiva-Merikakis (San Francisco: Ignatius Press, 1982), 32.

and exclusively turned toward the Word of God in the answering obedience of faith.

Her virginal consent becomes a maternal consent as she freely allows the divine initiative to make a new beginning in the Virgin Birth of her Son and she becomes Mother of Christ. Ultimately, the Mother of Christ becomes the Bride of Christ on Calvary wherein her free, faith-filled and now bridal consent to God's salvific will is brought to its highest achievement. Standing beside the Cross of Jesus, Mary receives in perfect faith and love the infinite fruitfulness flowing from the open wound in Christ's Heart. The new Eve receives the outpoured life and overflowing grace of the new Adam, intimately cooperating through her unrestricted *fiat* in his mission of redemptive love.[11]

As Virgin, Mother, and Bride of Christ, Mary becomes Mother of the Church from the seed of spiritual fruitfulness which the immaculate Bride received from her crucified Son: his Body given and His Blood poured out. As Virgin, Bride, and Mother, she gives birth to the Church again and again throughout the ages.[12]

Von Balthasar therefore, in his Marian theology, presents the Church with an archetype of her own life and love. Both Mary and the Church are fruitful precisely because of their virginal love. In the sacramental sign of the virginal birth, the Church is put in touch with the new birth of divine life of which

---

[11] Von Balthasar, *Theo-Drama*, vol. 3: *Dramatis Personae: Persons in Christ:* "Her cooperation, the work of her who serves both as a woman *and* as a creature, is not forgotten: it is integrated into his. Both redemption and preredemption spring from the same Cross but in such a way that she who is preredeemed is used in the Church's coming to be," 351.

[12] Von Balthasar, *Explorations in Theology II: Spouse of the Word*: "Mary, in giving birth spiritually and physically to the Son, becomes the universal Mother of all believers, for the Church as body is born of Christ and is herself Christ," 165. See also Hans Urs von Balthasar, Commentary on *Mary: God's Yes to Man: Encyclical letter, Mother of the Redeemer*, John Paul II, trans. Lothar Krauth (San Francisco: Ignatius Press, 1987): "Mary's abundantly effective faith, especially under the Cross, is, by her dying Son, made part of his actions in bringing forth the Church. This justifies the title 'Mother of the Church', bestowed on Mary by Pope Paul VI," 172.

she, like Mary, is Mother. Mary and the Church are each transformed into the Bride of Christ through an interior participation in the Passion, receiving the spiritual fruitfulness flowing from the pierced Heart of the Crucified. Finally, in this active receptivity Mary, and then the Church, become the productive womb of all Christian grace. Through the nuptial *fiat*, literally immaculate only in the Church's Marian archetype, Mary shares with the communion of saints her own archetypal experience as Virgin, Mother, and Bride of Christ.[13]

According to von Balthasar, Mary's bridal "yes" of bodily faith, which continues on in the Church as fruitful virginity, not only has implications for the Church, indeed, it is the Marian *fiat* that defines the Church. The *fiat* and redemption are so interwoven, so inseparably one, that the creature cannot say "yes" to God without being redeemed, but neither can the creature be redeemed without having somehow spoken his or her "yes." Mary's single "yes," her personal *fiat* in its unlimited availability to God's plan, sufficed for the incarnate Lord to say "yes" to all his creatures, and has become "by grace, the bridal womb, *matrix*, and *mater*" in and through which each creature can say "yes" to God, and by which "he also forms the truly universal Church."[14] Mary's *fiat*, therefore, like the *fiat voluntas tua* of the Lord, is vicarious; it is catholic: embracing the all of God's love for all of God's people; and it is archetypal.[15] Grounded in

---

[13] Von Balthasar, *Explorations in Theology II: Spouse of the Word*, 159-161. That the Church can bring forth Christ presupposes a subjective personal holiness of faith, hope and love realized in act. Mary, through her immaculate conception was able to make this act of holiness: this perfect archetypal response. Her womanly and receptive faith was enabled to fully correspond to the masculine seed of Christ in her *fiat* of surrender to God's Word and the Spirit of God who overshadowed her, 160.

[14] Hans Urs von Balthasar, *The Office of Peter and the Structure of the Church*, trans. Andree Emery (San Francisco: Ignatius Press, 1986), 206-207.

[15] Von Balthasar, *Das Katholische an der Kirche* quoted in *The Von Balthasar Reader*: "*In this fundamental act in the room at Nazareth, in this alone the Church of Christ is founded as Catholic. Its catholicity is the unconditional character of the* Ecce Ancilla ('*behold the handmaid*') *whose offer of infinite accommodation is the creaturely counterpart to the infinitely self-bestowing love of God*," 214.

Mary's archetypal *fiat* the bridal Church, like Mary, conceives, bears and gives birth to Christ.

An integral part of von Balthasar's Marian theology is the apostolic archetypes Peter, John, and Paul, who form in the Church, together with Mary, a necessary and indissoluble group of persons surrounding the human life of Christ.[16] Von Balthasar considers the Marian *fiat* as the foundational form, undergirding and sustaining the apostolic archetypes, for Mary's experience came first and thus wholly conditions the apostolic experience.[17]

The Church, therefore, coming forth from Christ "finds her personal center in Mary as well as the full realization of her idea as Church." Her Marian faith response to the Divine-human Bridegroom, is elevated in the Church to the status of principle and is coextensive with the masculine principle of Office and Sacrament in bearing the fruit of Christ for the world.[18] Knowing that all people are envisaged in God's plan, the Church can humbly know herself as the chosen representative of mankind before God "in faith, prayer, and sacrifice, in hope for all, and still more in love for all." As bride, in imitation of her Marian archetype, she turns to her Bridegroom so that she may serve as handmaid and give him back new offspring shaped in the form of Christ, as well as receive from her Head, "in the depths of their intimacy," the entire Trinitarian life.[19] Her whole disposition can only be a feminine dependence on God embodied in Mary's *fiat*.

Von Balthasar's Marian theology has a contemplative orientation. This is clear in his insistence that the first duty of the Bride-Church to her Bridegroom is the glorification of divine

---

[16] Hans Urs von Balthasar, *The Glory of the Lord*, vol. 1: *Seeing the Form*, trans. Erasmo Leiva-Merikskis; ed. Joseph Fessio and John Riches (San Francisco: Ignatius Press, 1983), 343.

[17] Ibid., 362.

[18] Von Balthasar, *Explorations in Theology II: Spouse of the Word*, 161. For a discussion of the "Marian Principle" see Hans Urs von Balthasar, *Elucidations*, trans. the Publishers (London: S.P.C.K., 1975), 64-72.

[19] Von Balthasar, *Explorations in Theology II: Spouse of the Word*, 183.

love. This divine love was poured into Mary's pure womb as the first-fruit of redemptive grace, and she fully responded with her *fiat* of faith and adoration.[20] It is this Marian receptivity and response to the Word of God which is the sole purpose of the contemplative life of the Church wherever it is found.

> The highest priority belongs, without exception, to our readiness to serve the divine love, a readiness that has no other end than itself, and that appears senseless to a world caught up in so many urgent and reasonable occupations.[21]

Like her Marian archetype, the contemplative desires to give a similar answer of obedience and adoration, a service of pure glorifying thanksgiving to absolute love. Like Mary, the contemplative identifies herself with the "innermost center of the Church where she is simply the bride in the presence of the Bridegroom." It is the life which Jesus praised in the Gospel, the life of Mary at his feet:

> Mary of Bethany can never be dispensed with. *Personam Ecclesiae gerit:* she represents in her special role, the Church herself. She actualizes in the world of human consciousness the inmost mystery of the nuptials between Christ and the Church, God and the world, grace and nature, a relation that is the mystery both of Mary's fecundity as mother and of that of the Church.[22]

Confirmation by St. Thomas Aquinas

St. Thomas Aquinas, in discussing the Marian *fiat*, seems to confirm von Balthasar's basic viewpoint. According to St. Thomas, Mary's *fiat* was necessary in order to show that a spiritual

[20] Hans Urs von Balthasar, *Love Alone*, trans. and ed. Alexander Dru (New York: Herder and Herder, 1969), 63-64.

[21] Ibid., 88.

[22] Von Balthasar, *Explorations in Theology II: Spouse of the Word*, 36.

marriage was being enacted between the Son of God and human nature. Mary's "yes" stood for the "yes" of all God's people thereby making it possible for every person to pronounce his own personal *fiat* and attain intimate union with the divine nature.[23] In commenting on the mystical meaning of the wedding at Cana, the Angelic Doctor teaches that Mary is present in the mystical marriage of the soul with God and that it is she who arranges the marriage, because through her intercession the soul is joined to Christ through grace. St. Thomas calls Mary *consolatrix* and *mediatrix*.[24] In his commentary on the Incarnation St. Thomas declares that Mary is so full of grace, that it overflows to us, and in this overflowing plenitude of grace Mary excels all the saints.[25]

From an evaluatory viewpoint von Balthasar's Marian theology is itself a critical evaluation of the Church's Mariology from the Patristic period right up to Vatican Council II.[26] He rethinks the unreflective faith of pre-critical times from the standpoint of the present historical situation which has passed through the Reformation and the Enlightenment. Rigorously reasoning through its lines of thought he shows the fundamental catholicity of the Marian *fiat* and the correctness of the development of the archetypal image of Mary as Virgin, Mother, and Bride. He notes the exaggerations which emerged through the centuries

---

[23] St. Thomas Aquinas, *Summa Theologiae*, 3a, 30, 1. In discussing the question "whether it was necessary to announce to the Blessed Virgin Mary that which was to be done in her," St. Thomas answers that "it was reasonable that it should be announced to the Blessed Virgin that she was to conceive Christ . . . in order to show that there is a certain spiritual wedlock between the Son of God and human nature. Wherefore in the Annunciation the Virgin's consent was besought in lieu of that of the entire human nature."

[24] St. Thomas Aquinas, *Commentary on the Gospel of St. John*, ed. James A. Weisheipl, O.P. (Albany, N.Y.: Magi Books, Inc., 1980), n. 343, n. 344.

[25] Ibid., n. 201; see also St. Thomas Aquinas, *Summa Theologiae*, (Blackfriars Summa) vol. 51, *Our Lady*, trans. and ed. Thomas R. Heath, O.P. (N.Y.: McGraw Hill, 1969), appendix 1, 93-95.

[26] Hans Urs von Balthasar, *Theo-Drama*, vol. 3: *Dramatis Personae: Persons in Christ*, 295-318.

and which were pruned in Chapter VIII of *Lumen Gentium*. He calls attention, however, to "the limits of the Council's Mariology" and calls it a minimalist presentation.[27] He then gives Mariology a new start by presenting his own triptychal view of Mary as a "dramatic character."[28]

Mary is a dramatic character, according to von Balthasar, because her Immaculate Conception locates her personal existence "between a paradisal (*supralapsarian*) existence and human life in its fallen state."[29] This must necessarily be so because the privilege of her Immaculate Conception freed her from any influence of sin yet she lived her human existence in the fallen world of sin. It is so, secondly, because her personal life is situated at the passageway between the Old Covenant of law and sin and the New Covenant of grace and Spirit.

> As a fleshly Mother she stands in direct continuity with the generations who descend from Adam via Abraham, whereas, as a virgin Mother, who became pregnant on the basis of her consent to the overshadowing Spirit, she signifies a hiatus and a new beginning.[30]

Finally, it is so because her existence lies in the eschatological tension between time and eternity. Although she herself has regained Paradise in her Assumption, as Mother of all the living she "gives birth to the Messiah-scion and his brothers in the birth-pangs of the Cross."[31] In von Balthasar's view,

> Mary's dramatic role emerges both from her center—as Christ's virginal Mother— and from the whole range of her being, which starts with supralapsarian humanity, embraces fallen and redeemed humanity and comprehends the

---

[27] Ibid., 317-318.
[28] Ibid., 318-339.
[29] Ibid., 319.
[30] Ibid., 328.
[31] Ibid., 334.

eschatological *status* of mankind. Her role is universal and in a certain sense (which we must analyze in more detail) coextensive with Christ's.[32]

Proposal for Future Development

Perhaps von Balthasar's Mariology with its in-depth penetration of the Marian *fiat* could be given even firmer ground by rooting it metaphysically in the participation metaphysics of St. Thomas Aquinas especially as it is being developed by contemporary Thomists.

According to St. Thomas's theory of the participation of being, God is *ipsum subsistens esse* and every finite creature participates in existence, proceeding in an ascending order. Whereas bodies participate only in being, souls participate according to their nature in being and life, and intellect participates in being, life and intelligence.[33]

Cornelio Fabro, probably the greatest expositor of Thomistic metaphysics, in commentating on the above statement says:

> In this metaphysical extension of the notion of participation all the constitutive relations of being are actualized, both with regard to structure and causality, up to their highest degree. This consists in the attainment of their ultimate goal, which is imitation and similarity in being, and most of all in the joint action of an inferior substance or faculty and a superior principle.[34]

With respect to the person of Mary could not this be restated in the light of the Immaculate Virgin Mother as the unique, most exalted of human persons in the plan of salvation? Her im-

---

[32] Ibid., 338.

[33] Thomas Aquinas, *In l. De Causis*, 1,19; ed. Saffrey 106, 11-13, quoted in Cornelio Fabro, "The Intensive Hermeneutics of Thomistic Philosophy: The Notion of Participation," trans. by B.M. Bonansea, *Review of Metaphysics* 27 (1974), 479.

[34] Ibid.

maculately conceived being participated, above all others, in the life and the being of God. Her *fiat* opened the door for fallen humanity to participate in her *fiat*, and to ascend to God by means of countless graces of imitation and similarity in being. Such a study might well deepen and fructify the Church's awareness of Mary as Mediatrix of All Graces and make a significant contribution to the discussion of the proposed dogma. As W. Norris Clarke mentions in the concluding remarks of his lecture on the metaphysical ascent to God through Thomistic participation, slightly adapted to fit "our metaphysical wings," it may be that the efficacy of the arguments is so inextricably involved in a profound existential commitment of the living dynamism of the spirit to a truly personal quest for the full intelligibility of the [Marian *fiat*] that it can remain opaque if one stands back in a purely detached, abstract, logical perspective. It may well be, as in Plotinus himself, that the strands of the metaphysical and the mystical quests are so tightly interwoven that they are fully separable only by violence. The quest for the hidden Center of the [universal Church] whose presence—or better, the exigency for whose presence—most of mankind seems to feel obscurely, dimly, and inarticulately in the ineffable recesses of their minds and hearts, may well have to be a quest of the whole person, of the whole being of a man or a woman.[35]

Two thousand years of Christian tradition bear witness to the abiding presence of the Mother of God at the heart and center of the Church. Perhaps the quest for the "full intelligibility" of the mystery of her *fiat*, as the hidden center of the universal Church, may need to be an interweaving of both the metaphysical and mystical strands, a quest "of the whole person, of the whole being of a man or a woman."

---

[35] W. Norris Clarke, *The Philosophical Approach to God* (Winston-Salem, No. Carolina: Wake Forest University, 1979), 38. In the adapted quotation the brackets replace "universe" in both instances.

Epilogue

In an interview with the Honorable Howard Q. Dee, former Philippines Ambassador to the Holy See, speaking of the proposed dogma of Our Lady as Co-redemptrix, Mediatrix of all Graces, and Advocate, Ambassador Dee submitted the following statement by His Eminence, Christoph Cardinal Schoenborn, O.P., the Archbishop of Vienna, Austria, from a paper which the Cardinal offered to the Fatima Symposium on the Alliance of the Two Hearts:

> Why is it that theology finds the center of its heart in the heart of a woman who is Jesus' mother? Mary is the guarantor of Christian realism; in her it becomes manifest that God's word was not only spoken but also heard; that God has not only called, but that man has also answered; that salvation was not only presented, but also received. Christ is God's word, Mary is the answer; in Christ God has come down from heaven; in Mary the earth has become fruitful. Mary is the seal of perfect creatureliness; in her is illustrated in advance what God intended for creation.

These words inspired the following insight in Ambassador Dee:

> In my simple understanding of what Cardinal Schoenborn is saying, the gift of redemption, freely and perfectly given must be freely and perfectly received. . . . In this light [Mary] is indispensable in God's plan for the redemption of man. She is indispensable not because God is incapable of redeeming us by Himself, but because He wants man, whom He has created with a free will, to cooperate freely in his own redemption. . . . The Redeemer needs man to cooperate in his own redemption.
>
> This role of coredemption was offered to Mary who was conceived without original sin. Only she could begin a new

blood lineage liberated from the slavery of sin, qualifying her alone to be Co-redemptrix, who like the paschal lamb must be unblemished. This offer was made by the Lord through the Angel Gabriel, and with her *fiat* she accepted on behalf of all mankind and became Co-redemptrix.[36]

The present writer is suggesting that the participation metaphysics of St. Thomas, underpinning von Balthasar's penetrating theological understanding of Mary's limitless *fiat* flowing from her unique creation as the Immaculate Conception, might provide a fresh foundational resource for the proposed dogma of Our Lady as Co-redemptrix, Mediatrix of all Graces, and Advocate.

---

[36] Interview with the Honorable Howard Q. Dee, former Philippines Ambassador to the Holy See, "Our Lady's Ambassador," *Inside the Vatican*, November 1998, 30-33.

Marian Coredemption in the Hagiography of the 20th Century

Rev. Stefano Manelli, F.F.I.

Fr. Manelli is Founder and Minister General of the Franciscan Friars of the Immaculate. He is internationally known for his distinguished preaching and biblical, Mariological scholarship. His biblical Mariology has recently appeared in English under the title: All Generations Shall Call Me Blessed.*

An interesting and well-documented theological essay on hagiography, recently published, has examined the living teaching of a group of twentieth century Saints on the Coredemption. It is a very timely essay and happily demonstrates that in the final century of the second millennium there has been "a hagiographical chorus... which, without respite, has occupied itself in singing in unison the sweetest glory of Mary our Mother Co-redemptrix and universal Mediatrix of all graces." It concludes, and with good reason, that the teaching of the Saints is a "teaching certainly no less valid and precious than that of astute theologians and professors of theology."[1]

The teaching of the Saints is a teaching of doctrine and

* Reprinted with permission from *Mary at the Foot of the Cross. Acts of the International Symposium on Marian Coredemption* (Ratcliffe College, Leicester, England, February 2000, translated from the Italian.

[1] S.M. MIOTTO, *La voce dei Santi e la "Corredentrice"*, in *Maria Corredentrice*, Frigento, IT 2000, vol. III, pp. 189-223.

virtue; it is a teaching of faith lived in a testimony pushed to the very limits of heroicity; it is a complete teaching including both orthodoxy and orthopraxis, which works towards *"the edification of the Body of Christ"* which is the Church (Eph 4:12).

One could also say that the teaching of the Saints is the teaching with the greatest possible guarantee for our Faith. Only the Saint, in fact, possesses the *sensus fidei* at the level of radical maturity in the practice of heroic virtue, and principally of the theological virtues: faith, hope, and charity. Perhaps no one like the Saint lives his Christian life with fullness and totality "in the light of faith under the guidance of the Church" (*in lumine fidei sub ductu Ecclesiae*), to use the ancient axiom of fundamental theology standing at the very foundation of the most guaranteed teaching of the Church.[2]

If it is true that an element of great force "in the passage of an article of Faith towards its dogmatic definition," as De Maria writes, "is the role of the People of God who, with their *sensus fidei* constitute the platform, one might say, of the concrete orthopraxis of a truth of the Faith,"[3] then it is licit to observe how much more decisive will be the role played by that elect portion of the People of God who are the Saints. Bartman, in his time, could write that "all the theologians speak of the *sensus fidei* as a valid argument, in determined conditions, for the certain discernment of divine Tradition, and was the teaching appealed to for the dogmatic definition of the Assumption."[4] We can add that so much more is the *sensus fidelium* of the Saints a

---

[2] On this point Gherardini notes precisely: "When theology is truly conducted '*in lumine fidei sub ductu Ecclesiae*', one could consider and define it as the *laboratory* of the ecclesiastical Magisterium" (B. GHERARDINI, *La Corredentrice nel mistero di Cristo e della Chiesa*, Rome, IT 1998, p.12). On the theme of the *sensus fidei* in Vatican II cf. LG 12, 35; PO 9; GS 52.

[3] M. DE MARIA, *Il "sensus fidei" e la "Corredentrice"*, in AA.VV., *Maria Corredentrice*, Frigento, IT 2000, vol. III, p.8. This brief, yet interesting historical-theological essay is useful in pointing out the current positive situation regarding the definibility of Marian Coredemption.

[4] B. BARTMANN, *Teologia Dogmatica*, Alba, IT 1958, p. 88

"valid argument" for the ecclesiastical Magisterium, that is, of those who, as affirms Miotto, offer the best guarantee of the most genuine *sentire cum Ecclesia*[5] and live every divine truth "with ardent and luminous, throbbing and adamant faith."[6]

It is for this reason that one ought to consider the thought of the Saints and the truth of their testimony as being of such great importance in regard to the truth of Marian Coredemption. The teaching of their sensus fidei cannot but have a theological value of the highest quality for the Church who, both instructing others and herself learning, traverses along the path of discernment and decision regarding the dogmatic definition of Marian Coredemption.

It is true that in the matter of the *sensus fidelium*, considered as a support of faith for the truth of Marian Coredemption, other fruitful elements are operative, such as that "geographically wide extension," remarks De Maria, "of Marian sanctuaries dedicated to Our Lady of Sorrows, the Co-redemptrix, located in every part of the world;"[7] such as the Liturgy and the piety of the faithful expressing the love and prayer of the People of God towards the divine Mother of Sorrows, our Co-redemptrix;[8] such as the movement *Vox Populi Mariae Mediatrici*, originating in the United States under the guidance of Mariologist Mark Miravalle in order to gather the signatures of those supporting the request for the dogmatic definition of Marian Coredemption;[9] such as painting and architecture,

---

[5] S.M. MIOTTO, *op, cit.*, p. 191

[6] Ibid., p.219. Cf. also F. OCARIZ, *Teologia Fondamentale*, Rome, IT 1997, p. 113.

[7] M. DE MARIA, *op. cit.*, p. 12

[8] Cf. A.B. CALKINS, *Mary as Co-redemptrix, Mediatrix and Advocate in the Contemporary Roman Liturgy*, in *Mary Co-redemptrix, Mediatrix, Advocate. Theological Foundations*, S. Barbara, CA, vol. I, pp.45-118; A. TRIACCA, *Maria "Corredentrice" dalla Liturgia Romana?*, in *Maria Corredentrice*, Frigento, IT 1998, vol. I, pp. 221-281.

[9] Cf. *Vox Populi Mariae Mediatrici*. International Update/Newsletter, Ohio. In a few years the movement for the Coredemption *Vox Populi Mariae Mediatrici* has already gathered the support of over 6 million of the faithful, 40 Cardinals, and around 500 Bishops from every continent. This is certainly a social fact of notable importance and value.

musical productions and the theater, preaching, publications and popular folklore.[10]

Reflecting on all this, one well comprehends how it is "impossible," quoting De Maria yet again, "not to recognize that devotion to the Co-redemptrix and Lady of Sorrows *ab antiquo* is a most precious patrimony of the living and operative faith of God's People. That faith has always spontaneously identified Our Lady of Sorrows with the Co-redemptrix, for it has been animated by that *sensus fidei* which gives the most secure understanding of the divine truth deep within the minds and hearts that are docile to the Spirit."[11]

In this rich patrimony of Faith, however, towering above all these elements, at the highest level of grace and of charisms, stands the teaching of the Saints on the Coredemption. They, indeed, in respect to faith, hope and charity, are the "most secure way," to borrow the expression of Vatican II, for the entire People of God and for theology, both by way of orthopraxis and orthodoxy. Miotto, on this point, well concludes his accurate study on the coredemptive doctrine of a group of Saints, saying: "The theology of Marian Coredemption could not have a better guarantee, a more exalted, precious support and confirmation than that of the hagiographical."[12]

In the light of such considerations one can understand even better the usefulness and value of the present research and synthesis on the Coredemption in hagiography, which draws on specialized studies already published, be it about a group of eight Saints and Blesseds (St. Gemma Galgani, Bl. Elizabeth of the Trinity, St. Pius X, St. Francis Xavier Cabrini, Bl. Bartolo Longo, Bl. Luigi Orione, St. Teresa Benedicta of the Cross, Bl. Josemaria

---

[10] Illuminating and pointed is the article prepared by a Marian study group, signed by NELLO CASTELLO, *Maria SS. Corredentrice. Una verità in cammino*, in *Palestra del Clero*, 76 (1997) 759-766.

[11] *Op. cit.*, p. 13.

[12] S.M. MIOTTO, *op. cit.*, p. 220.

Escrivà),[13] or be it specifically on St. Maximilian Mary Kolbe,[14] or St. Leopold Mandic,[15] Bl. Idelfonso Cardinal Schuster,[16] Bl. Pio of Pietrelcina,[17] Ven. Gabriel Allegra,[18] or Ven. James Alberione.[19]

This present essay is a work of synthesis and deals solely with the coredemptive thought of a group of Saints, Blessed and Venerable of the twentieth century. The first reason for this choice is the abundance of research and studies already done on the Saints and Blessed of previous centuries beginning with the patristic age.[20] The second reason is the significant fact that the thought of the Saints, Blessed and Venerable of the last century of Christianity's second millennium represents the maturest and most complete development of coredemptive doctrine both at the level of research and theological reflection, and of the purest and best guaranteed *sensus fidei*, that of the "elect" who are the most qualified among the People of God.

Obviously the research had also to be limited to a restricted number of twentieth century Saints, Blessed and Venerable and could not touch upon many other Servants of God without

---

[13] Ibid. pp. 192-218.

[14] L. IAMMARRONE, *Il mistero di Maria Corredentrice in San Massimiliano Maria Kolbe*, in AA.VV., *Maria Corredentrice*, Frigento, IT 1999, vol. II, pp. 219-256.

[15] P. STEMMAN, *Il mistero di Maria "Corredentrice" nella vita e negli insegnamenti di San Leopoldo Mandic'*, in AA.VV., *Maria Corredentrice*, Frigento, IT 1999, vol. II, pp. 257-276.

[16] P.M. SIANO, *Maria SS. "Corredentrice" nel pensiero del Beato Ildefonso card. Schuster*, in AA.VV., *Maria Corredentrice*, Frigento, IT 2000, vol. III, pp. 137-161.

[17] S.M. MANELLI, *Maria SS. Corredentrice nella vita a negli scritti di Padre Pio da Pietrelcina*, in AA.VV., *Maria Corredentrice*, Frigento, IT 1999, vol. II, pp. 293-314.

[18] L. MURABITO, *La Corredenzione di Maria nel pensiero del Venerabile Padre Gabriele M. Allegra*, in AA.VV., *Maria Corredentrice*, Frigento, IT 1999, vol. II, pp. 293-314.

[19] S.M. MANELLI, *Il mistero di Maria Corredentrice nel Venerabile Giacomo Alberione*, in AA.VV., *Maria Corredentrice*, Frigento, IT 2000, vol. III, pp. 163-188.

[20] For an overall vision cf. J.B. CAROL, *De Corredemptione Beatae Virginis Mariae*, Vatican City, 1950, 643 pages. For the Franciscan school in particular cf. the recent, magnificent volume: AA.VV., *Maria Corredentrice*, Frigento, IT 1998, vol. II, 318 pages. Regarding the Dominican school, the coredemptive thought of St. Louis M. Grignon and St. Alphonsus M. de Liguori, cf. AA.VV., *Maria Corredentrice*, Frigento, 2000, vol. III, pp...

prolonging what is already an over-long list. "In our twentieth century," wrote Miotto, "there has been a veritable constellation of Saints and Blessed, Venerable and Servants of God, who preached and wrote, proclaimed and defended the great doctrinal patrimony of Marian Coredemption and Mediation."[21]

Within this "constellation" of twentieth century Saints, Blessed, and Venerable, the present study focuses on selected exemplars, that is, six Saints, six Blessed, and two Venerable, who of the holy People of God are the most representative and significant. Treated here are both men and women, a Pope (St. Pius X) and Cardinal (Bl. Ildephonse Schuster), seven priests and religious (Sts. Maximilian Mary Kolbe and Leopold Mandic, Bls. Luigi Orione, Pio of Pietrelcina and Josemaria Escrivà, Vens. James Alberione and Gabriel Allegra), two lay faithful (St. Gemma Galgani and Bl. Bartolo Longo), a missionary (St. Frances Xavier Cabrini) and two contemplatives (Bl. Elizabeth of the Trinity and St. Teresa Benedicta of the Cross); from this group two are very young (St. Gemma Galgani and Bl. Elizabeth of the Trinity) and in all they represent seven different nations (St. Maximilian Mary Kolbe: Poland; St. Leopold Mandic: Yugoslavia; Bl. Elizabeth of the Trinity: France; Bl. Ildephonse Schuster: Germany; St. Teresa Benedicta of the Cross: Israel; Bl. Josemaria Escrivà: Spain; and the other eight: Italy).

This hagiographical representation, quite varied and extensive, even ethnically speaking, has its own particular value with regard to the affirmation of a divine truth which is part of our Faith, therefore to be upheld by all schools and currents of

---

[21] S.M. MIOTTO, *op. cit.*, p. 190. With regard to the Servants of God, "in order to recall, even if only in passing, some of the great number of Servants of God," writes Miotto, "we can point out Sr. Maria Mantonani, Cofoundress of the Little Sisters of the Holy Family, (+ 1934), who speaks expressly in accents of a most ardent faith of the *'most merciful Co-redemptrix'* and *'Queen of the Martyrs'*; and Fr. Mariano of Torino, OFM Cap., (+ 1972), the celebrated preacher and catechist who speaks of Mary Most Holy who 'does not add to the Redemption, but enters into the constitution of the Redemption itself...: she is the *Co-redemptrix* of the human race'" (ibid. 219-220).

thought, mentalities and traditions in the Church, since they are only Catholic in so far as they united with the pilgrim Church's perennial and universal doctrine as she presses towards eternity, where every truth will be unveiled and contemplated in its most pure essence, which is God Himself.

Let us now begin our rapid examination of the thought of the six pre-selected Saints, followed by the six Blessed and then by the two Venerable, each set arranged in chronological order according to their deaths. This conference offers brief summaries of their doctrine on the Coredemption. More extensive treatment and in-depth study on the thought of each one are available in the works cited throughout this essay. Our reflections and final conclusions will serve to explain clearly, by way of synthesis, the inner credibility, consistency and constancy of the doctrine of the Coredemption in view of its importance and fecundity for the life of the Church seeking always to discover and possess *"the whole truth"* (Jn 16:13).

The Saints
St. Gemma Galgani (+ 1903)

The teaching of St. Gemma Galgani on the Coredemption is expressed entirely in an ascetical-mystical context and terminology. This accords well with her character and is to be expected, given the extraordinary mystical experiences the Saint had of the mystery of Redemption, accompanied by mystical phenomena, spiritual and corporal, of the highest degree. Hers is, one might say, a soteriology eminently affective, characteristic of the so-called *theologia cordis*, permeated by the profoundest *sensus fidei* and by an intense, living, concrete suffering, united with the unspeakable sufferings which the Blessed Virgin of Sorrows must have endured in her mission as universal Coredemptrix.

In the first place, St. Gemma clearly affirms that the Incarnation of the Word was *redemptive*, and that the Blessed Virgin knew well, even from the Annunciation, the whole divine plan of the Redemption linked to the Son's Crucifixion: *"Oh what great sorrow,"* writes the Saint to her spiritual director, *"it must have been for the Mother, after Jesus was born, to think that they had to then crucify Him! What pangs she must have always had in her Heart! How many sighs she must have made, and how many times she must have wept! Yet she never complained. Poor Mother!"*[22] Her *"fiat"* (Lk 1:38), therefore, extends itself from Nazareth to Calvary, including within itself, operatively, even the mystery of the universal Redemption.

In the second place, and as a consequence, the Saint affirms the unity of the sufferings of the Mother with those of her Son and the impossibility of their disassociation. She writes that *"truly, then, when she sees Him being crucified... that poor Mother was transfixed by many arrows... Therefore my Mother was crucified together with Jesus."*[23] This affirmation of Our Lady's crucifixion *"together with Jesus,"* places Mary precisely at the heart of the Redemption worked by her Son. How are we to express this intimate and personal unity with Jesus of Mary, the Virgin of Sorrows, *"crucified together with Jesus,"* if not with the semantically and theologically simpler and more significant term

---

[22] S. GEMMA GALGANI, *Lettere*, Rome, IT 1979, p. 106.
[23] ibid.

Coredemption?[24]

In one of her dolorous ecstasies, moreover, St. Gemma confirms the reality of the indissoluble union between the Son and the Mother in suffering for the salvation of sinners on Calvary, when she exclaims: *"Oh wicked sinners, stop crucifying Jesus, because at the same time you are also transfixing the Mother."*[25] The *crucifixion* of the Son and *transfixion* of the Mother simultaneously constitute the salvific work of the Redeemer and Coredemptrix.

In two other marvelous, sorrowful ecstasies St. Gemma seems to take us further into the profounder and more interior area of "effecting" the Redemption by means of the sufferings of the Son and the Mother: *"Oh my Mother, where do I find you?"* exclaims the Saint in ecstasy, *"Always at the foot of the Cross of Jesus... Oh what pain was yours!... I no longer see one sacrifice only, I see two of them: one for Jesus, one for Mary!... Oh my Mother, if one were to see you with Jesus he would not be able to say who is the first to expire: is it you or Jesus?;"*[26] and in the second ecstasy she

---

[24] There are some who want to battle for the substitution of the term *co-redemptrix* with that of *associate* (cf. E.DAL COVOLO, *Maria SS.: "associata" a Cristo o "corredentrice"?*, in *Palestra del Clero*, 78 (1999) 607-612). But the fact that the term *associate in modern usage disguises* precisely Mary's *own specific role* in her most personal and *unique* cooperation in the Redemption immediately leaves the reader perplexed. Calling Mary Most Holy the *"Associate"* effectively says little or nothing in contrast with the title *Co-redemptrix*. The word *associate* is a word entirely generic, weak and dull (*associate*: to whom? to what? why? and in what manner?...), when one does not want to explain every time the term is used what he intends by it, the substantial content which the word *co-redemptrix* by itself and immediately makes clear, that is, that Mary Most Holy has been the associate of the Redeemer ("under Him and with Him" LG 56) as *active and immediate cooperatrix* (in actu primo) *in the very "effecting" of the Redemption and that this entails the "acquisition" of salvific grace then to be distributed* (in actu secondo) *to each redeemed soul.* But precisely this clarification in its entirety Dal Covolo does not mention, reducing thereby the association of Mary in the Redemption to a merely intenser and fuller participation than that of other men. As a result she is called *redeemed sister in the first place.* But from this, however, no clue is given as to how and for what reason she is also called "Mother."

[25] S. GEMMA GALGANI, *Estasi, Diario, Autobiografica, Scritti vari*, Rome, IT 1988, p. 24.

[26] ibid. p. 30

exclaims yet again: *"What compassion you show me, oh my Mother, to see you so every Saturday at the foot of the Cross!... Oh! I no longer see one Victim only, but there are two."*[27] In these two ecstasies St. Gemma could not have expressed with greater simplicity nor, at the same time, with greater force the reality of Christ's redemptive immolation and Mary's coredemptive immolation for the universal salvation: in the unity and uniqueness of the sacrificial offering, the immolation of each one appeared to the Saint as so real and concrete that she cannot claim to see *"one sacrifice only"* but *"two of them: one for Jesus, one for Mary!...,"* or in such a manner that she claims, not to see *"one Victim only, but... two."* The Mother's coredemptive immolation is, according to St. Gemma, configured by the two realities most expressive of the work of Redemption, namely the *sacrifice* and the *Victim*.

Nevertheless, we see St. Gemma climb even higher still when she exclaims: *"Oh my Mother, if one were to see you with Jesus he would not be able to say who is the first to expire: is it you or Jesus?"* This question of the ecstatic Saint is truly original, not to mention sublime. It reveals to us the enormous weight of the redemptive suffering which immolates the Son and the Mother, and which absolutely seems to precede with the Mother's sacrifice, as also the sin of Eve preceded that of Adam. Cornelio Fabro wrote well when affirming that "this can be considered a key-text"[28] for grasping Mary's coredemptive mission: an ontological mission, and not merely functional; an operative mission — always subordinate to the Redeemer, obviously: *"under Him and with Him,"* as states *Lumen Gentium* n. 56 — linked to the "effecting" of the one and same Redemption.

With regard to the Marian mediation and dispensation of all graces to every single person to be saved, St. Gemma has also left her teaching in another letter to her spiritual director, wherein

---

[27] ibid. p.34
[28] C. FABRO, *Gemma Galgani*, Rome, IT 1987, p. 104.

she describes one of her more ineffable Marian visions, that of the Coronation of the Blessed Virgin Mary, receiving from the Eternal Father a crown of "splendid gold, all aflame," with a special sign which indicated and glorified her who is "Dispensatrix of the treasures of Paradise."[29]

At this point we can also conclude with Miotto who writes: "St. Gemma's teaching on the Coredemption, in its simplicity and essence, is complete: Mary Most Holy is the *crucified victim with Jesus'* (the Co-redemptrix); Mary Most Holy is the 'Dispensatrix of the treasures of Paradise' (the Mediatrix of all graces)."[30]

Pope St. Pius X (+ 1914)

It has rightly been written that "the Pontifical doctrinal authority decorated by the halo of sanctity constitutes the maximum guarantee, in charismatic form, of pure truth suffused by the heights of charity."[31] With St. Pius X we actually find ourselves in the school of a great Pope and Saint who taught and defended the truth of Marian Coredemption, if not in a solemn form, still in that of the ordinary Magisterium which must also be accepted with "religious respect of will and of intelligence," according to the teaching of Vatican II (*L.G.* 25). In this manner Pope St. Pius X not only confirms the common, perennial teaching of the Church, but does so in a systematic, fixed way, thus creating a first-class instrument for inserting the title of Co-redemptrix into the official vocabulary of the Holy See.[32]

In his encyclical letter *"Ad diem illum,"* written to celebrate the fiftieth anniversary of the dogmatic definition of the Im-

---

[29] S. GEMMA GALGANI, *Lettere*, op. cit., pp. 214-215.

[30] S.M. MIOTTO, *op. cit.*, p. 195.

[31] ibid. p.200.

[32] It is important to note that as early as 1951 there was published a specific doctoral thesis in Marian theology on the coredemptive doctrine of Pope St. Pius X: L. PILLET, *La Corredenzione mariana nel magistero del beato Pio X,* Torino, IT 1951.

maculate Conception, Pope St. Pius X presents the mystery of the redemptive Incarnation as strictly, inseparably bound to the Blessed Virgin Mary's maternal and coredemptive mission, to her who, the Pope affirms, would have *"the task of guarding and nourishing the Victim, and of placing Him on the altar. From this is derived that communion of life and of sorrows between Mother and Son, sorrows to which, for both of Them in equal manner, can be applied the words of the Prophet: 'My life is consumed in sorrow, my years are passed in groaning' (Ps 30:1)."*[33]

Here the Pope speaks of the *"communion of life and of sorrows"* between Jesus and Mary stretching across the entire course of the Son's earthly existence, that is from the Annunciation to the Crucifixion, or, as St. Pius X says in his text, *"from the house of Nazareth to the place of Calvary."*[34] On Calvary, then, at the foot of the Cross, that communion of sorrows reaches its peak and the Blessed Virgin Mary, the Pope says, citing St. Bonaventure, *"so participated in the (Son's) sufferings that, if it were possible, she would have been most happy to suffer herself all the torments which were supported by the Son."*[35] In this teaching it is not difficult to grasp how Mary's coredemptive mission was ontologically united with the redemptive mission of Jesus, being always "under Him and with Him," as Vatican II precisely states (*L.G.* 56).[36]

The Pope's explanation then goes on to find in that *"communion of sorrows and of wills between Mary and Christ"* the root

---

[33] AAS 36 (1903-1904) 453.

[34] ibid. pp. 454-455.

[35] ibid.

[36] Gherardini comments incisively on this text of St. Pius X, speaking of "a 'communion' so perfect that it reaches the utmost limits of identification in the 'same suffering and will', joining Christ to Mary in effecting the same salvific work, precisely by designating Mary, as Mother of the Word Incarnate, and therefore in virtue of Him and subordinate to Him, able to *merit* together with Him that infinite treasure of redemptive grace. In virtue of this, as He is said to be Redeemer, so she can be said to be Co-redemptrix. With Him who repairs, so she is the Reparatrix. With Him who reconciles, so she is the Reconciliatrix. With Him who redeems, so the Co-redemptrix." B. GHERARDINI, *La Corredentrice in Cristo e nella Chiesa*, Rome, IT 1998, p. 116.

of grace by which the Blessed Virgin Mary concretely *"merited to become the most worthy Reparatrix of the sinful world* (Eadmer, *De excellentia Virginis Mariae,* c.9), *and therefore the Dispensatrix of all the treasures which Jesus merited for us with His bloody death.*"[37] This is a splendid, fundamental text.

It is important to note that Pope St. Pius X specifies the constitutive elements of the salvific mediation of Mary: namely the "reparation," equivalent to the Coredemption by which she paid the price in suffering and immolation to reacquire the grace lost by our first parents, and the "dispensation" of grace, equivalent to the universal Mediation for the distribution of every grace to each and every redeemed person to be saved. In the teaching of St. Pius X "the passage from *Reparatrix* to *Dispensatrix,*" so Miotto comments, "follows the lines of antecedent and consequent: being made the *Reparatrix* of the human race, as a result (*"atque ideo"*) Mary Most Holy rightly becomes the *Dispensatrix* of all the gifts which work toward the salvation and the sanctification of each man."[38]

On the basis of this logic, therefore, St. Pius X links orthodoxy and orthopraxis by inserting for the first time the term Co-redemptrix into three official documents of the Holy See. The first of these was issued by the Congregation of Rites, while the other two came from the Holy Office (today called the Congregation for the Doctrine of the Faith). In all three documents Our Lady is expressly called the *"merciful Co-redemptrix of the human race,"*[39] *"our Co-redemptrix,"*[40] and the *"Co-redemptrix of the human race.*"[41] Here is an exceptional fact surely relevant because it plainly shows that the Holy See itself found no difficulty in adopting a theological term at once binding in its im-

---

[37] Ibid. pp. 453-454.

[38] *op. cit.,* p. 201. See above, footnote 32, a specific study on the coredemptive thought of St. Pius X.

[39] AAS 41 (1908) p. 409.

[40] AAS 5 (1913) p. 364.

[41] AAS 6 (1914) p. 108.

plications and expressive of a Marian soteriology. Were this merely a matter of theological opinion, this would have occasioned bitter dispute, but in reality because it was common doctrine, it was peacefully accepted even in the highest ranks of the Church's hierarchy and teaching organs.

In summary, the classic doctrine on the Coredemption set forth in the ordinary Magisterium of Pope St. Pius X is complete. Mary's salvific mission has two phases of development: the first as Reparatrix who has coredeemed humanity with the Redeemer, the second as Dispensatrix who gives each man the graces of salvation and sanctification. The first was the historical, soteriological mission which extended from Nazareth to Calvary; the second is the metahistorical mission which will continue even to the end of time.

What has been set forth here finds a confirmation and guarantee also in the conclusion of the doctoral thesis of L. Pillet on Marian Coredemption in the teaching of St. Pius X: "The various aspects of this doctrine expressly treated by Pius X in his magisterial documents, whether directly (especially in the encyclical *Ad diem illum*), or by means of the Roman Congregations, show this doctrine to be at least objectively very probable, if not indisputably certain. He is to be placed among the supporters of Marian Coredemption as understood in the strict sense. Mary, according to the Pope, through her union with the sorrows, sacrifice and salfivic intentions of Christ, actively participated in the Redemption wrought by Him: she was *'our Co-redemptrix,' 'she became with Him the Reparatrix of the fallen world,' 'she merited for us, with an inferior merit* (de congruo), *but on the same redemptive plane, the self-same graces which Christ merited for us* de condigno.'"[42]

---

[42] L. PILLET, *op. cit.*, p. 60.

St. Frances Xavier Cabrini (+ 1917)

This Saint, a Foundress and ardent missionary among the immigrants, has left a patrimony of pure and profound faith both by her example and her teachings. In an anthology of sayings of Mother Cabrini arranged by the perceptive theologian Giuseppe De Luca,[43] we find a harvest of simple but essential doctrine, animated by a "theological faith," notes Miotto, "lived *ad intra* in that most intimate dynamic of the love of the Holy Spirit, manifested and radiated *ad extra* in the dynamic of that labor of love translated into works of charity, into the active apostolate, into that unwearied passion for the missions even to the end."[44]

Within the patrimony of her teaching there is contained a very precious pearl, that of her teaching on Marian Coredemption. Within God's salvific design, in fact, St. Francis Xavier Cabrini points out the centrality of Mary's presence who, given to us by Christ, *"is the Mediatrix between God and men, our most amiable Mother."*[45] With a very pertinent biblical reference, she defines Blessed Mary as the *"New Eve, true Mother of the living,"*[46] as the one *"chosen by God to be Co-redemptrix of the human race."*[47] From Eve to Mary, from the sinful mother to the Mother Co-redemptrix: these passages are explicit and enlightening. Mary's salvific mission is rooted in Genesis 3:15, that most celebrated biblical prophecy which presents the Mother and Son indissolubly united in the work of Redemption.

To this biblical reference, furthermore, Mother Cabrini wisely unites the reference to the Pontifical teaching which gives a sure basis and guarantee as infallible truth. In her times Pope

---

[43] G. DE LUCA, *Parole sparse della Beata Cabrini*, Rome, IT 1938.

[44] S.M. MIOTTO, *op. cit.*, p. 203. Very interesting is the rich biblical-symbolic intonation of Cabrini's thought (cf. ibid. p. 204, nt.40).

[45] *Parole sparse della Beata Cabrini*, edition cited, p. 164.

[46] Ibid. p. 169.

[47] Ibid. l.c.

St. Pius X was the principal Master in the Faith, and to him she expressly appeals when she explains the mystery of the Marian Coredemption, writing that *"if the glory of giving life to our Redeemer pertained to her, then also, as our Holy Father said so well, the office of guarding and preparing the Sacred Victim of the human race for sacrifice pertained to her as well. Mary was not only the Mother of Jesus in the joys of Bethlehem, but even more so on Calvary,... and there she merited to become our most worthy Coredemptrix. "*[48]

This too is a splendid page of doctrine and faith, exemplary by its simplicity of expression and by its essentially theological content. Mother Cabrini, with her strong and profound *sensus fidei*, sees Mary's salvific mission as Co-redemptrix as most strictly united with that of her divine Son. She sees the divine Mother as entirely consecrated, for the whole span of her life, to her Son's redemptive work for the salvation of the human race, she herself preparing "the Sacred Victim" to be offered on Calvary in a co-immolation so interior and personal, so real and matter of fact as to merit her becoming "the most worthy Coredemptrix."

In these affirmations of Mother Cabrini the truth of the Marian Coredemption is presented clearly and firmly in its substance, linked to its biblical roots, nourished by the Church's Magisterium, espoused to the serenity and security of faith which does not encounter any obstacles in believing and transmitting a doctrine which forms part of the Church's grand, perennial patrimony of Faith. From St. Frances Xavier Cabrini's teaching it is obvious she had no need to *defend* the truth of the Marian Coredemption. Quite the contrary. There was nothing to de-

---

[48] Ibid. p. 170. Pope St. Pius X wrote as follows: "Not only is praise due to the most holy Mother of God for having formed 'the material of the flesh of the only Son of God who had to be born with human members', and not only for having as such prepared a victim for the salvation of men, but she also had the task of guarding and nourishing the Victim, and of placing Him on the altar on the day established" (AAS 36 1903-1904, 453).

fend. She writes and speaks of this most precious truth of our Faith with the maternal concern of recommending to the Mother Co-redemptrix the entire work of the apostolate and of evangelization which she and her daughters were engaged in throughout the world.

Miotto writes in fact that for Mother Cabrini our Blessed Lady "is the Mother Co-redemptrix, united and inseparable from her Redeemer Son in her cooperation with the accomplishment and completion of the universal plan for salvation, always 'serving towards the mystery of Redemption under Him and with Him,' as Vatican II summarizes it (*L.G. 56*). This is the substance of a most genuine Marian soteriology, all in the key of the Coredemption, which we discover in the saintly Mother Cabrini's intrepid and ardent life of faith, who sailed forth without rest across oceans from one continent to another."[49]

St. Maximilian Mary Kolbe (+ 1941)

Pope Paul VI placed St. Maximilian Mary Kolbe "among the great Saints and enlightened spirits who have understood, venerated and sung the mystery of Mary"[50] and Pope John Paul II set in relief the prophetic vision and great value of St. Maximilian's life and Mariology for the Church today.[51] Consequently, St. Maximilian's Mariological doctrine has already been the subject of studies at the highest level of systematic research and scholarship.[52] With regards to his doctrine on the Marian Coredemption, in particular, there exists a detailed study

---

[49] *Op. cit.*, pp. 205-206.
[50] *Insegnamenti di Paulo VI*, Rome, IT 1971, vol. IX, p. 909.
[51] Cf. *Osservatore Romano* 8-9, XII, 1982.
[52] It is sufficient to refer to the weighty volume of the *Acts* of the International Congress held at Rome in 1984: *La Mariologia di san Massimiliano M. Kolbe*, Rome, IT 1985.

by L. Iammorrone.[53] The coredemptive thought of St. Maximilian Mary Kolbe is of great value for several reasons. He was our contemporary, and more importantly was a great mystic and Marian theologian, besides being such an extraordinary apostle and missionary of the Immaculate, called the *"Fool of the Immaculate,"*[54] and defined by the Ven. Fr. Gabriel Allegra, his contemporary, as *"Apostle of the end times,"*[55] thus recalling the thought of St. Louis Mary Grignon de Montfort.[56]

First, it must be stated that St. Maximilian not only spread and defended the truth of the Blessed Virgin Mary's universal Mediation, but wrote, prayed, and ardently longed for the solemn dogmatic definition of Mary as Mediatrix of salvation (= *Co-redemptrix*) and Mediatrix of all graces (= *Dispensatrix*). As a matter of fact, as soon as he knew that Pope Pius XI had named three commissions to study the definibility of Marian Mediation, he wrote an article in which he exhorted all to pray *"so that our Most Holy Mother might hasten the moment of the Solemn proclamation of this her privilege."*[57]

In addition to the eternal predestination of Mary with Christ

---

[53] This is one of the conferences given at the International Mariological Symposium *"Maria Corredentrice. Storia e Teologia,"* celebrated at Castelpetroso, IT Sept. 8-12, 1997, where twenty theologians coming from every part of the world participated (cf. S.M. Manelli, *Cronistoria del Simposio con rilievi, spunti e riflessioni,* in *Corredemptrix.* Annali Mariani 1966, Castelpetroso, 1997, pp. 133-171). The conference of Fr. L. IAMMORRONE, *Il mistero di Maria Corredentrice in san Massimiliano Maria Kolbe,* is found in AA.VV., *Maria Corredentrice,* Frigento, IT 1999, vol.II, pp. 219-256.

[54] One can profit by reading the life of this apostle synthesized by S.M. MANELLI, *"Folle dell'Immacolata",* Frigento, IT 1990, 120 pages.

[55] G. ALLEGRA, *Apostolo degli ultimi tempi,* in *Miles Immaculatae* 18 (1982) 156-162.

[56] ibid. p. 160, 162.

[57] ST. MAXIMILIAN MARY KOLBE, *Scritti,* Rome, IT 1997, n.1029 (quotations abbreviated: *Scritti* and the margin number).

according to the celebrated Franciscan thesis,[58] St. Maximilian also based the Holy Virgin Mary's coredemptive and distributive Mediation on the biblical-patristic foundation of Mary as the New Eve. Reflecting thus on the original fall of Adam and Eve, our first parents, St. Maximilian maintains that *"from that moment God promised a Redeemer and a Co-redemptrix saying: 'I will place enmities between thee and the Woman, and thy seed and her Seed; She shall crush thy head.'"*[59] *"The Fathers and Doctors of the Church,"* the Saint writes elsewhere, *"proclaim that She, the second Eve, repaired that which the first had ruined; that She is the channel of the divine graces, She is our hope and our refuge; that we receive the grace of God through Her."*[60] One easily discerns here the equivalence between the *reparation* and the Coredemption, in the contrast between the devastating action of the Eve of old and the salvific action of the New Eve: both *Eves* presented as protagonists, respectively, in the fall and ruin of humanity (the first Eve), and in their ransom and salvation (the second Eve).

It is clear from the writings of St. Maximilian that for him the most certain truth, the most secure and unquestionable doctrine, and therefore the least in need of demonstration, was that of the Marian Coredemption; both because of the very clear reference to the devastating work of the first Eve neutralized by the reparative work of the second Eve (Mary), or because of the very life of Our Lady utterly bound up with, spent, and consumed in an unbreakable union with that of her divine Son in the work of the universal Redemption from beginning to end, that is from the Annunciation to the Crucifixion, from Nazareth to Calvary.

On the other hand, it seemed to St. Maximilian that the

---

[58] "The participation of Mary in the redemptive work of her Son," writes Fr. Iammarrone, "is founded, according to Fr. Kolbe, in the eternal decree of Mary's predestination together with her divine Son.": L. IAMMARRONE, *op. cit.*, p. 221; cf. also pp. 223-247.

[59] *Scritti* 1069.

[60] *Scritti* 1029.

doctrine most in need of in-depth theological elaboration was that of the Marian Mediation involved in the distribution of all graces, a doctrine consequent on the Coredemption and which he links above all with the mystery of the ineffable union between the Holy Spirit and the Immaculate Virgin, a *spousal* union creating a perfect collaboration in the distributive economy of all graces for the salvation and sanctification of men.[61]

Nonetheless, St. Maximilian did take into account the complex theological discussions surrounding Marian Coredemption then in the process of being clarified and developed. He wrote that, *"Clearly, our relationship with Mary Co-redemptrix and Dispensatrix of graces in the economy of Redemption was not understood from the beginning in all its perfection. But in these, our times, faith in the Blessed Virgin Mary's mediation continues to grow more and more each day."*[62]

As for his thought specifically on the Coredemption, we can say in summary that St. Maximilian, in his reflections, profoundly grasped both the expressly Christological value of the Marian Coredemption and the pneumatological value of Mary's mediation of all graces; he affirms that "Mary, as Mother of Jesus the Savior, becomes Co-redemptrix, while as Spouse of the Holy Spirit she takes part in the distribution of all graces."[63] According to the Mariological thought of St. Maximilian it was the plan of God "that His own Mother, the Immaculate," so writes Fr. Domanski, "should take part in the work of the Redemption, as she had likewise taken part in the work of the Incarnation."[64] And the demonstration which St. Maximilian took from a study of Bittremieux affirms that ". . . as the first

[61] Cf. H.M. MANTEAU-BONAMY, *La dottrina mariana di p. Kolbe. Lo Spirito Santo e l'Immacolata*, Rome, IT 1977; G. BARTOSIK, *Rapporti tra lo Spirito Santo e Maria come principio della mediazione mariana, negli ultimi scritte (1935-1941) di s. Massimiliano Kolbe*, in *Miles Immaculatae* 27 (1991) 244-68.
[62] *Scritti* 1229.
[63] Ibid.
[64] G. DOMANSKI, *Il pensiero mariano di P. Massimiliano M. Kolbe*, Rome, IT 1971, p. 38.

Eve, by truly free choices, contributed to our ruin, in that she exercised a real influence, so also Mary, by her own actions, collaborated in the reparation....: in this is contained, in the proper sense of the term and presently in a perfectly evident manner, an authentic mediation."[65]

The doctrine of St. Maximilian shows itself logical and luminous in the solidity of its method and development: "In the thought of Fr. Kolbe," writes Fr. Iammarrone, "Christ is the *only* universal Mediator between humanity and the Father... Mary is chosen by God as Mother of the Son and thus Mediatrix of grace because she must accompany Him inseparably in the realization of the Redemption. Son and Mother labor together in originating the life of grace (Redemption and Coredemption) and in distributing that life to men."[66] Always retaining the complete subordination of the Mother with respect to the Son, the biblical-patristic reference to the first Eve with the first Adam once again pointedly and precisely delineates the opposing operations: that is, the operation of our ruin, which had as its absolute and primary effector the first Adam, with the first Eve as his relative and dependent co-operator and the operation of our salvation, which had as its absolute and primary Effector the second Adam, Jesus, with the second Eve, Mary, as His relative and dependent Co-operator.

This, according to St. Maximilian, is the plan of God. "In the divine plan of salvation," writes again Fr. Iammorrone, "Mary is the New Eve who collaborates together with the New Adam, Jesus her Son, in the Redemption of man. In Fr. Kolbe's thought Mary's cooperation is *subordinate* to that of Christ the Redeemer, but it is *immediate* and *proximate, active* and *direct*... Mary, in the thought of Fr. Kolbe, participated in the Redemption in the objective sense (that is, in the acquiring of salvation with her own, proper activity united and associated to that original ac-

---

[65] J. BITTREMIEUX, *De Mediatione universale B.M.V.*, in *Scritti*, l.c.
[66] *op. cit.*, p. 237.

tivity of the Son) and she participates in the Redemption in the subjective sense, that is, in the distribution of the graces of salvation to each person in the course of time right up to the coming of the Lord in glory," and in this way "Mary fully realizes her maternity with her maternal compassion on Calvary."[67]

From his thought taken as a whole, it is obvious that for St. Maximilian such doctrine on Mary's coredemptive and distributive mediation of grace is well founded and solid. As regards his personal experience, it cannot be considered anything less than superlative, when one remembers his terrible martyrdom in the death camp of Auschwitz, assimilating him in an extraordinary way to the coredemptive offering of the Blessed Mother. No one, in fact, is so close and so similar to the Co-redemptrix as the martyr. The supreme glory of the Co-redemptrix, in truth, is precisely that of being the *Queen of the Martyrs*. In this St. Maximilian has left us his orthodoxy (the doctrine on the Co-redemptrix) perfectly united with his orthopraxis (the most concrete imitation of the Co-redemptrix, in shedding one's own blood).

Master and Model of the doctrine and spirituality of Marian Coredemption: this is St. Maximilian Mary Kolbe.[68] Consequently, concerning the coredemptive and distributive mediation of Mary, one can say that, according to St. Maximilian, there is not so much to discuss, as there is much need to pray so that the Immaculate *"might hasten the moment of the solemn proclamation"* of this dogma on the part of the Church.

---

[67] Ibid. pp. 244,245,246.

[68] Very little has been written on the coredemptive spirituality of St. Maximilian, coredemptive insofar as he was a *martyr* and one who *suffered* (illness of tuberculosis and always generous in sacrifices without limit). Much indeed would have to be discovered and written in order to grasp deeply the vital bond uniting the Holy Martyr to the mystery of the Immaculate in her universal, coredemptive mission, and in order to make our own the school of life and its Marian spirituality in the coredemptive key which he has left us, and that so we might be ever more intimate and faithful children of her whom Jesus gave us on Calvary, not only as *Mother*, but also as *Co-redemptrix*, or, even better yet, as *Mother Co-redemptrix*, that is, who has left the *Co-redemptrix* as our very own Mother.

St. Leopold Mandic (+ 1942)

It has been written that St. Leopold Mandic "had a special attention to, a living interest in, and, one could add, a true and thoroughly personal passion for Mary Most Holy as 'Co-redemptrix of the human race'."[69] In effect, one could say that St. Leopold's life presents itself entirely in a coredemptive key, especially the forty years he spent exercising the ministry of Reconciliation. If indeed the Co-redemptrix co-operated in the reconciliation of humanity with God, then St. Leopold, as a confessor, did nothing else but "reconcile" men with God, freeing them from guilt, filling them anew with grace.[70]

And if it is true that the study of Our Lady, as one biographer writes, "was his favorite field of study throughout his life,"[71] and that he had it much at heart to "affirm the theological fundamentals of his Marian devotion," as writes another biographer, and sought to show himself always "theologically austere in his motivations,"[72] it is also true that his own particular passion for the mystery of Mary Co-redemptrix reached such a degree of fervor that he proposed writing a whole book or treatise on the truth of the Marian Coredemption. Further, one biographer specifies that St. Leopold "longed throughout his life to achieve this intention of writing a book on Our Lady to show her Co-redemptrix of the human race, the channel of every grace from the Lord."[73]

---

[69] P. STEMMAN, *Il mistero di Maria "Corredentrice" nella vita e negli insegnamenti di san Leopoldo Mandic*, in AA.VV., *Maria Corredentrice*, Frigento, IT 1999, vol.II, p. 259.

[70] It is a significant fact that the title of the first biography of the Saint reads as follows: P.E. BERNARDI, *Leopoldo Mandic*. *Santo della riconciliazione*, Padua, IT 1990; and Fr. STEMMAN could write that "it seems licit, therefore, to affirm the most intimate and vital proximity between Mary Co-redemptrix, *Mother of Reconciliation*, and St. Leopold, *minister of reconciliation* " (op. cit., p. 262).

[71] P.E. BERNARDI, *op. cit.*, p. 117.

[72] LORENZO DA FARA, *Leopoldo Mandic*. *L'umanità. La santità*, Padua, IT 1987, pp. 181,182.

[73] P.E. BERNARDI, *op. cit.*, p. 118.

From these assertions of his biographers it is clear, then, "how important it is to recognize the grounding of St. Leopold's thought in Marian Coredemption," writes Fr. Stemman, "considered *in actu primo*, that is, in the acquisition of saving grace, and considered *in actu secundo*, that is, in the distribution of grace to individual persons. One could also speak of Mary's coredemptive Mediation through the *acquisition* of grace, and Mary's *distributive* Mediation through the *distribution* of that grace."[74]

Unfortunately St. Leopold was unable to write the proposed book on Our Lady as Co-redemptrix. The continuous flow of penitents to his confessional rendered vain every desire and effort to recollect and concentrate himself in the study needed for writing. "It was truly a sin," writes one biographer, "because with his acute intelligence and his ardent love for Our Lady we would most certainly have been given a work of great value."[75]

At any rate, there is sufficient material to know St. Leopold's thought on the Coredemption. There are two volumes of the Saint's letters and writings wherein he maintains and confirms repeatedly the truth of Marian Coredemption.[76] It is enough to state that he repeats the expression "*Co-redemptrix of the human race*" thirteen times in his writings; at one point he even calls her "*our Redemptrix*";[77] and also at other times he uses equivalent expressions. And the basis of the Marian Coredemption, for St. Leopold, too, is found in the biblical-patristic thesis of the New Eve (Mary) and the New Adam (Jesus) who together restore that which the first Eve and first Adam together had destroyed: "*I believe,*" writes St. Leopold, "*in this dogma of the Catholic Faith: the most Blessed Virgin Mary is a second Eve, just as we believe that Christ the Lord is a second*

---

[74] P. STEMMAN, *op. cit.*, p. 261.

[75] P.E. BERNARDI, *work cited*, p. 119.

[76] P. TIETO, (care of), *Suo umile servo in Cristo*, vol.I, *Lettere*, vol.II, *Scritti*, Padua, IT 1992.

[77] *Scritti*, vol.II, p. 117.

Adam.[78] And on Calvary, in the act of accomplishing the universal Redemption, the New Eve, the Co-redemptrix, is proclaimed by the Redeemer to be *Mother* of all men gathered to form the one Church, the new People of God, and this *"according to the mandate given by the Son dying on the Cross."*[79]

However, his passionate effort to maintain the truth of Marian Coredemption had two particular and admirable goals: the first goal was that of "cooperating in some fashion," writes Fr. Bernardi, "in circling our beloved Mother's forehead with a new crown, that of the dogmatic proclamation: Mary universal Mediatrix of all graces."[80] How the true sons of Mary cannot but desire to glorify their divine Mother ever more and more!

The second admirable goal was that of obtaining, specifically from the Co-redemptrix, the longed for reunification or reconciliation between the Church of Rome and the Christian Oriental Churches, thus putting an end to the painful schism due to the work of Photius and Caerularius which for nearly a millennium has been tearing apart "the seamless garment" of Christ. This ecumenical intention of St. Leopold is truly novel, not to mention extremely precious. Some today would say that the truth of Marian Coredemption shows itself altogether anti-ecumenical, and therefore is better left aside or any further discussion of it dropped. Such a rationale, however, appears particularly grotesque confronted by the goal of St. Leopold and therefore is shown to turn the truth of the matter upside-down.

St. Leopold actually maintained that if the Co-redemptrix is she who, in union with the Redeemer-Son — "under Him and with Him," as Vatican II states (*L. G.* 56) — has been made the *Mother of reconciliation*, then she always continues to be the *Mother of every reconciliation*, including that of the schismatic Churches. The Co-redemptrix is she who *"mystically generated*

---

[78] Ibid. p. 179.
[79] Ibid.
[80] *op. cit.*, l.c.

us at the foot of the Cross," writes St. Leopold, *"by way of the most dreadful martyrdom that a mother's heart could ever know. We are truly sons of her tears."* "One grasps intuitively," reflects Fr. Stemman, "that for St. Leopold Marian Coredemption, far from separating us, serves rather to reunite all the redeemed even more and better in the one absolute Redeemer and Mediator, Jesus Christ (cf. II Tim 2:5)."[81] "The fruit of the Coredemption, in fact, has been our reconciliation with God in Christ."[82] Fr. Stemman then continues his commentary on the thought of the Saint: "From whom, in fact, come the graces of reconciliation if not from the Co-redemptrix - Mediatrix of all the graces of Christ's Redemption? Coredemption and reconciliation are always correlated. One cannot forget this. By traveling any other path one reaches a dead-end."[83]

St. Leopold was so thoroughly convinced of this truth that, in order to obtain the miracle of union of the Oriental Churches with Rome, he wanted to offer his entire self and life as victim in deference to the Co-redemptrix. He literally writes in his own hand: *"In truth, before God and the Blessed Virgin, confirming all by oath, I myself am obliged, in deference to the Co-redemptrix of the human race, to exert all my life's strength, in accord with the obedience I owe my superiors, for the redemption of all the dissident Oriental peoples from schism and error."*[84] And in 1927, above one of his images, he wrote this precious thought: *"I, friar Leopold Mandic Zarevic, firmly believe that the most Blessed Virgin, insofar as she was Co-redemptrix of the human race, is the moral foun-*

---

[81] P. STEMMAN, *op. cit.*, p. 269.

[82] Ibid, p. 274.

[83] Ibid, p. 275.

[84] Ibid, p. 269. The original text of St. Leopold in Latin is this: *"Vere coram Deo et Deiparae Virgini, interposita sacramenti fide, me obstrinxi in obsequium Corredemptricis humani generis, disponendi omnes ratione vitae meae iuxta oboedientiam meorum superiorum in redemptionem Orientalium Dissidentium a schismate et errore"* (*Scritti*, vol.II, p. 97). Such an offering to the Co-redemptrix he repeated many times (Cf. *Scritti*, pp. 142, 150, 165).

tain of all grace, since we have received all from her fullness.'[85] Fr. Stemman comments: "Here St. Leopold specifies logically and with brilliant lucidity the difference between the Coredemption and the *Mediation of graces*. Our Lady is Co-redemptrix, as St. Leopold understood it, and therefore is the *'moral fountain of all graces'*; that is to say, because the Immaculate was Co-redemptrix of humanity (*'insofar as she was Co-redemptrix of the human race'*), she has rightly become the *'fountain'*, the spring of grace and the Distributrix of all graces; she has become *Our Lady of graces*, and in this way is very dear to the People of God."[86]

The teaching of St. Leopold on the Coredemption appears like a work of art which is as attractive as it is ardent in his passion to suffer for the reunification of the separated Churches. The essential elements of the coredemptive and distributive Mediation stand out clearly and are well-defined in the Saint's thought. He "firmly believes" in the truth of Mary as *"Co-redemptrix of the human race."* May his "I firmly believe" be also our own.

St. Teresa Benedicta of the Cross (+ 1942)
(Edith Stein)

One of the richest and most significant spiritual works of St. Teresa Benedicta of the Cross, that is, of this "illustrious daughter of Israel," as Pope John Paul II defined her in his beatification discourse of Edith Stein at Cologne on May 1st, 1987,

---

[85] Here is the original text written by the Saint in Latin: *"Ego frater Leopoldus Mandic Zarevic credo et teneo Virginem Beatissimam Mariam, eo quod Corredemptrix humani generis, esse fontem moralem totius gratiae, nam ex plenitudine ipsius omnes nos accepimus"* (*Scritti*, vol. II, p. 124).

[86] *op. cit.*, p. 273.

is the theological essay on St. John of the Cross entitled *"Scientia Crucis."*[87]

The title alone of this work suggests a program of life illuminated and signed by the Cross, a title which promises to be an exposition, or more precisely, *the* exposition of that supreme science which gives the possession of the greatest love: love crucified, love which spurs and carries one to immolation: *"Greater love than this no man hath, that a man lay down his life for his friends"* (Jn 15:13).

One could well say that the life itself of St. Teresa Benedicta of the Cross was a book, a complete text on the *"Scientia Crucis."* One biographer of Edith Stein could not have profiled her life of suffering "from the University to the camp of Auschwitz"[88] any better than he did by following the dramatic series of persecutions and flights, tortures and imprisonments endured by Edith Stein up to her death in that camp of horrors, Auschwitz.

But the *"Scientia Crucis"* immediately calls to mind the mountain of the Cross, Calvary, and transports the soul, almost by impulse, to the foot of that Cross upon which was nailed our divine Redeemer, Jesus Christ. And there, at the feet of Jesus Crucified the soul finds her, the Lady of Sorrows—Co-redemptrix, Mary Most Holy, the Mother concrucified in Heart with her adorable Son. She is, one could say, the personification of that most elevated *"Scientia Crucis,"* that which called in theology "Marian Coredemption."

"As Co-redemptrix," wrote Fr. Miotto, "Mary Most Holy, transfixed and concrucified with Christ on Calvary, is a mirror of light especially for the victim souls who have conformed their life and death to Christ Crucified, *'renewing in themselves His*

---

[87] BL. EDITH STEIN, *Scientia Crucis su San Giovanni della Croce*, Rome, IT 1996. This work remained unfinished in its final part, but it has rightly been pointed out: "Edith Stein could be said not to have written the conclusion of her book *La Scienza della Croce*, but to have lived it profoundly, dying for the Cross": Sr. MARIA FRANCESCA PERILLO, *Edith Stein. Ebrea, carmelitana, martire*, in *Palestra del Clero* 78 (1999) 695.

[88] E. DE MIRIBEL, *Edith Stein. Dall'università al lager di Auschwitz*, Milan, IT 1987.

death.' St. Teresa Benedicta of the Cross, daughter of the He-
brew people, was one of these victim souls, chosen and beloved
by God, to relive the mystery of the Passion of Christ, prolonging in herself the compassion of the divine Mother and universal Co-redemptrix."[89]

St. Teresa Benedicta of the Cross, who achieved the highest
levels of philosophical formation, never treated of Marian
Coredemption directly. But she did know the doctrine and left
some traces of it here and there in her writings which touch
upon it thematically, sometimes even theologically and spiritually. From the more significant texts we have one which speaks
expressly of Mary Co-redemptrix engaged in the work of the
universal Redemption together with Christ her Son, with whom
she is bound *"uno eodemque decreto,"* that is, "by one and the
same decree," according to the formula adopted by Pope Pius
IX, or *"by a close and indissoluble bond,"* as it is expressed by
Vatican II (*L.G. 53*).

The brief text of St. Teresa Benedicta of the Cross is this:
*"Mary leaves the natural order and is placed as Co-redemptrix along-
side the Redeemer."* These few words are theologically dense and
luminous. They present Mary in the superior light of the mind
of God and of His loving plan. Mary, a human creature and
daughter of Adam by nature, nevertheless leaves *"the natural
order";* in other words she surpasses and transcends it because,
one could say, she belongs more to Christ than to Adam, more
to the second than to the first Adam.

Catholic theology, as a matter of fact, teaches us that the
Blessed Virgin Mary, and only she, in as much as she is Mother
of the Word Incarnate, belongs to the order of the hypostatic
union: "Mary Most Holy," writes the mariologist Domenico
Bertetto, "pertains, in the divine plan, to the *hypostatic* order,
that is, to the divine economy which gives us the hypostatic or
personal union of the divine Son with a human nature and which

---

[89] S.M. MIOTTO, *op. cit.,* p. 212.

is the supreme manifestation of the merciful liberality of God, over and beyond that divine economy, which gave us the status of *nature elevated* in our first parents, and in us the status of *nature fallen and redeemed.*"[90]

The Blessed Virgin Mary, therefore, *"leaves the natural order,"* says St. Teresa Benedicta of the Cross, and is inserted into a new order, an exceptional order, "an order unto herself (*a sé*)," states Fr. Miotto, "which constitutes her as the hinge between the natural and supernatural, as a 'theandric' being because she is the Mother of the Word Incarnate."[91]

In this new order of the hypostatic union, our Blessed Lady is associated with Christ the Savior with the mission of *"Co-redemptrix alongside the Redeemer."* This is how St. Teresa literally describes it, and her words also bring to light with sufficient clarity that Marian Coredemption, like the divine Maternity, does not pertain to the natural order; instead, the Coredemption being one with Mary is elevated with her into the order of the hypostatic union, placed therefore *"alongside the Redeemer."* And since there is only one Co-redemptrix, the Co-redemptrix is truly unique: the divine Mother Mary.

With the expression *"alongside the Redeemer"* one could perhaps be led to think of a complementarity between the Redeemer and the Co-redemptrix in the work of salvation. However, St. Teresa Benedicta well understands, to the contrary, that Marian Coredemption is a direct and immediate cooperation on the part of Mary, but as a result of being a co-operation it is always said to be subordinate and dependent on the sole Operator,

---

[90] D. BERTETTO, *Maria la Serva del Signore*, Napoli, IT 1988, p. 221. "Something that is ontologically new in Mary," writes Ragazzini, "is her *being elevated* - by reason of her Divine Maternity - *to participate in a new order of being: that of the Hypostatic Order*, superior to that of the order of grace, not to mention that of the natural order. Mother of Christ, subject of the Order of the Hypostatic Union, Mary herself really makes up part of that new and exceptional Order" (S. RAGAZZINI, *La Divina Maternità di Maria*, Frigento, IT 1986, p. 215; one should consult the entire, lengthy chapter: pp.214-238).

[91] *Op. cit.*, p. 213.

Jesus, the only, absolute *Redeemer*. In another place, as a matter of fact, the Saint calls Mary the *"Collaboratrix of Christ the Redeemer."*[92]

Furthermore, in relation to the Blessed Mary's spiritual Maternity St. Teresa Benedicta of the Cross offers a precious clue in which Marian Coredemption is intimately united to the spiritual Maternity with a connatural interdependence in the sense that her spiritual Maternity springs forth precisely from the Coredemption, and her Virginity, fecundated by the Cross, becomes the Maternity of grace (in harmony with Vatican II which calls Mary precisely "Mother in the order of grace": *(L.G.* 61). Here is the Saint's text, which is as brief as it is brilliant and dense in content: *"Under the Cross the Virgin of virgins became the Mother of grace."*[93] Virginity, Coredemption, Maternity: it is a marvelous triptych, a truly unique and splendid diamond with three faces. St. Teresa Benedicta presents to us "the Cross and grace," writes Miotto, "the Coredemption and Maternity: these are the coordinates of our regeneration in Christ and Mary."[94]

The Blessed
Bl. Elizabeth of the Trinity (+ 1906)

It has been rightly said that Bl. Elizabeth of the Trinity "gazes upon Mary essentially with the eyes of a contemplative soul."[95] Bl. Elizabeth of the Trinity, being an extraordinary contemplative soul, looked upon and spoke about the mystery of the Coredemptrix in a transfigured light, in a mystical key, which enters into the interior, which penetrates profoundly. "The knowl-

---

[92] EDITH STEIN, *Beata Teresa Benedetta della Croce*, Vita, Dottrina, Testi inediti, Rome, IT 1997, p. 110.
[93] Text reported by R. GIRARDELLO, *Edith Stein. "In grande pace varcai la soglia"*, Rome, IT 1998, p. 277.
[94] *op. cit.*, p. 214.
[95] R. MORETTI, *Introduzione a Elisabetta della Trinità*, Rome, IT 1984, p. 158.

edge of Mary Most Holy as Co-redemptrix beside the Redeemer," writes Miotto, "has a particular characteristic in Bl. Elizabeth, a characteristic most congenial to a contemplative soul like hers. This is the characteristic of most profound interiority, of most silent hiddenness."[96]

Bl. Elizabeth preferred to call Mary at the foot of the Cross the *Mother of Sorrows* and *Queen of the Martyrs,* and with her contemplative eyes she observes: *"This Queen of Virgins is also the Queen of Martyrs, but it is always 'into her Heart' that the sword passes. In her everything happened from within!... How beautiful it is to contemplate her during her long martyrdom, so serene in her majesty who at the same time breathes strength and sweetness... She remains there, nearby, at the foot of the Cross, strong and heroic."*[97]

The holy and elderly Simeon had predicted to Mary in the temple: *"And thy own soul a sword shall pierce"* (Lk 2:35). Bl. Elizabeth fixes her gaze on that *"sword"* which penetrates deep within the Heart, which transfixes Mary's soul, and almost in ecstasy she cries out: *"In her everything happened from within!"* The Gospels actually say very little about the inexpressible sufferings of the Queen of Martyrs. But they do let us know, however, with the words of the aged Simeon, that truly all would transpire in the interior, in her soul transfixed by the sword of sorrow. As a result Bl. Elizabeth desires to scrutinize the deep recesses of the Heart of the Co-redemptrix and Mother of Sorrows, and yet she knows well that Our Lady *"lived within her Heart with such profundity that the human gaze cannot follow her."*[98] Nonetheless, Bl. Elizabeth "does not stop at the superficial aspects of this mystery," writes Fr. Philipon, "but penetrates the interior of Mary's soul... and seeks, within the hiddenness

---

[96] *op. cit.*, p. 197.
[97] BL. ELIZABETH OF THE TRINITY, *Scritti*, Rome, IT 1967, p. 660 (cited here as: *Scritti*).
[98] *Scritti*, p. 659.

of her own soul, to reach into the very depths of the mystery of Mary."[99]

In this way Bl. Elizabeth helps us to understand and to discover that the mystery of Marian Coredemption unfolds and is consummated above all *"from within"* the soul of Mary, "in the solitude of the Virgin's soul," reflects Fr. Philipon, "in conversation with God alone, without doubt with the active participation proper to the life of men. But in order to accomplish a divine work the soul of the Co-redemptrix was ever more assimilated with the Soul of Christ, whether in the solitary places in the evening, on the mountain, or in the Garden of Gethsemani."[100]

In the mission of Mary Co-redemptrix, Bl. Elizabeth grasps also the mission of Mary's divine Maternity with regard to man, that is to say "the providential and unique function of Mary in the economy of salvation," as writes Fr. Philipon, in that she is "associated with the Omnipotent in His redemptive work" which develops during the earthly phase of His life until its consummation in the mystery of the Cross on Calvary. And in that she is associated "with the Son who now abides in glory and with the Holy Spirit, cooperating with Them to 'form Christ' in the souls of the baptized" during the heavenly phase until the end of history with His coming in glory.[101]

Bl. Elizabeth of the Trinity also deals with the extent of Mary's Maternity in relation to the God-Man, Jesus, and to all men, brothers of Christ. She distinguishes two phases of the Holy Virgin Mary's maternal mission: the earthly phase connected to the work of Redemption by her "effective" role (viz. the *acquisitive* Coredemption acquiring grace), and the heavenly phase

---

[99] M. PHILIPON, *L'inabitazione della Trinità nell'anima*, Rome, IT 1966, p. 144.

[100] M. PHILIPON, *La dottrina spirituale di Suor Elisabetta della Trinità*, Brescia, IT 1968, p. 162. Fr. M. Philipon, a great student of Bl. Elizabeth of the Trinity, has also authored a book of Marian theology, *Il vero volto della Madre di Dio* (Rome, 1952), containing marvelous pages on the mystery of Mary Co-redemptrix (ibid. pp. 63-82).

[101] Cf. M. PHILIPON, *L'inabitazione della Trinità nell'anima*, edition cited, 1.c.

connected to the work of Dispensation of redemptive grace in order to "form Christ" in every single person in the world (viz. the *distributive* Coredemption). In brief, the first is Mary's *coredemptive* Mediation, the second is Mary's *distributive* Mediation of saving and sanctifying grace.[102]

Bl. Elizabeth experienced and received fully of the fruits of Mary's maternal mission in both its coredemptive and distributive aspects. As Fr. Ragazzini wrote in a perceptive essay on Bl. Elizabeth and St. Maximilian Mary Kolbe,[103] the purification and elevation of the soul in the mystical life of Bl. Elizabeth are the fruit of Mary's coredemptive and distributive Mediation, since "Our Lady, in the soul, is the active Co-redemptrix, Mediatrix, and Dispensatrix of graces, because she is the Mother... And as such, with Christ, she communicates the spiritual life which, if it is true that that life necessarily comes from the fullness of Christ, then it also comes from the fullness of Mary. Grace is, therefore, Christian (of Christ), but is also Marian."[104]

That Bl. Elizabeth was entirely filled with Marian graces and, in particular, Mary's coredemptive grace, she herself offers a proof when, towards the end of her life, she rejoices because she finds herself assimilated to the Co-redemptrix in cooperating with Christ for the salvation of many. And she writes to her mother, exhorting her to rejoice because *"the Master has deigned to choose your daughter, the fruit of your womb, to associate her in His great work of Redemption."*[105] During her last retreat, leav-

---

[102] In both the earthly and heavenly phases, Bl. Elizabeth enjoyed the living and operative presence of Mary Most Holy who "appeared to her," writes again Philipon, "humble and faithful, associated with Christ, involved in the entire economy of salvation by the will of God" (*op. cit.*, 1.c.).

[103] S. RAGAZZINI, *Due grandi mistici mariani del nostro secolo: la Beata Elisabetta della Trinità e San Massimiliano*, Castelpetroso, IT 1995.

[104] Ibid., p. 25. Cf. also the pages wherein is described the maternal action of Mary on Bl. Elizabeth's path of purgation and elevation (ibid. pp. 34-35, 40-41, 46-47, 50-51, 54-55, 60-61, 66-71).

[105] *Scritti*, p. 456.

ing us breathtaking "teachings on the image of the Mother of Sorrows,"[106] she herself writes again, saying: *"With Jesus Christ I am nailed to the Cross... I suffer in my body that which is wanting to the Passion of Christ, for His Body which is the Church... The Queen stands at 'your right'... She walks along the way of Calvary, at the right of her Crucified King... He wants to associate His spouse in His work of Redemption."*[107]

Truly Bl. Elizabeth, who, thinking of her Crucified Spouse, said that she endured *"within herself a prolongation of His Passion,"*[108] could have said as well that she endured *a prolongation of the "compassion" of the Mother Co-redemptrix.* "Only mystical contemplation," writes Fr. Miotto, "translates the truth into living experience. In the most secret, interior depths, as was the case for Bl. Elizabeth regarding Marian Coredemption... this meant to live out the content of the mystery of Mary, prolonging it in her own humanity."[109]

Bl. Bartolo Longo (+ 1926)

St. Francis de Sales and, even more, St. Alphonsus dei Liguori were two Doctors of the Church who engaged themselves with talent and passion in being apostles to the faithful Christians by transmitting to them, in simple and clear language, the very rich patrimony of the truth of our Faith, of the most precious piety and most cherished devotion; they did all this in order to nourish the people's Christian life. St. Francis de Sales and St. Alphonsus dei Liguori desired *"to break the bread"* (cf. Lam 4:4) of the word of God so that all the faithful might eat of it at ease; and they did this by means of books and essays, devout writings and sacred songs which have formed the Christian people for

---

[106] So writes E. LLAMAS, *Messaggio mariano di Sr. Elisabetta della Trinità*, AA.VV., *L'esperienza mistica di Elisabetta della Trinità*, Napoli, IT 1987, p. 184.
[107] *Scritti*, p. 642.
[108] *Scritti*, pp. 456-7.
[109] *Op. cit.*, p. 199.

centuries and which continue to do so today and will continue from generation to generation.

Bl. Bartolo Longo had the soul of an apostle and the quality of a Christian giant. He too knew how to enter upon the missionary road to the people, the path of simple and essential catechesis and of a most popular Marian piety, so as to reach all and to teach even the most marginalized and abandoned persons how to pray.[110] He accomplished all this by means of the *Rosary*, by means of this admirable prayer and devotion which is, effectively, suited for all and is tailored, one might say, for all, especially for the simplest and least gifted persons.

It has rightly been pointed out that "the doctrinal outline of Bl. Bartolo Longo's Marian spirituality," writes Fr. Miotto, "is firmly based on the truth of the Maternity of Mary Most Holy as universal Co-redemptrix and Mediatrix of all graces, of which the Rosary is a most devout, pious, and prayerful expression in the hands of the people. One can say that the lifelong mission of Bl. Bartolo Longo as an apostle of Our Lady and of charity was this: to carry to the most needy the graces of Redemption *'by setting the world on fire with love for the Rosary.'"*[111]

The Rosary, in effect, in its three series of joyful, sorrowful, and glorious mysteries, presents for the pious reflection and contemplation of those praying the fundamental mysteries of salvation — the Incarnation, the Redemption, and the Glorification — in which Blessed Mary is, respectively, the divine and

---

[110] It has, in fact, been written on solid grounds, that Bl. Bartolo Longo "is to be counted among those few authors who sought to elaborate a popular Marian spirituality, directed above all to the most spiritually and materially abandoned classes" of people (S. DE FIORES, *Maria nell'esperienza negli scritti di Bartolo Longo*, in *Atti del Convegno storico*, Rome, IT 1983, vol.I, p. 137).

[111] S.M. MIOTTO, *op. cit.*, p. 206. Shortly after he writes that "this system of Marian spirituality can be said to have shaped and sustained the entire painful life of Bl. Bartolo Longo in the accomplishment of his great work of charity and in the erection of that stupendous work of architecture, the Marian Basilica of Our Lady of the Rosary at Pompei. Love for the lowliest and the suffering and love towards the divine Mother Co-redemptrix and Mediatrix were united in the mind and heart, the will and actions, the words and writings of Bl. Bartolo" (ibid. p. 207).

virgin Mother of the Word Incarnate (*the joyful mysteries*), the Co-redemptrix alongside the divine Son and Redeemer (*the sorrowful mysteries*), and the "Woman" assumed into Heaven as Queen and universal Mediatrix (*the glorious mysteries*). This most authentic and well-founded theological vision of Marian spirituality is certainly complete in the holy Rosary, and Bl. Bartolo Longo presented, offered, explained, and illustrated this in that book of doctrine and mediation, of piety and devotion, entitled *The Fifteen Saturdays of the Holy Rosary*. This work is, as of now, approaching its 90th edition with millions and millions of copies in many languages.[112]

The theme of Marian Coredemption obviously runs through page after page in this text, with invocations and reflections, thoughts and insights, allusions and explanations which, taken altogether, reveal the clarity and certitude of faith in the Blessed Mother as *universal Co-redemptrix* and *Mediatrix of all graces*. We can recall here, as an example, the prayer in which he calls the Blessed Virgin Mary *"our Co-redemptrix and Dispensatrix of graces"* with the invocation: *"O Holy Virgin, fulfill today your office of being our Co-redemptrix."*[113]

How moving are the pages in which Bl. Bartolo speaks of the immense sufferings of Mary Co-redemptrix! He comments on the Presentation of the Infant Jesus in the Temple, where the Madonna had the sublime strength to *"offer up her Son, the Only-Begotten, to death for us sinners,"* accepting that *"sword"* driven into her soul, which rendered her the *"Queen of Martyrs,"* more heroic than all the martyrs, because from that day on she was offering the Son to the Eternal Father, thinking of the future sufferings which He would have to endure.[114]

Bl. Bartolo then expounds upon the most sorrowful partici-

---

[112] *I quindici sabati del santo Rosario*, Pompei, IT 1996 (here cited it as: *I quindici sabati*). To know more about this precious book cf. A. L'ARCO, *Il Beato Bartolo Longo*, Pompei, IT 1987, pp. 76 ff..

[113] *I quindici sabati*, p. 62.

[114] Ibid. p. 98.

pation of the Co-redemptrix in the mysteries of the Passion of Jesus Crucified by considering and manifesting Mary of Sorrows *"with her Heart crucified on Calvary,"*[115] at the foot of the Cross, where *"that Divine Lamb and this innocent little Sheep reciprocally beheld and understood one another: one being tormented by the sorrows of the other."*[116] With acumen, Fr. Miotto reflects on this text, so saturated with divine sentiment: "It seems that the sufferings of Both — that of the Redeemer and that of the Co-redemptrix — were not adding one to the other, but were *uniting.*"[117]

Likewise moving, and vibrant with Easter joy, are Bl. Bartolo's reflections on the glorious mysteries of the Rosary, starting with the apparition of the Risen Jesus who first turned to His Mother. In that most joyful apparition the Risen Jesus wished to thank expressly His Mother for her *"bitter participation in all the sorrows, as Co-redemptrix of the human race,"*[118] for the realization of God's salvific plan. And finally, at the completion of her earthly life, the Mother of God, assumed body and soul into Heaven, was received in Paradise by the Son who placed her *"at His right above all the choirs of angels... associating her to Himself as His Mother, Spouse, and Co-redemptrix, as His Cooperatrix for the Redemption of the world and Queen of the universe."*[119]

The faith of Bl. Bartolo is integral. In his theological vision, permeated by the *sensus fidei*, the mission of the Co-redemptrix on earth and in Heaven runs through all the events of Blessed Mary's life, a life inseparable from that of her divine Son to whom she remains always bound "by a close and indissoluble union" (*L.G.* 53), actively and immediately cooperating with the Redeemer in the work of Redemption, always "under Him

---

[115] Ibid. p. 144.
[116] Ibid. p. 246.
[117] *op. cit.*, p. 208.
[118] *I quindici sabati*, p. 271.
[119] Ibid. p. 348.

and with Him" (*L. G:* 56), and placed in the heavens for eternity *"at His right... as His Mother, Spouse, and Co-redemptrix."*

Bl. Luigi Orione (+ 1940)

Great indeed was the apostolic activity of Bl. Luigi Orione, wider still his field of labor, and vaster yet still his projects of evangelization and charity towards others, especially towards the suffering and most needy. The preaching, teachings, and instructions of Bl. Luigi Orione resounded through cities and villages, from pulpits and Cathedrals, through squares and the streets, in churches and homes... Words of light, words of life, words of hope, words of eternity! Bl. Luigi Orione was an incredible apostle, wholly dominated by a most ardent, triple love toward Christ, Mary, and the Pope.

As for his love towards the Holy Virgin Mary one could gather page after page, as some have in fact already done.[120] These pages do not form a treatise of Mariology, much less do they constitute an academic or scholastic theological textbook on Mary. Quite the contrary. They are a treasure chest of pure and ardent faith in the mystery of Mary, a mystery explained and illustrated, studied and contemplated, and at times, one is tempted to say, sung and praised with enthusiasm, all by a believer whose love for his most sweet and heavenly Mother of God could never be contained.

Regarding the mystery of Marian Coredemption in particular, Bl. Orione left us no systematic treatise apart on the subject. However, he does speak of it many times in his usual ardent and luminous style, and he treats all its essential details as common doctrine, as certain, as a patrimony of Faith lived by the People of God, and more precisely as a Faith permeated by that *sensus fidei* which illuminates, guides, and leads every believer along the way of a truly Christian life, that is, along the road to salva-

---

[120] Cf., for example, the anthology *Con don Orione verso Maria*, Rome, IT 1987.

tion and sanctification.

The primary foundation upon which Bl. Orione bases the truth of Marian Coredemption is the biblical-patristic. Bl. Orione shapes his thought and teaching on the three *doublets,* involving as it were a kind of opposition and recirculation, found among the pages of the Bible and the Church Fathers, namely Adam and Eve, Jesus and Mary, Eden and Calvary. With these three figures Bl. Orione presents the work of our destruction and our salvation. Bl. Orione writes: *"Adam and Eve ruined us; Jesus and Mary save us."*[121] These are the first two doublets. The fall of humanity is linked to the moral collapse of the first couple, Adam and Eve; the salvation of humanity is linked to the Redemption wrought by the second couple, Jesus and Mary.

In this thought of Bl. Orione it is easy to find the double unity. First there is that of the moral collapse, wrought *together* by Adam and Eve, with diverse responsibilities: principally for Adam as head of the human race, secondarily for Eve as the instigator and co-sinner (*co-peccatrix*) with Adam. Secondly, there is that of the *Redemption* wrought *together* by Jesus and Mary, with diverse responsibilities: primarily by Jesus as the Redeemer, secondarily by Mary as the Co-redemptrix. Here one can also read the double unity: the effectors of the *moral collapse* were solely Adam and Eve, and the Effectors of the *Redemption* were solely Jesus and Mary.

The third figure of Bl. Orione is this: *"Eden and Calvary were the two culminating points in history, where occurred the two greatest events for humanity."*[122] This third *couplet,* as it were, with one dramatic event placed against the other, is a charming way to indicate even the geographic locale serving as historical theaters for the most important events in human history, namely that of man's devastating fall (*Eden*) and that of his Redemption (*Calvary*) wrought by the two opposing couples, the sinner and

---

[121] Ibid. p. 115.
[122] Ibid.

co-sinner (Adam and Eve) versus the Redeemer and Co-redemptrix (Jesus and Mary).

Fr. Miotto correctly observed that in the thought of Bl. Orione "revelation and history, geography and topography are linked in the creative and redemptive plan of God willed for humanity. Adam and Eve, Christ and Mary, Eden and Calvary, the Incarnation and the Redemption, all meet at the crossroads of the divine design, and the unfolding of this plan of salvific love is here shown in its primary human and divine protagonists, in its theological and soteriological dimensions, in its most basic historical and geographical aspects as realized in the time and space of our world."[123]

Another enlightened insight of Bl. Orione on the mystery of Mary Co-redemptrix is his teaching on the salvific mission of our Blessed Lady, constituted our universal Mother precisely because she is Co-redemptrix, proclaimed our *"Mother"* by Jesus Himself on Calvary (cf. Jn 19:25-26) exactly at the consummation of the most sorrowful Coredemption. Bl. Orione writes: *"If Mary were not to have suffered, I say this only in order to express my point, we could say that she was not completely our Mother... Mary is Co-redemptrix of humanity; she is our most tender Mother because she even wept, especially for this reason..."*[124]

The Blessed Virgin Mary, therefore, is our Mother because she was the *"Co-redemptrix of humanity."* This affirmation reveals that for Bl. Orione, too, the Maternity and Coredemption in Mary are correlative and interdependent. It is with the Coredemption that she regenerated us unto supernatural life, becoming in this way our true Mother, our "Mother in the order of grace," as Vatican II teaches (*L.G.* 61). Mary's Maternity, therefore, has been a coredemptive Maternity. And such a coredemptive Maternity, which had its ultimate consummation on Calvary, was the mission which Blessed Mary received and

---

[123] S.M. MIOTTO, *op. cit.*, p. 210.
[124] *Con don Orione verso Maria*, edition cited, p. 215.

welcomed for our salvation, this from the beginning, offering for this goal *"the secret tears of her entire life,"* as Bl. Orione puts it,[125] tears which mixed and became one *"with the Blood of our Crucified Lord,"*[126] in order to pay the ransom and restore our supernatural life.

His Marian teaching also treats the mediation of graces springing from the Coredemption, matrix of all salvific grace to be distributed to every person on the road to salvation. If Mary Co-redemptrix cooperated with Christ in the acquisition of the divine grace lost in Eden, then Mary Mediatrix cooperates with Christ in the distribution of that grace recuperated on Calvary. Concerning her mediation, Bl. Orione is quite aware of how St. Paul speaks of Christ as the *"one Mediator"* between God and man (I Tim 2:5), and he is careful, therefore, when explaining in what sense Blessed Mary is Mediatrix. He writes: *"If Christ, the God-Man, is the supreme and omnipotent Mediator* by nature, *Mary, the Mother of God, is Mediatrix* by grace, *as* by grace *she is omnipotent: her prayer is most efficacious and her Mediation infallible."*[127]

In accord with the tenor of these brief reflections on the coredemptive doctrine of Bl. Luigi Orione, we too can agree with Fr. Miotto who thus summarizes: "The outline of Marian Coredemption in the thought of Bl. Orione is complete in all its constitutive elements. In contrast to the first Eve, already at the dawn of human history, Mary Most Holy has been presented by God as the New Eve with the mission of *Co-redemptrix of humanity* and maternal Mediatrix of all graces for our salvation."[128]

---

[125] Ibid. p. 216.

[126] Ibid. p. 104.

[127] Ibid. p. 95; on the same page Bl. Orione also presents Mary Most Holy as *"our Advocate before God, our Mediatrix, our Ark of Salvation"*.

[128] *Op. cit.*, p. 211.

Bl. Ildephonse Cardinal Schuster (+ 1954)

Cardinal Ildephonse Schuster is an eminent figure both as a teacher and pastor. Hence, his teaching holds a particular authority, marked by the charism of doctrine and pastoral practice. *Orthodoxy* and *orthopraxis,* mutually supportive and strengthened by his vision of faith and apostolic fervor, are the distinctive marks of the person and mission of Bl. Schuster, Cardinal Archbishop of Milan.

The mariological doctrine of Cardinal Schuster, found profusely in his numerous books and writings, presents itself in perfect harmony with the perennial Marian theology of the Church. The *sentire cum Ecclesia* was a constant in all of Bl. Ildephonse's teaching, and especially his Marian teaching contained both in his monumental work in nine volumes, *Liber Sacramentorum,*[129] and in his other writings, but above all in his last work, *L'Evangelo di Nostra Donna,*[130] which is truly a testimony of love from his Marian soul.

As for the mystery of Marian Coredemption, it is enough to read only a little of his writings to grasp immediately that in the thought of Bl. Ildephonse Marian Coredemption is treated as common and certain Catholic doctrine.[131] The Blessed freely adopts the term Co-redemptrix and frequently calls Mary *Co-redemptrix of the human race* without any caveats or fears. The term Co-redemptrix appears without quibble throughout his catechesis and studies, his homilies and other writings. Moreover, the term is employed both precisely and appropriately in accord with its semantic structure and clear significance. That

---

[129] I. SCHUSTER, *Liber Sacramentorum. Note storiche e liturgiche sul Messale Romano,* Turin-Rome, IT 1928, vol. IX.

[130] I. SCHUSTER, *L'Evangelo di Nostra Donna,* Milan, IT 1954.

[131] As for Bl. Schuster's doctrine on the *Coredemption* cf. the profound and well-articulated study of P.M. SIANO, *Maria SS. "Corredentrice" nel pensiero del beato Ildefonso card. Schuster (+1954),* in AA.VV., *Maria Corredentrice,* Frigento, IT 2000, vol.III, pp. 137-161.

structure and significance is soteriologically most exactly expressive of the relation of the Blessed Virgin Mary to the Redeemer in accomplishing the universal redemption.

The coredemptive thought of Bl. Ildephonse is ever grounded on Sacred Scripture and the Liturgy. The Old and New Testaments are the primary basis of truth and the foundation of Faith. Bl. Ildephonse always moves in the light of Revelation. And so it is also for his teaching on Marian Coredemption. He relates it to the biblical contrast between the two Testaments: Eve—Mary, Adam— Christ. Listen to his brilliant insight while treating the Blessed Virgin Mary's Assumption into Heaven: *"Even in Heaven Mary exercises the office of being our Advocate, that office which Jesus entrusted to her on Calvary; this is so that the Redemption might completely repair the fall, even in superabundance. To Adam and Eve, sinners and the source of original sin in this world, God has countered with Christ and Mary, the Redeemer and Co-redemptrix of the human race."*[132]

Bl. Ildephonse also presents two other women of the Old Testament as figures of Mary Co-redemptrix. He speaks of Deborah[133] and Judith.[134] Regarding Judith the Cardinal writes expressly that she is especially *"suited for celebrating the glories of the 'Co-redemptrix' of the human race, of her who, to save the world from final ruin, did not spare herself nor her only-begotten Son, but with a perfect conformity to the will of God the Father, she also, as His Immaculate Mother, offered Him in sacrifice on the altar of the Cross."*[135]

Liturgically, on the other hand, Bl. Ildephonse explains in a very timely manner that the Marian celebration of Our Lady's Sorrows during Good Friday was a most ancient and significant celebration, for which, after many centuries, the date was fixed

---

[132] I. SCHUSTER, *Liber Sacramentorum*, edition cited, Vol. VIII, p. 181.

[133] Ibid. p. 239; regarding the interpretation of Deborah, see P.M. SIANO, *op. cit.*, pp. 141-143.

[134] I. SCHUSTER, *op. cit.*, edition cited, 1929, vol. VII, p. 90.

[135] Ibid.

on September 15th. To that celebration of Mary's Dolors on Good Friday was linked, *ab antiquo*, the piety of the Church who *"associated herself with Mary in mourning Jesus Crucified."*[136] Consequently, the Cardinal writes: *"The special devotion to the Sorrows of the Virgin, Co-redemptrix of the human race, was already within the soul of the Christian people many centuries ago."*[137] The feast of Our Lady of Sorrows on September 15th, however, was *"rather the feast of the triumph of the Blessed Mother who, at the foot of the Cross, precisely by means of her cruel martyrdom, redeemed the human race together with her Son, and merited the triumph of her exaltation above all the choirs of Angels and Saints."*[138]

With these words Cardinal Schuster expresses in maximal fashion the direct and immediate participation of the Blessed Virgin in the universal Redemption. Listen again to his culminating point: She, *"at the foot of the Cross, precisely by means of her cruel martyrdom, redeemed the human race together with her Son."* The word *"redeemed"* seems to say too much, but in reality one can also reinsert here the expressions of Vatican II which speak of the Holy Virgin Mary as being totally united to Christ "by an intimate and indissoluble bond" (*L.G.* 53), always "serving the mystery of Redemption under Him and with Him" (*L.G.* 56).

---

[136] Ibid. p. 89.

[137] Ibid. p. 89. "Of utmost importance," comments Fr. Siano, "is this simple and perfect equivalence which Cardinal Schuster establishes between the *'sorrows of the Virgin'* and the *'Co-redemptrix of the human race'.* This means that there is, in substance, an identity between the titles *Our Lady of Sorrows* (Addolorata) and *Co-redemptrix.* To grasp this brilliant equivalence between the titles: *Our Lady of Sorrows* and *Co-redemptrix* it is sufficient to understand immediately how the truth of Marian Coredemption was *'already'* rooted *'within the soul of the Christian people many centuries ago',* before the late middle ages! Therefore, (one sees that) it dates back to the times of the early Church, and discovers that Marian Coredemption is a truth belonging to the deposit of the Christian Faith from the beginning. This is marvelous. Thus the authoritative word of Cardinal Schuster provides solid historical-liturgical support for the *sensus fidei* of the Christian people who have always cultivated *'the special devotion to the Sorrows of the Virgin, Co-redemptrix of the human race'"* (P.M. SIANO, *op. cit.*, p. 154).

[138] Ibid. p. 90.

Other fundamental points on Marian Coredemption touch those privileges which depend on it, such as the spiritual Maternity, the Queenship, and the Mediation of graces by our Blessed Lady. Cardinal Schuster's teaching is consistent: Mary is our Mother, our Queen, our Mediatrix of all graces because she is the Co-redemptrix. Bl. Ildefonso's reasoning follows a clear logic: we are sons of Mary Co-redemptrix, since *"she regenerates us in God by her bitter martyrdom at the foot of her Son's Cross and thus becomes Mother of all men."*[139] In the most sorrowful Coredemption Mary regenerates us amidst the sorrows and travails of childbirth.

Regarding the Queenship of the Blessed Virgin Mary, Bl. Schuster teaches along the same lines that *"Mary is the Queen of the world because she is Co-redemptrix of the human race together with Jesus and for Jesus, on whom the Father conferred 'omnis potestas in coelo et in terra' (viz. 'all power in Heaven and on earth') after His Resurrection."*[140] And as to the Mediation of all grace, with equal surety and consistent logic, Cardinal Schuster leads us to understand that if the Co-redemptrix cooperated in the *acquisition* of the graces of Redemption, she too will be the one to dispose of them for *distribution*. The Cardinal, in fact, maintains that *"the Virgin distributes the treasures of Redemption as Queen, Mother, and Mediatrix."*[141] And the Marian prayer of the People of God linked to the Co-redemptrix, according to Bl. Ildephonse, is the prayer of the Rosary which is the expression of the faith and love *"which,"* says the Cardinal, *"the universal Church nourishes for her who is the Mother of God and of men, the Co-redemptrix of the human race."*[142]

At this point in our rapid-fire presentation of but a handful of the many texts of Bl. Ildephonse on the Co-redemptrix, there remains nothing else but to conclude with a cursory look at his

---

[139] Ibid. p. 93.
[140] Ibid. vol.VIII, p. 79.
[141] Ibid. p. 138.
[142] Ibid. vol. IX, p. 18.

last work written in 1954, the year of his death; a truly stirring "swan's song" about the Mother of God and Co-redemptrix. It is the Marian work entitled *L'Evangelo di Nostra Donna,* "in which," writes Fr. Siano, "the remembrance of the Coredemption acts, in some ways, as a counterpoint to the entire text which breathes exclusively the Gospel."[143] This is so because in his mature contemplation Bl. Schuster "had already grasped— and also had written — how the figure of Mary could not be detached from the shadow of the Cross."[144]

What is more, this precious text presents the life of Our Lady in the light of the culminating moments of her coredemptive vocation and mission on earth. At the *Annunciation,* the Virgin Mary adheres to *"the plan of the future Redemption,"*[145] *"with perfect knowledge of cause and with absolute free will,"*[146] in order *"to become the Mother of Jesus, and, after a time, the Genetrix of His Mystical Body, the Co-redemptrix of human progeny."*[147] At the *Presentation* of the Infant Jesus in the Temple she encountered the holy and aged Simeon who, writes Bl. Schuster, *"already discerns from afar the Cross planted on Calvary, and he foresees Mary Co-redemptrix at the foot of the Cross with her Heart transfixed by the sword... Mary heard the old man, understood, but did not utter a word. Her unbloody martyrdom began from that moment, but she kept silence, because the victim usually keeps quiet and does not speak."*[148] At the times for nurs-

---

[143] P.M. SIANO, *op. cit.,* p. 154.

[144] G. BASADONNA, *Cardinal Schuster,* Milan, IT 1996, p. 60.

[145] CARD. I. SCHUSTER, *L'Evangelo di Nostra Donna,* Milan, IT 1954, p.1 7.

[146] Ibid. 1.c.

[147] Ibid. p. 19.

[148] Ibid. p. 67. During the previous year of 1953, on the occasion of a Marian study week held at Milan from Sept. 14-18, Cardinal Schuster declared in his address that from the Marian week of study *"we can find another advantage: a better knowledge of the mystery of Our Lady. As Co-redemptrix, as Mother of Christians and Mother of the whole Christ: Christ the Head, Christ the Body. As Co-redemptrix the aged Simeon sees her. After he prophesied the passion of Christ, he immediately prophesied the passion of Mary: a union of two passions"* (in *Maria nell'economia della salute,* Milan, 1955, p. 16).

ing the Baby Jesus, Mary, while nourishing the Body of the divine Infant was nourishing her own soul as well because, writes Bl. Ildefonso, *"by hearing the* Logos, *who had come to teach, during all the times in which she was feeding Him, she was made ever more fit for her mission of Co-redemptrix of the human race.* "[149]

Of the work of Redemption in its consummation on Calvary, Bl. Schuster expresses himself with extraordinary emotion when treating the holocaust of Jesus and Mary, from whom a *"wave of mercy will descend to wash away the sins of all generations.* "[150] From the Redeemer and Co-redemptrix, in fact, comes the cleansing waters which wash away the original sin for the salvation of the world. This was the work of redemption in accord with the loving plan of God, and *"the mission of Mary Co-redemptrix,"* teaches Cardinal Schuster, *"entered maximally in that soteriological mystery.* "[151]

In conclusion, Bl. Schuster's coredemptive teaching constitutes a precious patrimony of Marian doctrine which he, a most eminent and qualified teacher of the People of God, has bequeathed to the Church. And in this twenty-first century which has begun with the confidence of *Crossing the Threshold of Hope*, as our Holy Father John Paul II has written, we can surely affirm, with Fr. Siano, that among "the voices of the Saints and Blessed, Venerable and Servants of God who have sung the glory of Marian Coredemption, the voice of Cardinal Schuster full of authority and sanctity will rise above the others confirming that so sweet truth about Mary Most Holy, *'Co-redemptrix of the human race.'"*[152]

---

[149] Ibid. p. 106. Fr. SIANO comments on this point: "This contemporaneous exchange of gifts between the Mother and the Son is most beautiful: while the Mother with her virginal milk helps the Son to grow in His Body which will serve for the redemptive offering, the Son helps the Mother to grow in her soul for her *'mission of Co-redemptrix of the human race'"* (*op. cit.*, p. 158).

[150] Ibid. p. 33.

[151] Cf. Ibid. pp. 122-123.

[152] *Op. cit.*, p. 161.

Bl. Pio of Pietrelcina (+ 1968)

It has been written, and rightly so, that "if there is an aspect of the mystery of Mary especially fitting to the life and work of Padre Pio of Pietrelcina, it is certainly the coredemptive aspect of the person and mission of the Immaculate in God's salvific plan of love."[153]

The mystery of Mary Co-redemptrix is present in the life and writings of Bl. Pio of Pietrelcina at the highest levels of mystical experience which he lived out in body and soul, and of the *theologia cordis* transmitted by him to his spiritual children in the language of that wisdom transcending by far a language limited to the solely notional and conceptual.[154]

Bl. Pio of Pietrelcina in the first place lived the mystery of Marian Coredemption in his exceptional mystical experience of the Passion of Christ Crucified, of which he bore the living and bleeding stigmata in his body for fifty entire years, from 1918 to 1968. He became an "imprinted reproduction of the wounds of the Lord," according to the happy expression of Pope Paul VI.[155] In this exceptional mystical experience he co-immolated himself with Christ, assimilating himself in a most extensive and profound manner to the Mother Co-redemptrix who immolates herself with the Son on the Cross in order to bring to pass the universal Redemption.[156] It has been written that "Padre Pio penetrated the sorrows of Mary and participated in them,

---

[153] N. CASTELLO, S.M. MANELLI, *La "dolce Signora" di Padre Pio*, Cinisello Balsamo, IT 1999, p. 119.

[154] On this theme cf. the more far ranging and elaborate study: S.M. MANELLI, *Maria SS.ma Corredentrice nella vita e negli scritti di Padre Pio da Pietrelcina*, in AA.VV., *Maria Corredentrice*, Frigento, IT 1999, vol. II, pp. 277-294; see also: N. CASTELLO, S.M. MANELLI, *La "dolce Signora" di Padre Pio*, edition cited, pp. 119-128.

[155] PAOLO VI, *Discorso*, Feb. 20, 1971.

[156] It has been written, with good reason, that in the life and writings of Bl. Pio "the transparent, close and indissoluble union of Mary Co-redemptrix and Mediatrix of all graces with Jesus the one Mediator between God and men is (found) everywhere" MELCHIORRE DA POBLADURA, *Alla scuola spirituale di Padre Pio da Pietrelcina*, San Giovanni Rotondo, IT 1978, p. 93.

mirrored them, relived them; as his soul had been a partaker in the sorrows of the Passion, so too he had the gift of participating in the sorrows of Mary."[157]

Into this area of mystical experience, however, the inexperienced are not allowed to enter nor are they in a position to speak of it. St. Bonaventure, the "Seraphic Doctor," teaches expressly that, with regard to the mystical, "those who are not experts and who do not wish to become experienced, must absolutely keep silent."[158]

What is more within the range of our intelligence, then, is the coredemptive aspect of Bl. Pio of Pietrelcina's active ministry. He exercised the ministry of the confessional for more than fifty years, administering the Sacrament of Reconciliation to such a vast family of penitents that Pope Paul VI called it, in yet another happy expression, a "worldwide clientele."[159] But to administer the Sacrament of forgiveness and of reconciliation between mankind and God means to operate on the same wavelength, so to speak, as the Marian Coredemption. In fact, Mary Most Holy, being united with the Redeemer — "under Him and with Him," as Vatican II teaches (L.G. 56) — reconciled humanity with God through the sacrificial offering consummated on Calvary; and after Calvary she continues unceasingly to reconcile man to God with her Mediation and Distribution of all the graces of Redemption. Consequently, she is proclaimed the Mother of universal reconciliation.

The spiritual director of Bl. Pio of Pietrelcina, Fr. Benedict of San Marco, once told Bl. Pio in a letter of spiritual direction that his particular vocation was a "vocation to coredeem" by

---

[157] A. NEGRISOLO, N. CASTELLO, S.M. MANELLI, *Padre Pio nella sua interiorità*, Rome, IT 1997, p. 58. Of considerable importance and interest would be a comparative study of the mystical experience and coredemptive thought of Bl. Pio and St. Veronica Giuliani (Cf. Sr. MARIA FRANCESCA PERILLO, *Il mistero di Maria Corredentrice in santa Veronica Giuliani*, in AA.VV., *Maria Corredentrice*, Frigento, IT 1999, vol. II, pp. 169-217).

[158] St. BONAVENTURE, *Apologia Pauperum*, c.9, n.27; VII, 303.

[159] *Discorso*, Feb. 20, 1971.

means of the daily trials, battles, sufferings, and toils coming from the exercise of his ministry. And in reference particularly to his work as a confessor, it has been accurately observed that "in the ministry of reconciliation, Padre Pio prolonged or, in a certain sense, actualized the fruitfulness of grace of Marian Coredemption which 'restores the supernatural life in souls' (*L.G.* 61). In fact, the divine grace acquired by the Redeemer and the Co-redemptrix in the *'effecting'* of the Redemption is here distributed and applied to every soul in need by means of the sacramental absolution given by Padre Pio to his penitents."[160]

To understand Bl. Pio's "vocation to coredeem" better, one must also consult his writings, of primary value where he speaks of the Co-redemptrix in the salvific mystery. And one recognizes immediately that his discourse is not theoretical or notional, but reflects instead the most profound and moving characteristics of the *theologia cordis*, of theology lived at the level of ascetical and mystical experience, one which gives a knowledge of the mystery characteristically sapiential and experiential, as St. Bonaventure explains.[161]

The pages in which Bl. Pio speaks of the Blessed Virgin Mary's sorrows are exceedingly numerous.[162] In these pages the figure of Our Lady of Sorrows is present in her immense coredemptive suffering, and she is seen walking along the way to Calvary *"immediately behind Jesus... burdened with her own cross."*[163] A cross for Jesus, a cross for Mary. It is of value here to recall the insight of Arnold of Chartres who speaks of a double

---

[160] N. CASTELLO, S.M. MANELLI, *work cited*, pp. 127-128. It should also be noted that Bl. Pio frequently recalled Our Lady of Sorrows to his penitents in giving them the sacramental penance of reciting seven Hail Mary's to Our Lady of Sorrows, "and sometimes he could not succeed in finishing the word *Addolorata* (*Our Lady of Sorrows*) without an outburst of tears!" (ibid. p. 123).

[161] Cf. St. BONAVENTURE, *Questio disputata de perfectione evangelica*, Q.1, conclusion.

[162] Cf., for example, the first volume of the *Epistolario*, San Giovanni Rotondo, IT 1992, pp. 213, 345, 384, 601, 639, 993 (here cited as: *Ep.*).

[163] *Ep.* I, p. 597.

altar on Calvary: "one in the Heart of Mary, the other in the Body of Christ. Christ sacrificed His flesh, Mary her soul."[164] And Bl. Pio recommends to all *"to keep always right behind this Blessed Mother, to walk always close to her, since there is no other road which leads to life, except the one trod by our Mother."*[165]

When Bl. Pio wants to describe the sufferings of Our Lady of Sorrows, he finds a very valid point of reference in his very own suffering, be it moral or physical, a suffering so terrible as to dry up every tear and to petrify him in sorrow.[166] For this reason in contemplating Our Lady's sorrows he can expand his soul and say: *"Yes, now I understand, oh Jesus, why in admiring You Your Mother did not weep beneath the Cross,"*[167] because *"by the excess of sorrow, she remained petrified before her crucified Son"*;[168] and on another page of sublime contemplation touching his own measureless sorrows and those of Our Lady, he exclaims movingly: *"Now I seem to be penetrating what was the martyrdom of our most beloved Mother (...). Oh, if all people would but penetrate this martyrdom! Who could succeed in suffering with this, yes, our dear Co-redemptrix? Who would refuse her the good title of Queen of Martyrs?"*[169]

The words "dear Co-redemptrix" express most exactly the soteriological value of the Blessed Virgin Mary's maternal mission in the tones of a pure *theologia cordis*. She coredeemed humanity by offering the divine Victim, her Son Jesus, in the bloody immolation of the Cross, and co-immolating herself with Him in order to "restore supernatural life to souls" (*L.G.* 61), became

---

[164] ARNOLD OF CHARTRES, *De septem verbis Domini in cruce*, 3, PL 189, 1694. This is a text quoted recently by Pope John Paul II in a catechesis on the *Marian Coredemption* on Oct. 25, 1995.

[165] *Ep.* I, p. 602.

[166] So he writes, for example, in a letter: *"Oh God, what torture I feel... Would that I could at least have the satisfaction of pouring out this interior martyrdom with tears. The sorrow is immense and has overwhelmed me."* (ibid. 993).

[167] ibid.

[168] *Ep.* III, p. 190.

[169] Ibid., p. 384.

in this way our "Mother in the order of grace" (*L.G.* 1.c.).[170] She *"gave birth to us in sorrows,"* affirms Bl. Pio. She is, therefore, the Mother Co-redemptrix. She desires to raise her children and, what is more, to make them grow even unto the stature of Christ. She is, therefore, the Mother *Mediatrix and Dispensatrix of all graces,*[171] always "associated with Jesus in applying the fruits of the Redemption to souls," as Fr. Melchior da Pobladura writes.[172] The Co-redemptrix reacquired the grace lost. The Mediatrix distributes the grace reacquired. There is an operative continuity between the Coredemption and Distribution of saving grace. And, according to the teaching of Bl. Pio of Pietrelcina, we should be eternally grateful to *"our dear Co-redemptrix"* and to our *"Mediatrix and Dispensatrix of all graces."*

Bl. Josemaria Escrivà (+ 1975)

Bl. Josemaria Escrivà was an extraordinary apostle of our times and for all times. He was preoccupied with carrying the People of God to the highest realms of universal sanctity in accord with the "Work of God" *Opus Dei*, for which he battled and suffered, sacrificed and consumed himself without respite even to the very end of his life, always retaining the wealth of two precious treasures: that of his "supernatural sense and his most human cordiality."[173]

---

[170] The following is well stated: "As to the words *'dear Co-redemptrix'*, it is important to verify how for Padre Pio of Pietrelcina the term *Co-redemptrix* serves also to efficaciously explain the truth of the compassion and transfixion of Mary Most Holy in the universal work of Redemption. Here mystical theology, too, supports the usage of the term *Co-redemptrix*, already common in Mariology and in the Church for centuries, used even by the Sovereign Pontiffs, and particularly by Pope John Paul II" (N. CASTELLO, S.M. MANELLI, *work cited*, pp. 126-127).

[171] Bl. Pio himself wrote these expressions on a little memorial image for his 50th anniversary as a priest, calling Our Lady precisely the *"most sweet Mother (mamma) of priests, Mediatrix and Dispensatrix of all graces"* (reported by FERDINANDO DA RIESE, *P. Pio da Pietrelcina crocifisso senza croce*, Foggia, IT 1991, p. 428).

[172] MELCHIORRE DA POBLADURA, *op. cit.*, p. 96.

[173] *Colloqui con Monsignor Escrivà*, Milan, IT 1987, p. 14.

In the vast literary production of Bl. Escrivà, Our Lady's presence is constant and luminous. Every aspect of the Church's Marian doctrine occupies its place of importance and animates Bl. Escrivà's faith which he transmitted to his children spread throughout the world. Hence, the mystery of Marian Coredemption could not be absent from the Blessed's instruction and piety.

"Among the Marian writings of Bl. Escrivà," notes Fr. Miotto, "there is a page of splendid meditation in which a beautiful synthesis of Marian Coredemption is presented, drawing particularly upon the Gospel events of the *Presentation* of the Infant Jesus in the Temple and of the *Crucifixion* and *Death* of Jesus on Calvary, but also confirmed and guaranteed by the Pontifical Magisterium, especially the teaching of Pope Benedict XV."[174]

Bl. Escrivà views the scene of the Presentation of the Infant Jesus in the Temple in the light of the immense love of the Blessed Virgin Mary. He writes: *"Recall the scene of the Presentation of Jesus in the Temple. The aged Simeon says to Mary, His Mother: 'Behold this Child is set for the fall, and for the resurrection of many in Israel, and for a sign which shall be contradicted; and thy own soul a sword shall pierce that, out of many hearts, thoughts may be revealed' (Lk 2:34-35). The immense charity of Mary towards humanity accomplished, above all in her, the affirmation of Christ: 'Greater love than this no man hath, that a man lay down his life for his friends'(Jn 15:13)."*[175]

In this commentary of Bl. Escrivà's on the shocking words of the holy old Simeon to Mary, we learn that between the Redemption and the Coredemption there is a communality in that *"greater love."* The gift and immolation of life for the salvation

---

[174]S.M. MIOTTO, *op. cit.*, p. 215. On Bl. Escrivà's doctrine of the *Marian Coredemption*, cf. also: F. DELELAUX, *Nel dolore invocare e imitare Maria Corredentrice*, in *Eco del Santuario dell'Addolorata,* Castelpetroso, IT 1995, n.3, pp. 6-8, n.4, pp. 3-5.

[175]JOSEMARIA ESCRIVA, *Amici di Dio. Omelie*, Milan, IT 1978, pp. 318-319.

of humanity, says the Blessed, was common to both the Son and the Mother, to the Redeemer and the Co-redemptrix: a *bloody* immolation for the Redeemer, an *unbloody* immolation for the Co-redemptrix.

Consequently, according to the teaching of Bl. Josemaria Escrivà, between the Redeemer and the Co-redemptrix there was effected a union of sufferings terminating at *fusion* in the total immolation of both. With her indescribable coredemptive sufferings, then, Mary Most Holy was brought *"to fuse herself,"* as the Blessed writes, *"with the redeeming love of the Son,"* offering all her *"immense suffering — like a sharpened sword — which pierced her most pure Heart."*[176] In this *fusion* of love in her immolation with the Son — an immolation which *"pierces the soul"* — one must understand all the personal, direct, and immediate participation of the Co-redemptrix in the work of the universal Redemption.

At this point in his reflection, Bl. Escrivà cites the Papal teaching which constitutes the highest guarantee and certitude for every truth of the Faith. He finds here the clearest and most solid confirmation. In his subtle and deep reflection, in fact, he refers to the thought of Pope Benedict XV who speaks, perhaps as no other Pope ever has, of the Marian Coredemption. Pope Benedict XV states that Our Lady's presence at the foot of the Cross on Calvary was "not without divine design. In truth Mary suffered, and almost died with her suffering and agonizing Son. She renounced her maternal rights over her Son... and as far as what depended upon her, she immolated the Son to placate the divine justice in such a way that one can rightly say she, with her Son, redeemed the human race."[177]

Reechoing the teaching of other Popes before and after Benedict XV as well, Bl. Escrivà reflects and comments in this manner: *"The Supreme Pontiffs have rightly called Mary 'Co-*

---

[176] Ibid. pp. 318-319.

[177] BENEDICT XV, Encyclical Letter *Inter sodalicia*, March 22, 1918 (AAS 10 1919, 182).

redemptrix'. At that point, together with her Son who was suffering and dying, she suffered and almost died; at that point she abdicated her maternal rights over her Son for the salvation of humanity and immolated Him, insofar as she was able, in order to placate the justice of God; thus one can rightly say that she redeemed the human race together with Christ. In this fashion we are in a better position to understand that moment of the Lord's Passion which we should never grow tired of meditating upon: Stabat iuxta crucem Jesus Mater eius, *'Now there stood by the Cross of Jesus His Mother' (Jn 19:25).* "[178]

In analyzing the core of Bl. Josemaria's reflection we can say that:

— *rightly* do the Supreme Pontiffs call Mary "Co-redemptrix"

— Mary, in truth, suffered and almost died with her crucified Son

— Mary abdicated her maternal rights over her Son

— Mary, insofar as she was able, immolated her Son

— Mary redeemed the human race together with Christ

— Mary is the unique Co-redemptrix *"standing beside her Son"* on Calvary.

In the thought of Bl. Escrivà, this is the graphic panorama of the universal Redemption willed by God and worked out by Christ the Redeemer in His own Blood, in union with the Mother Co-redemptrix transfixed by the "sword" of sorrow, associated and united to Him in "a close and indissoluble bond" (*L.G.* 53) in order to serve "the mystery of Redemption under Him and with Him" (*L.G.* 56), with that "fusion" of supreme love in total immolation.

And now we turn to yet another reflection of the Blessed. If it is true that the *felix culpa* of which the celebrated *Easter praeconium* speaks obtained for us the gift of the divine Redeemer and Savior, then it is also true that it obtained for us the

---

[178] *Op. cit.*, p. 318.

gift of the Mother Co-redemptrix and omnipotent Mediatrix. The Blessed himself writes: "Felix culpa, *sings the Church: Oh happy fault because it has obtained for us such a great Redeemer. Oh happy fault, we can also add, which has merited us to receive Our Lady as Mother. Now we no longer have anything to fear, nothing must alarm us, because Our Lady, who is crowned Queen of heaven and earth, is the omnipotent intercessor before God. Jesus cannot deny anything to Mary, nor to us, children of His very own Mother.*"[179]

Here we can also conclude with Fr. Miotto who writes: "The Coredemption and Mediation shape the universal Maternity of Mary respectively in its phase of *'travailing in birth... in pain'* (cf. Rev 12:2) on Calvary at the foot of the Cross (cf. Jn 19:25-27), and in the phase of the nursing and growth of children most in need of maternal care and sustenance until they reach the Kingdom of Heaven, leaving this world of *'thorns and thistles'* (Gn 3:18). This is the truth of the Christian life in a soteriological light, a life made more amiable by the maternal presence of the Co-redemptrix and Mediatrix who desires to save and sanctify all of her children, all of her Son's little brothers."[180]

The Venerable
Ven. James Alberione (+1971)

Ven. Alberione is a brilliant Founder and extraordinary apostle of the twentieth century, a genius and charismatic pioneer in the field of evangelization by modern means to the entire planet. He was also a theologian, an orator, and a very prolific writer, teacher, and guide to generations of religious and laity.

Among his writings, his Marian works occupy a central and consistent place and, claims Roatta, he "set forth the profoundest

---

[179] Ibid. p. 319.
[180] *op. cit.*, p. 218.

portraits of the Virgin Mother."[181] Ven. James Alberione wrote an entire Marian trilogy, plus another Marian text dedicated to the Queen of the Apostles,[182] not to mention a rich series of articles and notes.

On the subject of Marian Coredemption Ven. Alberione has left us a complete doctrine in lessons and chapters of true and accurate Marian soteriology. All of this he presents in simple but certain language, with solid and clear theological method, expounding certain and commonly held truth, without hesitation or discussion as to the probability of such statements. Ven. James presents and illustrates the Coredemption and Mediation of Our Lady as a truth of Faith, even if not yet defined, but nonetheless a living doctrine in terms of the *sensus fidei* of the People of God and a genuine *sentire cum Ecclesia*.[183]

Ven. James confirms in a clear and precise synthesis that the Blessed Virgin Mary *"cooperated in the acquisition of grace, and therefore she is Co-redemptrix; she exposes our needs to God, and therefore she is Mediatrix of grace; she loves us and communicates the divine mercy to us, and therefore she is our spiritual Mother."*[184] This is the theological paradigm of the *coredemptive, distributive* and *maternal* Mediation of Mary Most Holy. In a few lines Ven. James shows the specific, constitutive elements and consequences of Mary's cooperation in the *acquisition* of redemptive graces as Co-redemptrix, in her *dispensation* of redemptive grace as *Mediatrix*, and in the *maternal care* of her children as *spiritual Mother*. Here a theologian has spoken, one who sought to cat-

---

[181] G. ROATTA, *Presentazione* for the work of G. ALBERIONE, *Pensieri*, Rome, IT 1972, p. 47.

[182] The trilogy carries the title of *Maria nostra speranza*, in three distinct volumes: *Le grandezze di Maria, Feste di Maria Santissima*, Albano, IT 1954 (3rd ed.), *Mese di Maggio*, Rome, IT 1938; adjoined to these is the text *Maria Regina degli Apostoli*, Rome, IT 1948.

[183] On the theme of the *Marian Coredemption* according to the doctrine of Ven. Alberione, cf. the extensive and accurate study: S.M. MANELLI, *Maria Corredentrice nel pensiero del venerabile Giacomo Alberione*, in AA.VV., *Maria Corredentrice*, Frigento, IT 2000, pp. 163-188.

[184] G. ALBERIONE, *Le grandezze di Maria*, edition cited, p. 42.

echize, one who knew how to *"break the bread"* of the word of God for the faithful (cf. Lam 4:4).

His explanation continues, simply and convincingly, with regard to Marian Coredemption. The Venerable writes concisely: *"Co-redemptrix. She cooperated with Jesus Christ the Redeemer, though in a secondary and dependent mode, in saving us from eternal damnation."*[185] With these words Ven. Alberione specifies that the *Marian Coredemption* is *"secondary and dependent"* with respect to the primary and absolute Redeemer; he maintains that the Coredemption served in the very reopening of the doors to the Kingdom of Heaven, that is to say, the Co-redemptrix cooperated in the very *"effecting"* of the universal Redemption.

In the second volume of the Marian trilogy — *The Feasts of Mary* — the Venerable presents the truth of Mary Co-redemptrix with other reflections made from different perspectives. He writes as follows: "Let us consider why Mary is not remembered in the Gospels during the glorious episodes of her Son (i.e. the transfiguration, the triumphal entry into Jerusalem, etc.), but her presence is recalled on Calvary. She knew her office and her mission: she accomplished these most faithfully, even to the very end, by cooperating with the Son as Co-redemptrix. She prepared the Host for sacrifice; and now behold her offering and immolating it on Calvary."[186] Here one immediately understands how the coredemptive mission was fundamental for Mary from the very moment of the Incarnation of the Word and Redeemer. She knew well from the Annunciation and, even more so, from the words of the aged Simeon, that she "would have to share in the pains because (she was) Co-redemptrix."[187] Furthermore, in order to offer Jesus as Victim "she had disposed and offered herself to become Co-redemptrix."[188]

---

[185] Ibid.

[186] G. ALBERIONE, *Le Feste di Maria*, edition cited, p. 54.

[187] G. ALBERIONE, *Brevi meditazioni per ogni giorno dell'anno*, Rome, IT 1952, vol.I, p. 438.

[188] Ibid. vol.II, Rome, IT 1965, p. 328.

We find even more insights which enrich the theme of the Marian Coredemption in the third volume of Alberione's Marian trilogy, the *Month of Mary*. Recalling the sacrifice of Abraham, Ven. Alberione writes that "more perfect than Abraham who completely prepared the sacrifice of his son according to the divine will, Mary felt in her Heart, with her voluntary presence, the sorrows of Jesus in the Crucifixion, the Agony, the Death; she suffered beyond words, and with profound charity she offered the Blood of Jesus and her own pangs in payment to the heavenly Father."[189]

In this text we find a particular item of great worth in the expression "she offered the Blood of Jesus and her own pangs in payment to the heavenly Father." Here Alberione clearly displays Mary's active and immediate cooperation in the very "effecting" of the Redemption, by giving the personal contribution of "her own pangs in payment to the heavenly Father," that is, by paying off, she too, the price of ransom with "her own pangs" united to "the Blood of Jesus." There is a divine union here between the Redeemer and the Co-redemptrix in working out the universal Redemption.

And as a support to this doctrine, Ven. James cites the magisterial text of Pope Benedict XV, considered so expressive and decisive in presenting the active and immediate cooperation of the universal Co-redemptrix: "Mary," states Pope Benedict XV, "as far as what depended upon her, immolated the Son... in such a way that one can rightly say she, with her Son, redeemed the human race."[190] If this is the doctrine of the Church, this is also the doctrine of Ven. Alberione who presents, explains, and communicates it to the People of God as a secure truth from the patrimony of our perennial and immutable Faith.

In his volume on Mary, Queen of the Apostles, Ven. Alberione adds other brilliant points of reflection on Mary Co-

---

[189] G. ALBERIONE, *Mese di Maggio*, edition cited, p. 69.
[190] BENEDICT XV, Encyclical Letter *Inter sodalicia*, March 22, 1918.

redemptrix in a chapter dense with Marian doctrine and spirituality, with a particular emphasis on the bond that runs between the Marian Coredemption and the active apostolate, or, put more precisely, between the work of Mary as *Co-redemptrix* and as *Co-apostle* which is in harmony with the apostolic work of the *Pious Society of St. Paul.*[191]

"*As Jesus in the Garden of Gethsemani agreed to offer Himself,*" writes the Venerable, "*so too Mary gave her consent to the immolation and, insofar as it stood within her power, she immolated her Son. Her consent was in a different mode, but similar to that given for the Incarnation... And the union of wills and intentions and sorrows between Mother and Son never came to be interrupted throughout Their lives; and much less was that union broken on Calvary... As a result of that union of sorrows, wills and intentions between Mary and Jesus Christ, Mary became Reparatrix and our Co-redemptrix and the Dispensatrix of the fruits of the Cross... The Redeemer is Jesus alone. Jesus is the principal Mediator by office; Mary is the secondary and associated Redemptrix to this great work by the divine will.*"[192]

The intimate union between the Redeemer and the Co-redemptrix through Their lives (a union "*of wills, of intentions, and of sorrows*"); the dynamic rapport between the Reparatrix-Co-redemptrix who acquired the fruits of Redemption, and the Dispensatrix who distributes the fruits of the Cross; Jesus as the one Redeemer "*by office,*" Mary as "*the secondary and associated Redemptrix... by the divine will.*" These are the constitutive and supporting elements of Marian Coredemption as analyzed in-depth and argued logically and consistently, with theological precision, in Ven. Alberione's writings. They are founded on Revelation, on Tradition and on the Papal Magisterium, on the

---

[191] "Fr. Alberione," wrote Todaro, "puts in a logical rapport Mary, Queen of the Apostles, and the apostolate of social communication" and he presents "the doctrine on Mary, Queen of the Apostles, as he transforms it into an new pastoral principle" (L. TODARO, *Maria Regina degli Apostoli*, Rome, IT 1994, pp. 96, 110).

[192] G. ALBERIONE, *Maria Regina degli Apostoli*, edition cited, pp. 110-111.

Liturgy and the *sensus fidelium* of the People of God. The theological thought of Alberione is luminous and solid, profound and clear, even in its simple style: the doctrine of Marian Coredemption makes up part of the patrimony of the Church's Faith, it belongs to the timeless theology of the Church, and is rooted in the Church's living *sensus fidei* which has always loved the Mother of God and Co-redemptrix.

Let us conclude summarizing the thought of Ven. James on the Blessed Mother: She *"suffered in union with Jesus the Redeemer; she was Co-redemptrix. She knew that this was her mission, to give worthy satisfaction for sin, to reopen Heaven, to save mankind. She fulfilled this, her office, from Jesus' crib even to Calvary, and to Jesus' Sepulcher."*[193]

Ven. Gabriel Mary Allegra (+ 1974)

Friar Minor, missionary in China and celebrated biblical scholar, Ven. Gabriel Allegra supported and defended the truth of Marian Coredemption and Mediation by demonstrating authoritatively the dogmatic definibility of the universal Coredemption and Mediation of all graces.[194]

The thought of Ven. Gabriel Allegra on Marian Coredemption reveals itself as theologically "clear and integral,

---

[193] G. ALBERIONE, *Brevi meditazioni per ogni giorno dell'anno*, edition cited, vol.I, pp. 452-453.

[194] On the coredemptive doctrine of Ven. Allegra, cf. the extensive study of L. MURABITO, *La Corredenzione di Maria nel pensiero del venerabile Padre Gabriele Allegra*, in *Maria Corredentrice*, Frigento, IT 1999, vol. II, pp. 195-314. The particular devotion of Ven. Allegra towards Our Lady of Sorrows dates back to his family upbringing (cf. ibid. p. 305); the Venerable attributed his religious, priestly and missionary vocation to Our Lady of Sorrows; the Venerable began his translation of the Bible into Chinese on April 11, the feast of Our Lady of Sorrows (Good Friday), and in the Statutes of the Biblical Studium in China he decreed that the "the heavenly Patroness of the Biblical Studium is the Mother of Sorrows" (ibid. p. 297).

luminous and harmonious," says Fr. L. Murabito,[195] particularly rich in its biblical authority and spiritual intonation. Above all on this subject of *biblical authority*, "Fr. Allegra," continues Murabito, "insists that, read well, Scripture teaches the entire design of God about Mary: her predestination to be the Mother of the Word Incarnate, her Coredemption at the foot of the Cross, her sweet office of Mother of the Church, her victory over the dragon, participating in the glory of her Risen Son."[196]

With significant expression, for example, Ven. Allegra calls Our Lady the "new Eve-Co-redemptrix," to indicate with clear biblical reference that the first Eve was the cause (secondary) of our fall with the first Adam (primary cause), while the second Eve has been the cause (secondary) of salvation with the second Adam (primary cause): He, the new Adam-Redeemer, she the "new Eve-Co-redemptrix."[197] With another expression, no less clear, the Venerable writes that *"the Mother of the Word Incarnate was also the Co-redemptrix, the new Eve, as Jesus was the new Adam."*[198]

Elsewhere on other pages of his Marian writings Ven. Gabriel Allegra speaks of the *"mystery of the Immaculate-Mother-Co-redemptrix"*[199] and calls Our Blessed Lady the "Sorrowful Mother-Co-redemptrix,"[200] and again: "our Co-redemptrix,"[201] thus employing the term Co-redemptrix with great freedom,

---

[195] Ibid. p. 300. The author adds that Ven. Allegra "treats of Mary Mediatrix and Co-redemptrix in a little volume published at Peking in 1944, published by 'Collectanea Commissionis Synodalis', under the title 'De doctrina Sancti Bernardini Senensis circa universalem Mediationem Gratiarum Beatae Mariae Virgnis'" (ibid. 1.c.).

[196] *op. cit.*, p. 300.

[197] G.M. ALLEGRA, *Il Cuore Immacolato di Maria*, Acireale, IT 1991, p. 76; cf. also IDEM, *Madre mia, fiducia mia!*, Catania, IT 1958, p. 10, 37. On the Mariological sense of the more important Old and New Testament prophecies, cf. also G.M. ALLEGRA, *Vaticini mariani dell'Antico Testamento e dell'Apocalisse XII*, Castelpetroso, 1996.

[198] G.M. ALLEGRA, *Madre mia, fiducia mia!*, edition cited, p. 42.

[199] Ibid. p. 5.

[200] Ibid p. 43.

[201] G.M. ALLEGRA, *Il Cuore Immacolato di Maria*, edition cited, p. 132.

without any reserve or preoccupation over the dangers of such usage, which presently some would like to describe as presumptuous, risking to obscure the term *Redeemer.* On this point the decisive affirmation of Ven. Allegra is authoritative; he writes: *"I firmly believe and with all my strength I will preach to the rest of the faithful that the title of Co-redemptrix is theologically exact in explaining the part that Mary had in the work of our salvation."*[202] This is the word of a great biblical scholar, one who is about to be honored at the altars.

Ven. Allegra expounds the truth of the term Co-redemptrix and its theological significance in terms of a balanced and secure Marian soteriology: that is, the term Co-redemptrix signifies the dependent participation, nonetheless direct and immediate, of the Blessed Virgin Mary in the work of the universal Redemption: *"Mary's cooperation in our Redemption,"* writes the Venerable, *"is such that Mary merited the title Co-redemptrix,"*[203] above all because *"she intimately united herself to her dying Son on the Cross as our Co-redemptrix,"*[204] and thus she was united with Him by means of that maternal *compassion* which *"intimately unites us to the dying Christ... The Compassion constitutes the Coredemption."*[205] And again: to be the Co-redemptrix means to be a "partaker of all the mysteries of the Son on earth," explains Fr. Murabito, "a partaker of the definitive battle and eschatological triumph of Jesus,"[206] according to Ven. Allegra.

He structures the Marian Coredemption, therefore, entirely in terms of the intimate and total union between the divine Son and Mother, between Jesus the Redeemer and Mary the Co-redemptrix. It is in the union of both their sorrows offered to-

---

[202] G.M. ALLEGRA, *Fasciculus Florum*, Quaderno, IT Nov. 18, 1939, in *Archivio della Vice Postulazione.*

[203] G.M. ALLEGRA, *I sette dolori di Maria*, Castelpetroso, IT 1995, p. 30.

[204] G.M. ALLEGRA, *Il Cuore Immacolato di Maria*, edition cited, p. 132.

[205] G.M. ALLEGRA, *De Compassione Matris Mariae*, in *Meditazione*, 1944, in *Archivio della Vice Postulazione.*

[206] L. MURABITO, *op. cit.*, p. 311.

gether that the universal Redemption is effected. *"The afflictions of Mary and those of Jesus,"* the Venerable stirringly writes, *"were but one affliction which made two Hearts to suffer... The Compassion of Mary increased the suffering of Jesus and the Passion of Jesus was the source of Mary's sorrows. This double offering redeemed the world."*[207]

Furthermore, Ven. Gabriel also points to the celebrated Franciscan thesis of the predestination of the Blessed Virgin *"together with her Son from all eternity. Jesus is the King, and Mary the Queen of the universe; Jesus is the Redeemer, Mary the Coredemptrix,"*[208] and at that fixed moment, *"when the fullness of time arrived"* (cf. Gal 4:4), the Immaculate Conception became *"the Mother of the mystical Body of the Lord, in virtue of the 'fiat' of the Annunciation, of the Coredemption on Calvary and of the glorious Assumption."*[209]

Regarding the doctrine of the absolute primacy of Christ and Mary, Ven. Allegra "knew well," Fr. Murabito points out, "that not a few theologians ignored the Franciscan and Scotistic doctrine on the Incarnation and absolute predestination of Christ together with Mary," and yet the Venerable, as early as 1945, noticed: *"I hear that the exegetes and biblical theologians are ready to direct themselves towards the doctrine of the absolute Primacy of Christ...;"*[210] and Fr. Murabito adds that the Venerable was already speaking of the "necessity to make known to the faithful the doctrine of the predestination of Mary in the mystery of Christ and the pilgrim Church and in history, because this doctrine sheds the most light on the doctrine and mystery of Mary Mediatrix and Co-redemptrix."[211]

---

[207] G.M. ALLEGRA, *I sette dolori di Maria*, edition cited, pp. 30-31. Ven. Allegra, as one can see, did not hesitate to affirm that the offering of the *compassion* of Mary also *"redeemed the world"*.

[208] G.M. ALLEGRA, *Madre mia, fiducia mia!*, edition cited, p. 11.

[209] Ibid. p. 27.

[210] G.M. ALLEGRA, *Il Primato assoluto di Cristo*, in *san Paolo e Duns Scoto*, Palermo, IT 1966, p. 36.

[211] L. MURABITO, *op. cit.*, p. 314.

As to the thorny problem of ecumenism, in particular, the Venerable suffered and lamented because, to cite Fr. Murabito again, "the theologians, whether under the influence of protestantism or just lacking conviction of the transcendent dignity of the Mother of God and of her mission in the Church, were becoming silent, when they were not directly denying this or that prerogative of the Immaculate Mother. From this arose their more or less open opposition to the doctrine of the universal Mediation and Coredemption of Mary."[212] Ven. Allegra, to the contrary, and in perfect accord with St. Leopold Mandic, was thoroughly convinced that "the Immaculate Mother, the Mediatrix and Co-redemptrix, would be the Victor of the ecumenical battle because, as he would say, the Immaculate will triumph."[213]

The doctrine of Ven. Allegra on Mary Immaculate, universal Co-redemptrix and Mediatrix-Dispensatrix of all graces, is filled with light, is anointed with inspiration, is solid in its structure, grounds a most lively hope for the whole Church and for all humanity. The Immaculate Co-redemptrix and universal Mediatrix is an entirely maternal Heart for us.[214]

Conclusion

Fr. Miotto, concluding his accurate study on the Coredemption in the hagiography of the 20th century, could write that this "rapid survey of coredemptive thought in the life and teaching of a group of Saints and Blessed from our twentieth century in Christian history confirms and comforts us with that affirmative chorus hailing the saving and fruitful truth of

---

[212] G.M. ALLEGRA, *Peregrinantibus et iter agentibus*, Macao, 1970, p. 41.

[213] L. MURABITO, *op. cit.*, p. 313.

[214] Regarding the particular connection which Ven. Allegra establishes between the Co-redemptrix and the Immaculate Heart of Mary, cf. Fr. Murabito: *op. cit.*, pp. 309-313.

Marian Coredemption as a living part of the deposit of our Faith *ab antiquo*."[215]

This conclusion, comprehensive and compelling, equally serves to conclude our hagiographical research embracing a larger number of Saints, Blessed and Venerable, all exclusively belonging to the twentieth century. And this resounding chorus of voices, though but a handful with respect to the much larger number of living "elect" of the twentieth century, are a chorus more than sufficient to impress us profoundly with the certainty of the truth of Marian Coredemption which, for the "elect," admitted of no reservations, much less arguments or negations of any kind. We speak here of that certainty of faith and sureness of truth which only the Saints succeed in communicating with their living *sensus fidei* substantiated by prayer and contemplation, doctrine and spirituality, heroic virtue and mystical experience.

In view of the hagiographical landscape here depicted one can immediately assert that the doctrine of Marian Coredemption in the thought and experience of the twentieth century Saints, Blessed and Venerable is evident in all its richness, immensity, and solidity. The teaching and catechesis, the studies and research, the writings and sayings, the cult and piety, the action and contemplation centered on the mystery of the divine Mother Co-redemptrix had free rein in the lives of the Saints and Blessed, the Venerable and Servants of God who lived in the last century of the second millennium of Christianity. Even the variety of Saints examined represents a wide spectrum. Saints young and old, men and women, consecrated religious and lay-faithful, missionaries and contemplatives, with the presence also of a great Supreme Pontiff, Pope St. Pius X.

It has been authoritatively asserted by T. Koehler that the twentieth century has been a "century of Mariology."[216] More

---

[215] S.M. MIOTTO, *op. cit.*, p. 218.

[216] T. KOEHLER, *La storia della Mariologia*, Vercelli, IT 1974, IV 183.

precisely, perhaps, one could say that the twentieth century has been the century of "coredemptionists," and in particular of the Saints and Blessed, Venerable and Servants of God, all upholding the Coredemption, loving and singing, venerating and defending that so delightful truth of Marian Coredemption with speech and writing, virtues and works, veneration and devotion. They demonstrate that Marian Coredemption is a precious patrimony of the perennial Faith of the pilgrim Church as she makes her way towards the Kingdom of Heaven.

Of particular importance and beauty in this Marian review of hagiography is the fact that the opening and closing of the twentieth century are linked by two stigmatists: St. Gemma Galgani who died in 1903, and Bl. Pio of Pietrelcina who died in 1968 and was beatified on May 2nd, 1999. It is a significant fact, especially if we consider the very expressive and tight-knit association stigmatization has with the Coredemption-transfixion of Mary Most Holy in relation to the Crucifixion of the Redeemer.

Another significant fact is the flowering of studies on the Co-redemptrix. Especially during the last decade of the millennium, this has occurred at the highest levels of research,[217] reanimating the languishing field of Mariology then in a truly pitiable state: "After Vatican Council II," Laurentin bluntly maintains, "biblical and theological criticism was reduced to the status of a skeleton or an ectoplasm."[218] The theme of the

---

[217] For the first half of the century it is sufficient here to cite the fundamental work of J.B. CAROL, *De Corredemptione Beatae Virginis Mariae*, Vatican City, 1950, pp. 643; for the rest of the century, cf. in addition to the wealth of bibliographical data throughout the review *Marianum*, the two volumes *Mary Co-redemptrix, Mediatrix, Advocate, Theological Foundations*, Santa Barbara, CA, 1995 vol. I, 1997 vol. II, and the three volume study *Maria Corredentrice*, Frigento, IT 1998 vol. I, 1999 vol. II, 2000 vol. III; cf., finally, the instructive work of B. GHERARDINI, *La Corredentrice in Cristo e nella Chiesa*, Rome, IT 1998, and the study of A.M. AVELLA, *L'Addolorata nostra Madre Corredentrice*, Castelpetroso, IT 1999.

[218] R. LAURENTIN, *Maria chiave del mistero cristiano*, Cinisello Balsamo, IT 1996, p. 5.

Marian Coredemption is now sparking the vitality of Mariology for all areas of orthodoxy and orthopraxis,[219] notwithstanding the opposition and objections raised by the anti-coredemptionists, always hyper-cautious.[220]

The present essay on the Coredemption in hagiography, in any case, is not only indicative, but even more assertive, both in respect to the validity of the coredemptive doctrine theologically speaking, and in respect to the vitality of the cult and devotion towards Our Lady of Sorrows-Co-redemptrix on the part of the most elect portion of the Church made up by the Saints and Blessed, Venerable and Servants of God, as well as that army of unknown saintly souls among the People of God. This hagiography, peopled by great Masters of the Faith (one thinks of Pope St. Pius X, Bl. Ildephonse Schuster, and Ven. Gabriel Allegra), as also by simple and humble souls (like St. Gemma Galgani and St. Frances Xavier Cabrini), by apostles and contemplatives (such as Bl. Bartolo Longo, Bl. Orione, Ven. Alberione, and Bl. Elizabeth of the Trinity), and by martyrs and extraordinary mystics (like St. Maximilian Mary Kolbe, St. Teresa Benedicta of the Cross, and Bl. Pio of Pietrelcina), gives us the highest and best tested guarantee of orthodoxy and orthopraxis for every truth of the Faith, and, in this case, the truth of Marian Coredemption.

From this hagiographical exposition of the Coredemption one can cite the tranquil ownership and the ordinary, uncontested use of the term Co-redemptrix in its simpler, more essential semantic connotation and theological content, namely that of Mary's subordinate and dependent, yet direct, immediate, active and exclusive participation in the very "effecting" of the Redemption in its primary and fundamental phase, that of the

---

[219] See in particular S.M. MANELLI, *Una finestra aperta sul terzo millennio: la "Mediazione materna"*, in AA.VV., *La Corredentrice in Cristo e nella Chiesa*, Quaderno Mariano, Castelpetroso, IT 1999, pp. 19-27.

[220] Cf. A. APOLLONIO, *Il "Calvario teologico" della Corredenzione mariana*, Quaderno Mariano, Castelpetroso, IT 1999.

acquisition of the universal redemptive grace on the part of the sole and absolute Redeemer. With the title Co-redemptrix one then associates that of Dispensatrix of redemptive grace, distributed to each person, in the second phase of Redemption, i.e., of the application of grace according to divine plan in the economy of salvation. The Coredemption, in its historical, earthly phase, and the Dispensation of graces, in its heavenly phase, are shown united, we could say, in the maternal Mediation, consisting in the spiritual and universal Maternity of Our Lady, for all men "still on pilgrimage," as Vatican II states, "and placed among dangers and anxieties, until that time when they are conducted into the blessed Fatherland" (L.G. 62).

There now remains nothing else but to conclude by glorifying Almighty God for the gift of His "elect" who live "in lumine fidei sub ductu Ecclesiae," and radiate the pure and timeless Faith of divine Revelation, guaranteeing it with their lives and works, their words and writings, "to the edification of the Body of Christ," which is the Church (Eph 4:12). It is the "elect" whom the Church displays to humanity as resplendent models, conformed to Him who is "full of grace and of truth" (Jn 1:14); they are the masters and builders of the Christian life of faith; they are the ones sustaining and guaranteeing the *sensus fidei* of the holy People of God on pilgrimage toward the Kingdom of Heaven.

Theologians fare badly, as a result, by paying in their studies and research but scant attention to the teaching of the Saints and, on the other hand, not holding their writings and instructions in great esteem. The teaching of the Saints endures and lasts like their sanctity. A single written expression from the likes of a Bl. Pio of Pietrelcina, who calls Our Lady of Sorrows "yes, our dear Co-redemptrix," or the offering of one's life in a vow to the "Co-redemptrix of the human race" as did St. Leopold Mandic, form a school of Faith for age after age. And what about the teachings of Bl. Orione, Bl. Schuster, Bl. Escrivà, Ven. James

Alberione and Ven. Gabriel Allegra who unanimously taught others to call Mary "Co-redemptrix of the human race"?[221] Their teaching of the truth about Marian Coredemption, guaranteed by their lives of faith with the practice of heroic virtue, is a teaching of light and life which leads to eternal salvation.

The Saints, Blessed and Venerable, recognized as such by the Church (which first rigorously scrutinizes their writings and then recognizes their heroic virtues), are in reality the highest and most vital guarantee of the truth at the maximum levels of grace and charisms. And in regard to doctrine and spirituality they constitute the most fertile and living, secure and enlightened teaching for all mankind. Vatican II states that they are the "most secure way" in our pilgrimage of faith from earth to Heaven (*L.G.* 50).

So it is that in learning the truth of Faith about Marian Coredemption from the school of the life and doctrine of the Saints and Blessed, Venerable and Servants of God, we find ourselves along that "most secure way" of the life of faith and of the *sentire cum Ecclesia.* And for this reason let us always give thanks to God and to the Mother of God Co-redemptrix!

---

[221] What, then, is to be said of the term *Co-redemptrix* used by the Supreme Pontiffs? We recall St. Pius X who first introduced the term into the documents of the Holy See; we recall Pope Pius XI who used it more than a few times in his discourses; we recall, above all, Pope John Paul II who has used it a good six times. Gherardini rightly teaches that "once 'co-redemptrix' makes its appearance in any pontifical document whatsoever, it has a weight by far superior to the same 'co-redemptrix' on the lips of a theologian, even if he were a new St. Thomas Aquinas" (*op. cit.* p. 115).

Mary Co-redemptrix: Doctrinal Development and Ecumenism

By Dr. Scott Hahn

Dr. Scott Hahn is a Professor of Theology and Scripture Studies at the Franciscan University of Steubenville. He is an internationally recognized author and speaker in Apologetics, Ecumenism and Scripture Studies. **

Divine providence often furnishes Catholic converts with ironic stories about the twists and turns on their journeys home to the Catholic Church. In my case, as a former Protestant minister, with deep anti-Catholic convictions, it was my Saul-like crusade against Mary that was wondrously transformed by God's grace into a deep filial love for the Mother of God. As they say, the bigger they come, the harder they fall—in love.

But if, prior to my entry into the Church at Easter, 1986, I had encountered a movement like Vox Populi Mariae Mediatrici ("The Voice of the People for Mary Mediatrix"), I would have been quite appalled, my worst suspicions confirmed. Indeed, I can almost hear myself loading the cannon, "What do you mean, Mary as 'Coredemptrix, Mediatrix of all graces, and Advocate for the people of God?' At last, proof positive that Catholics

* Originally printed in *Contemporary Insights on a Fifth Marian Dogma: Mary Co-redemptrix, Mediatrix, Advocate, Theological Foundations III,* (Queenship, 2000).

supplant Christ's prerogatives with Mary!" For many years, I considered Marian doctrine and devotion to be symptomatic of a mortal infection within Catholics; indeed, it represented what was most wrong with Catholics. I initially opposed the definition of the dogma, for various reasons, but mostly because I feared that it would only add to the confusion already out there.

Yet as a teacher, I had to ask myself, what's the best thing to do when you come across confusion? You dispel it. And the best way to do that is to get in line with the Church, proclaim what the Pope proclaims, and then explicate it—the job of a theologian.

Paradoxically, my former anti-Marian views have resulted in an appreciation for the common objections frequently raised against the Church's teachings about Mary, as well as the prospect of a new Marian dogma being defined by the Pope. As an Evangelical, the one overarching reason why I opposed Catholic teaching about Mary was that I believed that it undermined the perfect work of Christ, and robbed Him of His glory. Today, the one overarching reason why I embrace the Church's teaching is that I now see Mary as the perfect work of Christ, and greatest revelation of his glory. She no more steals the Son's glory than the moon steals the sun's.

In view of the potholes and detours I have encountered along the road to Rome, perhaps it would be useful to clarify how this Evangelical came to accept the Church's teachings, and to explain why I would welcome a definition of a new Marian dogma, if that is what Pope John Paul II decides to do.

The Gospel Of Jesus Embodied In Mary

Jesus announced the gospel, and then proceeded to fulfill it. But the gospel didn't change the second Person of the Trinity. The eternal Son did not gain a single drop of glory for himself—after living, dying, and rising as a human—which he lacked beforehand. God did not create and redeem the world in order to get more glory, but rather to give it. There is no tug-of-war between the Creator and His creatures. The Father made and redeemed us through the Son and the Spirit, but they did it for us—starting with Mary, in whom it was accomplished not only first but best.

Do we thus detract from Christ's finished work by affirming its perfect realization in Mary? On the contrary, we celebrate his work, precisely by focusing our attention on the human person who manifests it most perfectly.

Mary is not God, but she is the mother of God. She is only a creature; but she is God's greatest creation. Just as artists long to paint one masterpiece among their many works, so Jesus made his mother to be his greatest masterpiece. To affirm the truth about Mary would not detract from Jesus, although not to affirm it could.

Of all creatures, Mary is directly related to God by a natural bond of covenant kinship, as the Mother of Jesus, to whom she gave her own flesh and blood. This bond is what enables us to share the New Covenant grace of Christ by adoption. Furthermore, Jesus was legally bound by his Father's law ("Honor your father and mother") to share his honor, as her son, with Mary. Indeed, he fulfilled this law more perfectly than any son has ever done, by bestowing the gift of his divine glory upon her. And we are simply called to imitate him.

Salvation Is A Work-Sharing Dynamism

Pope John Paul II has stated: "God in His deepest mystery is not a solitude, but a family, since He has in Himself fatherhood, sonship, and the essence of the family, which is love." The work of salvation is the work of all three Persons of the Holy Trinity. Our redemption thus assumes Trinitarian and family proportions.

The first Person of the Trinity is now our Father (Jn 20:17), because of the saving work of the Son, who is "the firstborn among many brethren" (Rom 8:29), and so the Holy Spirit is "the Spirit of sonship," who causes us to cry "Abba, Father" (Rom 8:15). This is what is unique and definitive about the Christian religion; it is the gospel of God sharing his family life and love with mankind. And it all began with the gift of Mary as mother; she obeyed the Father by bearing his Son in the power of the Holy Spirit—for us.

The Apostle Paul spoke of the mystery when he stated: "We are God's co-workers" (1 Cor 3:9). How is this? Can't God accomplish redemption by Himself? Of course he can. But since He is a Father, his job is raising up mature sons and daughters, by making us co-workers. And his work is our redemption, which he shared in an unparalleled way with Mary—to whom God entrusted such tasks as feeding his Son with her own milk, singing him to sleep, and accompanying him all the way to the cross where she gave her sorrowful yes to his self-offering. In short, the Father willed that his Son's entire existence as a man would hinge, so to speak, upon the ongoing *fiat* of Mary. Can there be a more intimate "co-worker"?

Being a disciple, a co-worker, with Jesus takes effort. At times, it takes suffering. One passage that seemed to have escaped my attention as a Protestant was St. Paul's rather curious line, "I rejoice in my sufferings for your sake, and in my flesh I complete what is lacking in Christ's afflictions for the sake of his body, the Church" (Col 1:24). Cradle Catholics may remember with some fondness being told (in the event of an unsuccessful team try-out, a skinned knee, or a broken heart) to "offer it up." This simple phrase holds the key that unlocks the mystery of our coredemption. By consciously uniting our sufferings to our Lord's redemptive sufferings, we become co-workers. By uniting her heart to his, especially at Calvary, the Blessed Mother became the co-worker par excellence.

This understanding is echoed in the *Catechism of the Catholic Church*: "The motherhood of Mary in the order of grace continues uninterruptedly from the consent which she loyally gave at the Annuciation and which she sustained without wavering beneath the cross, until the eternal fulfillment of all the elect." However, Mary's divine maternity did not end with her Son's Resurrection and Ascension, nor even after her Assumption; as the *Catechism* states: "Taken up to heaven she did not lay aside this saving office, but by her manifold intercession continues to bring us the gifts of eternal salvation…Therefore the Blessed Virgin Mary is invoked in the Church under the titles of Advocate, Helper, Benefactress, and Mediatrix" (CCC 969, citing *Lumen Gentium* 62). It is significant that the Catechism describes Mary's divine motherhood as a "saving office," which it then uses to explain her rather remarkable titles. But what is meant by the phrase "saving office"?

Mary's "Saving Office": Maternal Mediation

Pope John Paul II has used these titles repeatedly (along with "co-redemptrix") throughout his pontificate. He has also found just the right formula to make it possible for the Catholic world not only to believe them, which it already does, but to grasp them with both head and heart—and to celebrate them. As a well-trained theologian in his own right, the Pope has introduced the compact phrase "maternal mediation" into the common currency of the Church's theological vocabulary. And it seems to capture the very heart of Marian doctrine and devotion.

As an Evangelical, I rushed to the one verse that seemed to snuff out this seemingly heretical spark: St. Paul's categorical assertion that Christ is the only "mediator between God and man" (1 Tim 2:5). How dare we refer to Mary's maternal mediation, or call her "Mediatrix"?

First of all, the Greek word used here for "one" is *eis*, which means "first" or "primary," not *monos*, which means "only" or "sole." Just as there is one mediator, there is also one divine sonship, which we all share – by way of participation—with Christ (*filii in Filio*, sons in the Son). Christ's mediation does not exclude Mary's, but rather establishes it, by way of her participation.

Furthermore, the Epistle to the Hebrews explains Christ's high priesthood in terms of his being the firstborn Son of God (Heb 1:6-2:17), which serves as the basis for our divine sonship (Heb 2:10-17), as well as our priestly sanctity and service (Heb 13:10-16; 1 Pet 2:5). Once again, there is no tug-of-war between us.

As firstborn Son in God's family, Jesus mediates as the High Priest between the Father and his children; whereas Mary mediates as queen-mother (see 1 Kg 2:19 and Rev 12:1-17). This is what her maternal mediation is all about. For the Father, Mary mothers the Son. For us sinners, she mothers our Savior. And for her Son, she mothers his siblings. When it comes to Mary's role in God's saving plan, "mother" is not only a noun but a verb, and hence an office.

As the Mother of God and his children, Mary shows us how to glorify the Father, not by groveling, but by receiving the gift of his Son in the fullness of the Spirit. That is how God's sovereign grace enables us to share in his glory, and so become "partakers of the divine nature" (2 Pet 1:4). So if you want to judge how well a person grasps the gospel in its essence, find out how much they make of having God as their Father—and Mary as their Mother.

Judging by this standard, I would say that Pope John Paul II appreciates the gospel as much as any other man of our time. And his magisterial insight into maternal mediation may well prove decisive.

Christ Merited Mary's Capacity To Merit

If merit is understood as a purely economic term, it's untrue and offensive; but if it used in a familial sense, it is as natural as an inheritance, or an allowance. What father begrudges his kids the gifts he gives them? Or resents those whom he rewards? As St. Augustine wrote: "When God rewards us for our labors he is only crowning his work in us" (CCC 2006).

According to the Catechism, it is "God's fatherly action" that enables us to merit: "Filial adoption, in making us partakers by grace in the divine nature, can bestow true merit on us as a result of God's gratuitous justice. This is our right by grace, the full right of love making us 'co-heirs' with Christ" (CCC 2008-2009).

Christ has merited our capacity to merit—which he confers on us with the grace of his divine sonship and the life of his Spirit. Indeed, Jesus did not merit a single thing for himself, since there was nothing needed. Thus, he only merits according to our need.

Where does God the Father show the world just how much his Son really merited? In each one of us, to be sure, but most of all in Mary. Unlike the rest of us—in whom there is often a yawning gap between what we want and what God wants—with Mary, there is no gap. By the gift of an infinite grace, Mary attained the goal of the covenant: a perfect interpersonal union of divine and human wills. With Mary, the ideal and the real are one and the same.

Mater Et Magistra

What role does the magisterium play in all this? It is misleading to reduce the role of the magisterium to an adversarial courtroom, where theologians are on trial before bishops, who must hand down the verdicts—unless the Pope is needed to render a final decision, as Chief Justice of the Supreme Court. While the magisterium certainly has a judicial role in the Church, its nature and purpose is more properly evangelistic and prophetic. Indeed, Jesus Christ formed and empowered the magisterium to serve as his apostolic body for preaching and teaching the Good News to a world that has grown tragically accustomed to bad news.

The magisterium is the most consistent prophetic voice of the Church in the world. It speaks with the authoritative voice of our Lord, who faithfully keeps his pledge to Peter and his key-holding successors (Mt 16:17-19). Jesus also guides the papal magisterium to penetrate further into the vast depths and riches of the sacred deposit of faith, so that the plenitude of truth will always be proclaimed with purity and power. Jesus guarantees this charism of infallibility with his own omnipotent love. It is not human oppression, but divine light.

This understanding of the magisterium is reflected in the way the two previous Marian dogmas were proclaimed, since around the time of the definiton of the dogma of papal infallibility itself. Neither the Immaculate Conception in 1854 nor the Bodily Assumption in 1950 were defined to counter heresy or resolve a long-standing doctrinal debate. Rather they were defined for the evangelistic purpose of proclaiming the gospel, as it is perfectly embodied in God's mother and ours. In a world torn apart by unbelief and sin, Mary thus stands as a living sign of how God restores his family.

Shortly after the Assumption was defined, Archbishop Fulton Sheen wrote that this dogma actually pointed to yet another: "There is one more truth left to be defined, and that is that she is the Mediatrix, under her Son, of all graces. As St. Paul speaks of the Ascension of Our Lord as the prelude to His intercession for us, so we, fittingly, should speak of the Assumption of Our Lady as a prelude to her intercession for us. First, the place, heaven: then, the function, intercession." The previous Marian dogmas, then, set up a trajectory which seems to lead (not by logical necessity, of course, but by fittingness) from the personal identity of the Blessed Virgin to Mary's maternal role in the Church, the family of God.

Providence arranged that Vatican II was not to be primarily a dogmatic, but a pastoral, council. The Council Fathers decided not to define a new Marian dogma. Instead their treatment of Mary was set in an ecclesial context, as the crowning chapter of *Lumen Gentium*, the "Dogmatic Constitution on the Church." While Mary's co-redemptive role as Mediatrix and Advocate was reaffirmed, it was not defined as such (LG 62). Perhaps the definitive truth of Mary was not to be laid hold of until the elevation of Pope John Paul II, a shepherd for whom the proposed dogma is anything but alien.

Bad For Ecumenism?

Theology itself is a true science: its subject matter consists of divinely revealed mysteries. Down through the centuries, many of the doctrinal seeds that were planted by Christ and the apostles have blossomed into dogmas, as defined by the magisterium. In this manner, theology has developed over time, as other sciences do, but each in its own distinctive way.

Scientists formulate and test various theories, some of which are proven with enough certitude to be renamed laws (Newton and gravity); others are discarded as unworkable hypotheses. Thus, laws become the markers of scientific progress. Similarly, the definition of dogma serves as the mark of theological progress.

Dogma is the perfection of doctrine, and doctrine is nothing other than the Church's teaching and preaching the gospel truth, as Jesus commissioned and empowered her to do. If the Pope chooses to define this Marian dogma, he will be doing much more that teaching the world a valuable lesson in theology—he would be using his God-given charism to fulfill his apostolic mission to preach the gospel to all nations (Mt 28:18-20).

Throughout the history of the Church, the definition of dogmas have stimulated the apostolic and theological energies of some of her best minds, especially when a definition became the occasion of controversy. More recently, many Protestants, including the late Max Thurian of Taize, France, objected strenuously after hearing rumors that Pope Pius XII was about to define the dogma of Mary's Assumption. Where is that in the Bible? (Incidentally, Max Thurian died a Catholic priest on the feast of the Assumption, 1996).

Authentic ecumenical progress is not simply the result of our own human energies. Even more, it is not caused by compromise, on either side. "Here it is not a question of altering the deposit of faith," writes Pope John Paul II, "changing the meaning of dogmas, eliminating essential words from them, accommodating truth to the preferences of a particular age…The unity willed by God can be attained only by the adherence of all to the content of revealed faith in its entirety" (*Ut Unum Sint*, 18).

Ecumenical unity thus requires a special grace and the word of God, who acts for the sake of his family. Accordingly, we should not expect him to work apart from but through the Mother he gave us to serve as the symbol and source of family unity.

It may be significant, in this connection, that experts often trace the rise of Catholic ecumenism back to the early 1950s. This immediately followed the definition of the Assumption and celebration of a Marian Year in 1954 as the centenary of the definition of the Immaculate Conception. If ever there was a time when Catholic ecumenism could have been expected to go into a deep freeze, it would have been that decade. But instead of a chill, Catholics and Protestants experienced the start of a great thaw.

As we begin the third millennium, I believe that God wants to use Mary to bring a deep grace of conversion to all Christendom, not only Protestant and Orthodox, but Catholic as well. This fits with the Holy Father's call for authentic ecumenism to be based on a "dialogue of conversion." More than commitees, this requires saints; instead of mere compromises, the courage of our convictions.

Perhaps our best model is Mother Teresa, who was universally beloved as a saint – now mourned and missed—by all peoples.

More than any other woman of the past century, she exemplified the grace of Marian devotion and service.

Not inconsistently, she was also an indefatigable supporter of the proposed Marian dogma, "Mary is our Co-redemptrix with Jesus," she wrote. "She gave Jesus his body and suffered with him at the cross. Mary is the Mediatrix of all grace. She gave Jesus to us, and as our Mother she obtains for us all his graces. The papal definition of Mary as Coredemptrix, Mediatrix and Advocate will bring great graces to the Church."

Detractors of the dogma tend to fall into two groups: those who believe it, but simply don't think the time is right to define another dogma, at least this one; and those who don't believe it, and may even feel embarrassed by it. Having found myself in both groups at different times, I understand their concerns, and still feel a real sympathy with them.

At the same time, however, I see another kind of opposition surfacing, especially in certain sectors of the media, that almost borders on deceit. For example, a false report was circulated that a Marian lobby is pressuring the Pope to make Mary the fourth person of the Godhead. Or more recently, it was falsely reported that the Pope's official spokesman had announced the Pope's opposition to the new Marian dogma.

It reminds me of the old saying, "The only way to beat a dogma is with a stigma."

Whatever our disagreements, these are "family matters" more than political issues. Indeed, we all should resist the temptation to reduce such matters to ecclesiastical politics, or to respond to our honest differences by impugning motives. How wrongheaded it is to strive after Mary's honor in a way that would dishonor her.

While I am not naïve, I am hopeful, but only because of the Father's desire to pour out his supernatural power to unite all of his children around his Son and "our common mother" (*Redemptoris Mater* 25). That is why I would welcome a new Marian dogma, if the vicar of my Lord should choose to define one. Having recently celebrated the Jubilee of the Incarnation, how fitting indeed would be a dogma celebrating the role and full identity of the Woman who made the Incarnation possible.

For more information regarding the
Vox Populi Mariae Mediatrici movement, please contact:

Vox Populi Mariae Mediatrici
98765 Annapolis Rd.
Hopedale, OH, USA 43976
e-mail: voxpopuli@1st.net
1-740-946-7777
Fax: 1-740-946-7778